Options pricing

An international perspective

Options pricing

An international perspective

Gordon Gemmill

McGRAW-HILL BOOK COMPANY

London · New York · St Louis · San Francisco · Auckland · Bogotá
Caracas · Hamburg · Lisbon · Madrid · Mexico · Milan · Montreal
New Delhi · Panama · Paris · San Juan · São Paulo · Singapore · Sydney
Tokyo · Toronto

Published by
McGRAW-HILL Book Company Europe
Shoppenhangers Road, Maidenhead, Berkshire, SL6 2QL, England
Telephone (0628) 23432
Fax (0628) 770224

British Library Cataloguing in Publication Data

Gemmill, Gordon, T.
Options Pricing: International Perspective
I. Title
332.64

ISBN 0-07-707497-1

1 2 3 4 5   CUP   9 5 4 3

Typeset by Computape (Pickering) Limited, North Yorkshire
and printed and bound in Great Britain at Cambridge University Press

To Gerda

CONTENTS

Preface

This book is aimed at the middle ground: between those excellent, but mathematically difficult, treatments that are available and those books with many words (but few ideas) on how to make a fortune with options. It should not only provide an accessible review of the subject, starting at the simplest possible level, but should also have sufficient detail on applications to be relevant for professionals. Examples are drawn from European and American markets, providing an 'international perspective'.

The book is divided into three parts. Part One is concerned with 'basics'. If you know something about options, then I suggest that you skim the first chapter. However, the second chapter on strategies should be of interest. Part Two is concerned with 'valuation of stock options'. It is the theoretical core of the book. Individual chapters deal with arbitrage bounds, the binomial and Black/Scholes methods, necessary adjustments to the methods in order to value stock options realistically and whether the underlying assumptions of the models are likely to invalidate them. A good comprehension of Part Two should enable the reader to solve new valuation problems as they rise. Part Three is concerned with the 'valuation of use of options on various other kinds of asset'. There are separate chapters on currencies, stock indices, portfolio insurance, interest rates, warrants/convertibles and commodities. This part concludes with chapters on 'exotic' options such as those on average rates, and whether option markets operate efficiently and have any impact on the markets for the underlying assets.

I have not been able to find a unified, up-to-date and accessible treatment of these topics, even though the subjects are well developed in the literature. Some chapters have sections that are more difficult to follow, and these are indicated with a star. Their omission should not affect continuity. There are also appendices to several of the chapters, containing results which, although not central to the argument of the book, will be of interest to some readers.

A suite of programs that implements most of the models in this book can be obtained from the author. A set of exercises is also available on request.

Options are fun, but they are often misunderstood, and I hope that some of their intellectual excitement may be gained by the reader.

Acknowledgements

I would like to thank the following people for offering comments on chapters and providing information: Kevin Connolly, Paul Dawson, Alfred Kenyon, Jenny Tanner, Stephen Taylor, Patrick Thomas, Xavier Trabia and two anonymous referees. No doubt some errors remain, but there would have been many more without their help. I would also like to thank my colleagues at the City University for giving me the time to complete this work.

PART ONE

Basics

1
Introduction

A whole book on options may seem rather 'excessive'. Are they not just contracts which allow for the purchase or sale of an asset at a fixed price at some future date? Not quite. The agreements just described would be forward contracts. Options are different because they give the holder the choice of whether to go through with the fixed-price deal or not. The holder of an option can simply abandon the deal if that is desirable, whereas the holder of a forward contract is obliged to complete the deal.

One person's right is another person's constraint. 'Freedom for the pike is death for the minnow.' If the holder of an option benefits from the right to abandon it, the issuer (or writer) of an option must suffer the consequences. There are two sides to every deal and risks in options are quite different, depending on which side you are on. The buyer can only *lose* what has been paid for the option, the premium, because the option can be abandoned. On the other hand, the writer of an option can only *gain* the premium and no more, but can lose a very much larger sum of money. Pay-offs are asymmetric.

DEFINITION   *An option is a contract which confers the right but not the obligation to buy or sell an asset on a given date at a predetermined (exercise) price.*

UNIQUE FEATURE   *An option may be abandoned and the buyer just loses what was paid for it.*

There are options to buy assets, known as *call* options, and options to sell assets, known as *put* options. The puts are less common than the calls and are more difficult to comprehend. Investors usually want the right to buy something. On the other hand, producers of commodities, such as farmers, are very interested in guaranteeing their selling prices and so are naturally oriented towards the purchase of put options. One way to remember the terms call and put is to think that the first 'calls' for the asset, while the second 'puts' it on the market.

The following gives an example of a call option on a share. It is 2 January and Mr Optimist is still suffering from the New Year celebrations. He has ulcer problems. This makes him think of buying some shares in a pharmaceutical company, Glaxo, which is well known for its ulcer drugs. The current share price is 850 pence. For £850 he could therefore buy 100 shares. Alternatively, in order to have a more exciting new year, he could buy a larger number of call options on Glaxo. He believes that a share price of more than 900 pence is likely by the end of March. His broker informs him that, for a cost of 50 pence per share, he can buy call options with an exercise price of 850 pence and a life of three months. For £850 he is able to buy options on 1700 shares.

What does Mr Optimist stand to gain or lose? If his view is correct and Glaxo's price rises, then he will eventually exercise his call options. For example, if the share price were to rise to 920 pence, then exercising his right to buy at 850 pence would give him a pay-out of 70 pence per share. Since he paid 50 pence per option, his new profit would be 20 pence per share. If Glaxo shares were to rise only to 900 pence, then exercise of the options would pay 50 pence

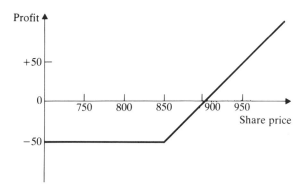

Figure 1.1   Profit at maturity on purchased Glaxo call

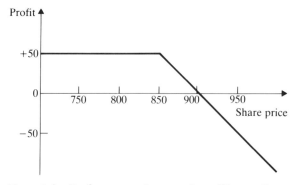

Figure 1.2   Profit at maturity on written Glaxo call

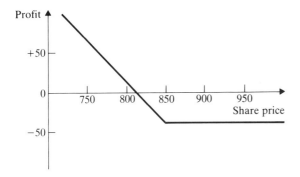

Figure 1.3 Profit at maturity on purchased Glaxo put

gross, which would be a profit of zero after deducting the cost. Nevertheless, even if Glaxo shares only rose to 851 pence, it would pay Mr Optimist to exercise. That way he could at least recoup 1 penny per share, to set against the 50 pence per share cost of the options. However, if Glaxo fell below 850 pence, he would not exercise: it would be irrational to go ahead and buy at 850 pence if the market price were less than that.

Mr Optimist's potential profit is illustrated in Fig. 1.1. At a share price of less than 850 pence he loses the whole outlay of 50 pence. Above 850 pence he claws back the loss until, above 900 pence, he makes a profit.

The seller (or 'writer') of the Glaxo option can only gain what the buyer loses and so faces the profit diagram of Fig. 1.2. He or she can only gain a maximum of 50 pence, but can lose much more. The seller's view must be that Glaxo is unlikely to exceed 900 pence in March.

Now suppose that there is another character, Mr Pessimist, who takes a rather negative view of Glaxo's prospects. He could have sold the call to Mr Optimist, but that would have entailed high risk. Instead he can buy a put

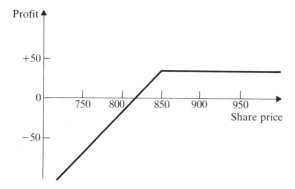

Figure 1.4 Profit at maturity on written Glaxo put

option, with an exercise price of 850 pence, maturing in March and costing 35 pence. Mr Pessimist rubs his hands with glee at the thought of the Glaxo price falling below 815 pence, the break-even level for this strategy (see Fig. 1.3).

Once again the writer has the mirror-image of the pay-out to the buyer. The latter can only lose 35 pence on the purchased put, while the former can only gain 35 pence at most on the sold put, as shown in Fig. 1.4.

1.1   A cautionary tale

Writers of options on shares are typically professionals who control their risks. Often they are 'covered' because they already own the shares on which call options are written. If the share price rises and the options are exercised, they deliver the shares. Small investors are mostly buyers of 'naked' options, i.e. options that are not covered in any way. They also prefer to buy calls rather than puts, finding it psychologically easier to have the right to buy than the right to sell.

In the Crash of October 1987, the buyers of put options made huge gains and the writers of these options lost. One disaster (out of many) at the time related to a schoolboy, aged 13, who had written naked puts on the FTSE 100 share index in London. He was unobtainable (at school) during the day and by the time he had been located his account was more than £1 million in deficit. Needless to say, he could not pay. This not only indicates the risk of being an option writer, but it also indicates the need for adequate back-office controls by a broker.

1.2   Early exercise

Some options give the buyer an additional right. The option may not only be exercised at the maturity date, but also on any date before then. These are known as *American* options. Options that do not allow such early exercise are known as *European* options. The source of this terminology is obscure. One cannot help thinking that it was invented by an American who found Europeans to be rather inflexible. Most options that are traded on exchanges the world over are American, but many of the off-exchange ('over-the-counter') deals are for European options.

Since an American option gives an extra right, it must be worth at least as much as a European option and could be worth more. Later in the book we shall examine the circumstances in which it is worth more.

1.3   History and markets

Option contracts on commodities, such as wheat, have been used by merchants since the middle ages. Sometimes it suited a merchant to make a simple fixed-price forward contract, but at other times it was safer to have the option to back out. In the nineteenth century forward contracts became standardized with respect to the quality of the goods and the time of delivery. By 1865 futures contracts had developed in Chicago. These are highly standardized forward contracts that are traded on an exchange and have a central bank or 'clearing house' to manage the counter-party credit risks. Similar standardization of options did not occur, there being any number of exercise prices. If the price of wheat was $100 on one day, then 3-month options would be written with an exercise price of $100. If the price was $101 on the next day, then 3-month options would be written at an exercise price of $101. This proliferation of exercise prices and maturities prevented the development of a secondary market in which the options could be repurchased or resold.

Standardization of exercise prices and maturities had to await the opening of the Chicago Board Options Exchange (CBOE) in 1973. The Chicago Board of Trade wanted to trade futures on shares, but was denied authorization by the Securities and Exchange Commission (SEC), so it switched to options and established the CBOE. Exercise prices were standardized in bands, such as $39, $40 and $41 if the current stock price was $40. Maturities were set in 3-month cycles, such as March, June, September and December, with two or three maturities quoted at any one time.

Some typical CBOE quotes for options are given in Fig. 1.5, which is an extract from the *Wall Street Journal*. Exercise prices are shown down the page, with maturities across the page. Thus, on 23 September 1991 there were options on IBM at exercise prices from $90 to $125 with maturities from October to January. The actively traded options would be those 'near the money', i.e. near to the current share price of 104\frac{1}{2}$. At an exercise price of $105, October calls cost 2\frac{1}{8}$ and October puts cost 2\frac{7}{16}$. Although they are quoted per single share, the options on this exchange relate to 100 shares. Hence the purchase of an April call at 2\frac{1}{8}$ would cost $212.50 and give the right to buy 100 shares.

The CBOE is by far the world's largest options exchange, but options are traded on several stock exchanges in the United States, including the American Stock Exchange (AMEX), the Philadelphia Stock Exchange, the Pacific Stock Exchange and the New York Stock Exchange. In Europe, the European Options Exchange (EOE) in Amsterdam was established in 1978 and the London Traded Options Market (LTOM) at the same time. The latter was established at least partly to prevent the entrepreneurs in Amsterdam from 'stealing' the trade in options on London shares. In the late 1980s options exchanges were started in many European countries, including Switzerland (SOFFEX), France (MONEP), Germany (DTB) and Sweden (OM). In the far-east time zone options are traded by exchanges in Osaka, Tokyo, Sydney and Singapore. Figure 1.6 gives a selection of prices from some of the European exchanges in September 1991.

Table 1.1 indicates the most important stock options traded by exchanges around the world in July 1991. Figure 1.7 gives an indication of the relative

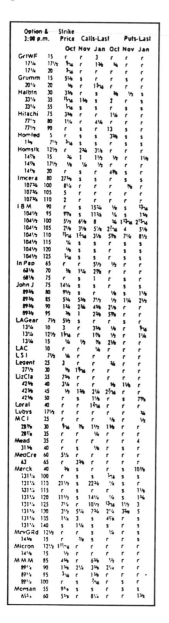

Figure 1.5 Extracts of CBOE prices

Source: Wall Street Journal Europe, 23 September 1991. Reproduced with permission

DTB, Frankfurt

	Calls (Kauf)				Puts (Verkauf)			
Str.	B	A	L	V	B	A	L	V
Daimler 12							Schluß: 714,30	
Oktober								
650	69,10	70,50	68,00	30	0,80	1,00	–	–
700	25,00	25,50	25,00	396	5,50	6,00	5,60	533
750	3,40	3,70	3,60	489	34,10	34,50	34,60	235
800	0,70	0,80	0,70	48	83,10	84,90	84,50	77
November								
650	72,50	78,00	–	–	1,80	2,40	2,20	74
700	32,10	32,30	33,00	104	8,50	8,90	8,50	443
750	8,20	8,50	8,30	254	35,10	35,70	35,50	168
800	1,00	1,50	1,30	23	83,00	84,90	--	–
Dezember								
700	40,10	42,40	40,10	53	11,50	12,00	11,70	247
750	14,80	15,00	14,50	158	36,10	37,50	36,10	181
800	3,90	4,00	4,00	173	83,10	85,00	84,20	31
850	0,80	1,10	1,00	85	132,00	140,00	--	--
März								
650	95,00	98,00	95,00	15	5,70	7,00	6,50	34
700	56,50	59,00	56,50	22	16,10	17,50	16,50	166
750	28,10	29,30	28,10	34	38,00	41,50	40,00	30
Deutsche Bank 14							Schluß: 640,70	
Oktober								
550	92,50	96,00	–	–	0,40	1,00	–	–
600	45,10	46,50	46,50	33	1,20	1,50	1,50	332
650	8,30	8,80	8,50	595	12,10	13,00	13,30	113
700	0,70	0,90	0,90	27	57,10	59,00	58,50	21
November								
550	95,50	101,00	--	–	0,40	1,60	–	–
600	51,00	52,50	–	–	3,10	3,20	3,20	89
650	14,80	15,10	15,10	123	15,50	16,50	16,00	79
700	2,80	3,00	2,80	34	56,00	58,50	59,00	3
Dezember								
550	101,00	104,00	–	–	1,10	1,80	1,80	4
600	57,50	58,40	58,00	64	4,80	5,40	5,10	60
650	22,00	22,30	21,50	266	18,20	20,00	19,00	26
700	5,80	6,20	6,30	89	57,50	58,80	58,00	33
März								
600	70,70	74,00	70,30	106	7,60	8,80	–	–
650	38,00	38,50	38,50	43	22,10	25,00	22,10	5
700	14,50	15,00	14,50	17	57,00	62,00	–	–

Call = Kauf, Put = Verkauf, Str. (Strike) = Basispreis, B = Bid (Geld),
A = Ask (Brief), L = Last (letzt geh. Kurs), V = Volume (Umsatz)
S = Settlement (Abrechnungskurs), C = Closed (Schlußkurs)
O = Open int. (Offene Kontrakte), G (gmt) = Uhrzeit

EOE, Amsterdam

Serie		Uitoef.-prijs	Om-zet	Lgste koers	Hgste koers	Slot-koers
abn amro 39,30						
c	okt	37,50	21	2,10	2,30	2,10
c	okt	40,00	33	0,30	0,40	0,30
c	jan	37,50	10	2,70	2,70	2,70
c	jan	40,00	47	1,20	1,20	1,20
c	jan	42,50	32	0,40	0,40	0,40
c	apr	40,00	18	1,70	1,80	1,80
c	apr	45,00	13	0,40	0,40	0,40
c	j93	37,50	20	4,10	4,30	4,30
c	j93	40,00	20	2,60	2,80	2,60
c	j94	32,50	70	8,30	8,50	8,20a
p	okt	40,00	10	0,80	0,80	0,80
p	jan	37,50	44	0,40	0,40	0,40
p	jan	40,00	24	1,00	1,10	1,10
p	j93	37,50	588	1,10	1,20	1,20
aegon 111,80						
c	okt	115,00	50	0,60	0,60	0,60
c	okt	125,00	11	0,20	0,20	0,20
c	jan	110,00	66	5,70	6,00	5,70
c	jan	115,00	72	3,00	3,30	3,10
c	jan	120,00	17	1,10	1,40	1,40
c	j94	110,00	10	15,80	15,80	15,80
p	okt	115,00	24	3,30	3,60	3,30
p	jan	110,00	85	1,90	2,20	2,00
p	jan	115,00	29	4,10	4,70	4,20
p	apr	115,00	10	4,20	4,20	4,20
p	j93	110,00	101	4,80	5,00	5,00
p	j94	110,00	38	6,80	7,00	6,80
ahold 83,00						
c	okt	80,00	10	3,50	3,50	3,50
c	jan	85,00	101	2,50	2,80	2,60b
p	okt	85,00	15	2,70	2,70	2,70
p	jan	80,00	26	1,20	1,50	1,50
akzo 120,10						
c	okt	110,00	20	10,50	10,50	10,50
c	okt	115,00	86	5,00	5,40	5,50b
c	okt	120,00	172	1,80	2,50	2,20b
c	okt	150,00	105	0,10	0,10	0,10
c	jan	125,00	138	1,80	2,30	2,00
c	apr	110,00	50	13,80	13,80	13,80
c	apr	120,00	38	6,50	6,80	6,50
c	apr	125,00	23	3,50	3,50	3,50
c	o92	180,00	26	0,50	0,50	0,40a
c	o94	135,00	12	10,20	10,90	10,50b
c	o95	80,00	30	42,00	42,00	41,60a
p	okt	115,00	66	0,50	0,60	0,50
p	okt	120,00	201	1,80	2,20	1,90a
p	okt	125,00	47	5,00	5,40	5,30
p	jan	105,00	34	0,50	0,70	0,70
p	jan	110,00	30	1,00	1,30	1,00
p	jan	115,00	25	2,30	3,00	2,60
p	jan	120,00	33	4,40	4,90	4,40
p	apr	110,00	25	1,70	1,70	1,70
p	apr	125,00	36	7,50	8,00	7,60
p	o94	135,00	52	19,50	20,00	20,00

MONEP, Paris

VALEURS		OPTIONS D'ACHAT							
	Prix d'exercice	SEPTEMBRE				DECEMBRE			
Cours de la valeur		+ Haut	+ Bas	Dernier	Volume	+ Haut	+ Bas	Dernier	Volume
Accor	800	.27	.22	26	37.1.....	....	....	....	.....
	840	.....	.....	....	....	38	.26,50	.32	315.....
824	880	.....	.....	....	....	24	.20	.20	.80
	920	.....	.....	....	....	13,50	.11,50	.12	148.....
Alcatel Alsthom	560	.48	.47	47	..4	61	.61	.61	.20
	600	.10	...7,50	..8	128.....	34,50	....32....	....32....	.42
607	640	.....	.....	....	....	14,50	.13	.13	251.....
Axa	1000	...2	...1	..1,50	40	....	.....	.....	.....
960		.....	.....	....	....	....	.....	.....	.....
B.S.N.	960	...4,90	...4	..4	12	41	.37	.40,70	.10
	1000	.....	.....	....	....	16,90	.16,90	.16,90	.15
953		.....	.....	....	....	....	.....	.....	.....
Bouygues	600	.....	.....	....	....	....	.....	.....	.....
	680	.....	.....	....	....	..9,50	...9,50	...9,50	...2
607		.....	.....	....	....	....	.....	.....	.....

LTOM, London

		CALLS			PUTS		
Option		Oct	Jan	Apr	Oct	Jan	Apr
Alld Lyons	600	62½	82½	92½	14	24	32½
(*644)	650	32½	54½	67½	32½	47½	49½
	700	15	35	47½	75	78½	81½
ASDA	60	9½	13½	17½	5	6½	9
(*64)	70	5¾	10	13½	10½	13½	14½
	80	2¾	6	8¼	17½	18½	19½
Brit. Airways	160	25½	28½	34½	1	3½	6½
(*184)	180	8½	15	21½	4¼	10½	12½
	200	2½	6½	13	17	21½	24½
SmKl Beecham A	700	68½	–	–	2	–	–
(*762)	750	29½	53½	72½	11½	24	29½
	800	7¾	28	47½	39½	47½	52½
Boots	390	29½	37	49	1¾	7½	9½
(*415)	420	9½	20½	31	11½	18½	23
	460	1¾	7	15½	46½	46	48
B.P.	300	30½	34½	38½	¾	3¼	6
(*329)	330	7½	15	20½	6½	12½	17¼
British Steel	120	9	11½	14½	1¼	4	5¾
(*127)	130	3¼	6½	9	5	8½	10
Bass	977	26	–	–	20½	–	–
(*978)	1000	–	33½	53½	–	58	61½

Figure 1.6 Extracts of prices from some European Options Markets
Sources: Die Welt (DTB), *Algemeen Dagblad* (EOE), *Financial Times* (LTOM), *Agence Economique et Financière* (MONEP). Reproduced with permission

Table 1.1 Volume statistics for main stock options markets in December 1991 and annual totals

AMEX	**Dec. vol.**	Newell Company	7333
Phillip Morris Companies Inc.	227 977	Maytag Corporation	7107
Amgen	161 250	**Total Dec. 1991**	**140 691**
Glaxo Holdings plc	132 761	**Jan.–Dec. 1991**	**1 864 025**
RJR Nabisco Holdings	102 793		
Walt Disney Co.	93 608	**Oslo Stock Exchange**	**Dec. vol.**
Total Dec. 1991	**2 978 853**	Norsk Hydro	59 900
Jan.–Dec. 1991	**31 829 444**	Saga Petroleum	36 610
Australian Options Market	**Dec. vol.**	Bergesen B	30 260
Broken Hill Proprietary Co. Ltd	230 018	Den Norske Bank	2550
M.I.M. Holdings Ltd	61 698	**Total Dec. 1991**	**130 870**
Western Mining Corp.	51 667	**Jan.–Dec. 1991**	**1 466 102**
Fosters Brewing Group	48 974	**Pacific**	**Dec. vol.**
National Australia Bank	44 726	Compaq Computer Corp.	99 202
Total Dec. 1991	**738 051**	Microsoft Corp.	77 138
Jan.–Dec. 1991	**9 171 951**	Advanced Micro Devices Inc.	62 451
CBOE	**Dec. vol.**	Sun Microsystems Inc.	43 303
IBM	668 577	Nike Inc.	28 608
UpJohn	135 828	**Total Dec. 1991**	**885 741**
Walmart	115 647	**Jan.–Dec. 1991**	**13 361 780**
General Electric	108 381	**PHLX**	**Dec. vol.**
General Motors	100 338	Home Depo	92 647
Total Dec. 1991	**3 517 696**	Fanny Mae	59 222
Jan.–Dec. 1991	**45 255 301**	Waste Management	43 592
DTB	**Dec. vol.**	Time Warner	40 815
Volkswagen	144 969	Security Pacific	38 358
Daimler Benz	92 911	**Total Dec. 1991**	**776 234**
Siemens	73 319	**Jan.–Dec. 1991**	**7 799 348**
Deutsche Bank	67 329	**SOFFEX**	**Dec. vol.**
Thyssen	25 797	Swiss Bank Corp.	52 449
Total Dec. 1991	**527 966**	Union Bank of Switzerland	42 840
Jan.–Dec. 1991	**9 810 072**	Roche Holding	36 090
EOE	**Dec. vol.**	CS Holding	22 032
Phillips	129 346	Swiss Re-Insurance	19 591
Royal Dutch	55 343	**Total Dec. 1991**	**237 437**
Unilever	41 934	**Jan.–Dec. 1991**	**4 460 140**
ING	30 537	**Stockholm OM**	**Dec. vol.**
KLM	30 061	Ericsson	83 342
Total Dec. 1991	**420 175**	Electrolux	20 213
Jan.–Dec. 1991	**6 993 357**	Astra	18 510
LTOM	**Dec. vol.**	SE Banken	15 595
Asda	20 386	Trelleborg	8088
British Gas plc	11 726	**Total Dec. 1991**	**175 212**
Glaxo Holdings plc	10 795	**Jan.–Dec. 1991**	**4 074 330**
Sears plc	10 524		
Hanson plc	9596	**Top equity warrants in Dec.***	
Total Dec. 1991	**484 598**	(secondary market)	
Jan.–Dec. 1991	**6 772 177**	Casio Computer	$181.8m.
MONEP	**Dec. vol.**	Sanwa Shutter	180.3m.
Alcatel Alsthom	29 082	Misawa Homes	81.1m.
ELF Aquitaine	20 153	Seiren Co. Ltd	75.4m.
Michelin	17 794	Fuji Oil	60.7m.
Peugeot	13 479	**Top index warrants in Dec.***	
Eurotunnel	12 689	(secondary market)	
Total Dec. 1991	**206 893**	BZW FTSE call 18.06.93	$110.0m.
Jan.–Dec. 1991	**2 389 122**	BZW FTSE call 18.06.93	93.0m.
NYSE	**Dec. vol.**	BZW FTSE call 18.12.92	89.2m.
Telephonos de Mexico S.A. De C.V.	13 673	BZW FTSE put 18.06.93	83.5m.
Nymex Corporation	11 959	BZW FTSE call 18.06.93	77.9m.
Campbell Soup Co.	8450	* *Source:* Euroclear	

(The volume figures above are for individual equity options only and do not provide a total for the exchange as a whole)

Source: Futures and Options World, February 1992.

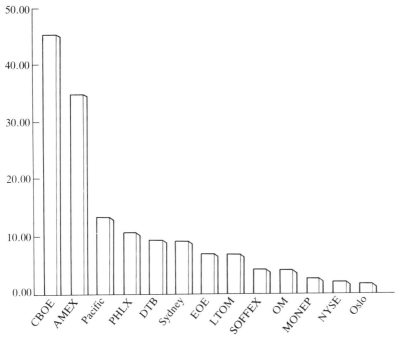

Figure 1.7 Total stock options volume by market in 1991
Source: Adapted from data in *Futures and Options World*, February 1992. Reproduced with permission

importance of the different exchanges, based upon volumes of stock options in the first seven months of 1991. The dominance of the CBOE and AMEX is not surprising, but the activity on the other options markets is considerable. Volumes for options on indices, currencies, interest rates, etc., will be given in the relevant chapters later in the book.

1.4 Market organization and margining

Trading on most exchanges is by open outcry on a large floor, but the latest exchanges, such as the SOFFEX and DTB, are totally electronic, with screen-based bids and offers.

As already discussed, although the buyer of an option has limited liability, the writer can lose an unlimited amount if the asset price moves unfavourably. To make sure that writers are always able to meet their obligations, exchanges require them to lodge enough capital with the clearing house to cover one day's potential loss. Such money, which may be in the form of treasury bills or other assets on some markets, is known as *margin*. This system of margining is, in principle, the same as that used by futures markets, except that only the writer of the option has to lodge it, and not the buyer. In practice, the margining on options exchanges has tended to be more severe than on futures markets, although this is changing. The clearing house asks for margin from its members (the brokers on an exchange), who, in turn, ask for margin from their clients.

1.5 Transactions costs

Transactions costs are of two kinds. Firstly, there is the implicit cost of the bid/ask spread, i.e. the difference between the buying and selling prices. Secondly, there is the explicit cost of commission and exchange fees. We shall consider these in turn, using a hypothetical example.

Suppose that in London the price of shares in company XYZ is 400 pence bid and 405 asked. There are call options with two months to maturity at exercise prices of 360, 400 and 440 pence. The quotations on the market for these calls are given in Table 1.2. The 360 option is said to be *in-the-money*, because its immediate exercise would give a pay-out of $400 - 360 = 40$ pence. The 400 option is *at-the-money* and the 440 option is *out-of-the-money*.

The buyer of a 360 option would pay 85 pence, but would only obtain 80 pence if it were immediately resold. Implicitly there is a 2.5 pence asking spread and a 2.5 pence bid spread, i.e. about a 3% cost in buying and a 3% cost in selling. The at-the-money 400 option has a spread of 3 pence (1.5 pence on each side) and the out-of-the-money 440 option has a spread of 2 pence (1 penny on each side). We see therefore that options that are further out-of-the-money have smaller bid/ask spreads in absolute value, but in percentage terms the bid/ask spread increases: it is 6% for the 360 option, 7% for the 400 option and 18% for the 440 option. The share itself has a bid/ask spread of 5 pence, the same as the 360 option, but that is only 1.2% of the share price.

On top of the bid or ask spread, an investor will need to pay a commission to the broker. In London this is typically 1.85% on the first £5000 of any deal, 1.25% on the next £5000, and 0.5% thereafter.

An example may help to place these implicit and explicit costs of trading options in perspective. Suppose I buy 100 of the $E = 400$ call options on XYZ. This option is quoted in pence per share, but is traded on 1000 shares. I would pay 43 pence per share on 100×1000 shares, i.e. £4300, plus a broker's

Table 1.2 Example of call prices on XYZ with bid/ask spread

Exercise price	Bid	Ask
360	80	85
400	40	43
440	10	12
Share price:	400	405

commission of 1.85%, i.e. £79.55. The total cost would therefore be about £4380, of which £150 was the ask spread and £80 the commission. These are London costs, but costs elsewhere are similar.

1.6 An informal example of valuation: a housing option

The most interesting question concerning an option is, 'What is it worth?' This example should help by demonstrating the factors that need to be considered in answering the question.

To the east of London is an area called Docklands, which is in the middle of redevelopment. The British love to speculate on housing, and throughout the land prices boomed in 1987–8 and slumped in 1990–1, particularly in Docklands.

Suppose that a builder in Docklands offers me, now, the right to buy an apartment that is to be completed in one year's time. I know that the fair value today for such an apartment is £100 000, because there are equivalent apartments being traded regularly at that price. The option would give me the right to buy at £102 000. Interest rates are 10% for one year. Rents are £4000 per annum. What would be a fair price for the option?

My first reaction is to estimate the chance that prices will be above £102 000 in one year's time. If that probability is zero, then the option is worthless. However, even if I expect prices to fall to, say, £99 000, there may still be a chance that they will exceed £102 000, thus giving the option some small value. The longer the option has to run, the greater this chance.

There are two ways by which I could guarantee to own an apartment in one year's time:

1. I could buy a completed one now at a cost of £100 000 (S) and let it for a year at a rent of £4000 ($\hat{D}$) paid in advance. The net cost today would be £96 000.
2. I could pay a premium of C for the option to buy at £102 000 (the exercise price, E). To make sure that I had £102 000 in one year's time in order to exercise the option, I would need to invest £92 727 today at 10% interest. £92 727 is the present value of £102 000, which we shall denote PV(E).

Which strategy is better? Both guarantee me the apartment, but if prices fall the option strategy guarantees me at least £102 000 from the risk-free investment. It follows that the option strategy must be worth at least as much as the direct-purchase strategy, and probably more. The immediate purchase strategy costs $S - \hat{D}$ today. The option strategy costs $C + $ PV(E) today. Hence we have,

$$C + \text{PV}(E) \geq S - \hat{D}$$

or

$$C \geq S - \hat{D} - \text{PV}(E).$$

In this example we therefore have,

$$C \geq £100\,000 - £4000 - £92\,727$$

hence

$$C \geq £3273.$$

The option to buy the apartment is worth at least £3273. If prices are volatile, it may be worth much more than that.

Of course, this calculation assumes that £100 000 is a fair price for the apartment today, which it may not be in a market so opaque as that for housing. Nevertheless, the example shows that the value of a call option depends on the:

- asset price (S) +
- dividends or rents $(\hat{D})$ −
- time to maturity (t) +
- exercise price (E) −
- interest rate (r) +
- volatility of asset price (σ) +

The plus and minus signs indicate whether the call option rises (+) or falls (−) in value as the different factors increase.

1.7 Summary

The most important distinguishing feature of an option is that the holder can choose whether or not to exercise it at maturity. Options are of two kinds: calls, giving the right to buy; and puts, giving the right to sell. The fixed price on the contract is known as the exercise price or striking price. Issuers of options are known as writers. The cost of an option is known as the premium. The buyer of an option can only lose the premium, at worst. The writer of an option can only gain the premium, at best. Options that allow early exercise are known as American options (cf. European options).

There are options on all the important types of financial asset, i.e. shares, currencies, bonds, etc. The factors on which the value of an option depends are simple to define. They are: the asset price; any dividends, rents or coupons on the asset over the life of the option; the time to maturity; the exercise price; the interest rate; and the asset–price volatility. Being more precise about the value of different kinds of option is a subject that will occupy much of Parts Two and Three of this book.

2
Simple valuation and strategies

We saw at the end of the last chapter that it was relatively easy to obtain a 'ball-park' estimate of the value of an option. In this chapter we begin by examining the traditional approach to valuation, which is based upon the 'intrinsic' and 'time' values of an option. We then go on to discuss trading strategies, such as straddles and spreads, using a 'building-block' approach. Finally, we unravel a complicated offer on gold made by Mocatta Metal, which was headlined by the *Financial Times* as 'A costly way of squeezing out risks'. An understanding of the 'building blocks' helps to reveal the true nature of the deal being offered.

2.1 Traditional valuation

On 21 February 1990 the share price in London of the oil company, BP, was 339 pence. Options were available for late April and late July, approximately two and five months away, respectively. The sterling interest rate was 15%.

Table 2.1 allows you to fill-in your views for the value of calls and puts on BP at exercise prices of 300, 330 and 360 pence. Taking the 330 April call as an

Table 2.1 Outline table for guesstimates of BP option prices on 21 February 1990

Exercise price	Calls		Puts	
	April	July	April	July
300				
330				
360				

Note: Share price = 339; interest rate = 15% p.a.
April maturity is 2 months; July maturity is 5 months.

15

example, what would you be willing to pay for the chance that the BP price will be above 330 pence on, or before, late April? Note that the options are American: they can be exercised at any time until maturity, even immediately if so wished.

The possibility of immediate exercise places a minimum *intrinsic value* on some of the options. For example, the 330 calls must be worth at least 9 pence, because they give the holder the right to buy immediately at 330 pence, when the share could be sold today at 339 pence. Similarly, the 300 calls must be worth at least 39 pence, because they give the holder the right to buy at 300 pence. The 360 calls have no intrinsic value. Turning to the puts, the 360s must be worth at least 21 pence, as the holder could buy the share in the market at 339 pence and sell immediately by exercising the options at 360 pence. By contrast the 330 and 300 puts have no intrinsic value: their exercise would result in a loss.

Any extra value that an option has above the intrinsic value is known as its *time value*. This is related to the chance that the share price will move favourably, resulting in an increase in the value of the option. Table 2.2 gives the actual market prices for BP options on 21 February, together with their intrinsic/time values in brackets.

Consider, first, the 330 options. The April 330 call costs 19 pence in the market, of which 9 is intrinsic value so the remaining 10 is time value. Participants are therefore willing to pay a net 10 pence for the chance that BP will rise in price by late April. For the July 330 call they are willing to pay 18 pence for that chance, the larger value reflecting the longer period over which the share price could rise.

Now turn to the 360 calls. The chance that BP will rise to that level by late April is small: it is reflected in the price of 6 pence. Even by July that chance is only valued in the market at 14 pence. On the other hand, the 360 puts are well into-the-money and 21 of their total price of 29 pence comprises intrinsic value.

Table 2.2 Market prices for BP options on 21 February 1990

	Calls		Puts	
Exercise price	April	July	April	July
300	43	46	2	5
	(39/4)	(39/7)	(0/2)	(0/5)
330	19	27	7	14
	(9/10)	(9/18)	(0.7)	(0/14)
360	6	14	26	29
	(0/6)	(0/14)	(21/5)	(21/8)

Note: Brackets enclose calculated (intrinsic/time) values.
Source: Prices from *Financial Times.*

Finally, consider the 300 calls. They are deep-in-the-money, having large intrinsic values and small time values. The 300 puts have the converse character: there is little chance that they will pay off, so they have no intrinsic value and time values of only 2 (April) and 5 (July).

As the intrinsic values are obvious, options pricing is all about time values. The perceptive observer may now ask whether the time values show some simple pattern? The answer is a qualified 'yes': yes, there is a pattern, but no, it is not particularly simple. The longer an option has to run, the greater the chance of share prices moving favourably. Hence time values reflect maturity and potential share-price moves. They are also affected by interest rates, because the more an option costs, the more interest that is forgone.

2.2   Building blocks: put/call/forward combinations

Options may be combined to give a great variety of potential risks and returns. In this section we shall treat each option as a simple building-block with which more complicated structures may be made.[1]

In Chapter 1 we examined how pay-outs at maturity depended on the share price. Here we shall consider the *slopes* of the pay-outs. Buying a call gives a constant pay-out until the share price reaches the exercise price, after which it gives a 1 pence pay-out per 1 pence more of share price. Thinking in slopes, the purchased call can be described as a $\{0, 1\}$ instrument. Conversely, the sold call is a $\{0, -1\}$ instrument. These are illustrated in Fig. 2.1.

Buying a put gives a $\{-1, 0\}$ slope profile and selling a put gives a $\{1, 0\}$ slope profile, as shown in Fig. 2.2.

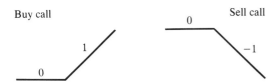

Figure 2.1   Building blocks for calls

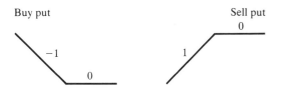

Figure 2.2   Building blocks for puts

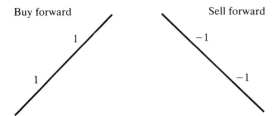

Figure 2.3   Building blocks for forward contracts

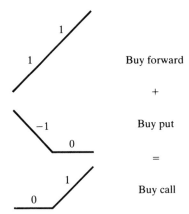

Buy forward

+

Buy put

=

Buy call

Figure 2.4   Buy forward + Buy put = Buy call

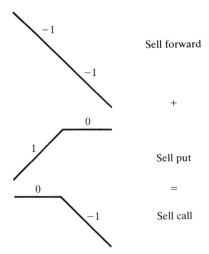

Sell forward

+

Sell put

=

Sell call

Figure 2.5   Sell forward + Sell put = Sell call

In addition to the options, strategies may make use of the underlying asset, which we assume to be a share. In order to deliver a share at a particular date in the future, an investor may borrow the capital and buy the share today (spot); alternatively, the investor may make a forward contract for delivery.[2] As this avoids the complication of borrowing and lending terms, we shall make use of forward contracts rather than shares as our building blocks. Buying a forward contract gives a $\{1, 1\}$ profile and selling it gives a $\{-1, -1\}$ profile, as shown in Fig. 2.3.

We have three instruments with which to build strategies—calls, puts and forwards—but with any two of them the third can be replicated. Consider a purchased call, which has a $\{0, 1\}$ profile. A $\{0, 1\}$ result can also be achieved by combining a forward buy $\{1, 1\}$ and buying a put $\{-1, 0\}$, as shown in Fig. 2.4. Similarly, selling forward and selling a put produces the same profile as selling a call, as shown in Fig. 2.5.

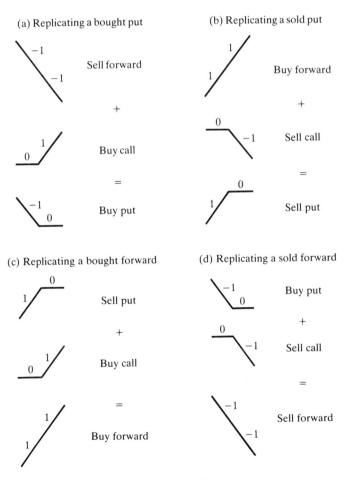

Figure 2.6 Replication of puts and forward contracts

Figure 2.6 indicates, in a similar way, how a bought put $\{-1,0\}$, a sold put $\{1,0\}$, a bought forward $\{1,1\}$ and a sold forward $\{-1,-1\}$ may be replicated.

The reader should now be thinking in terms of 'pay-off profiles' and be ready to examine strategies that require the use of more than one option.

2.3   Spreads and straddles

A *spread* is a position constructed with more than one option; for example, buying a call at one exercise price and selling a call at another exercise price. A *straddle* is a spread that uses both puts and calls; i.e. it is a special kind of spread. The different kinds of spread can be classified as:

- *vertical*, if they use options for a single maturity but at different exercise prices, e.g. buy an April 330 call and sell an April 360 call;
- *horizontal*, if they use options at a single exercise price but at different maturities, e.g. sell an April 330 call and buy a July 330 call; and
- *diagonal*, if they use options at both different maturities and different exercise prices, e.g. buy an April 330 call and sell a July 360 call.

These terms derive from the way in which options are listed in the newspaper. Exercise prices run vertically down the page, while maturities stretch horizontally across the page.

Because a spread may require the use of several options, it is not always clear whether it should be called a 'short' spread or a 'long' spread. We shall adopt the convention that a short spread is one in which the lowest-exercise-price option is sold. If it is a time spread with only one exercise price, then we define it as short if the nearest option is sold. Our presentation begins with vertical spreads.

2.3.1   VERTICAL SPREADS

2.3.1.1   *A mildly bullish strategy: the bull spread*

If an investor is 'bullish' the simplest strategies to follow are (in order of increasing risk): buy the share (or forward contract); buy a call option; and sell a put option.

If an investor is willing to forgo some of the upside potential in order to cut the downside risk, he or she may use a *bull spread*. This requires the purchase of a call at a low exercise price (E_1) and the sale of a call at a higher exercise price (E_2), as shown in Fig. 2.7(a). Alternatively, exactly the same pay-off may be obtained by buying the put at the low exercise price and selling the put at the higher exercise price, as shown in Fig. 2.7(b).

Table 2.3 illustrates a bull spread using the BP data from Table 2.2 and the spread is plotted in Fig. 2.8. Buying the 330 April call costs 19 pence and selling the 360 April call pays 6 pence, so the total cost of the position is 13 pence. Should the share price finish below 330 pence, then the bought 330 call would

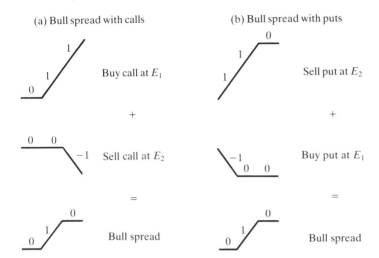

Figure 2.7 How to construct bull spreads

Table 2.3 Profit at maturity from 330/360 bull spread in BP
Buy 330 call for 19, sell 360 call for 6, net cost = 13

Stock price at maturity	Pay-out on 330	Pay-out on 360	Initial cost	Profit
300	0	0	− 13	− 13
330	0	0	− 13	− 13
343	13	0	− 13	0
360	30	0	− 13	17
390	60	− 30	− 13	17

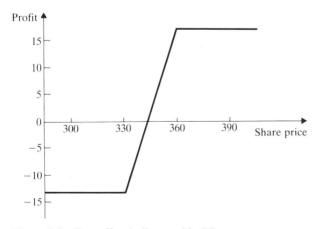

Figure 2.8 Pay-off to bull spread in BP

be worthless, the sold 360 call would have no pay-out and the net position would be a loss of the initial cost, 13 pence. However, should the bullish view be correct and the price rise to 360 pence, the 330 call would pay 30, the 360 call would not pay-off and a net profit of $30 - 13 = 17$ pence would result. The greatest potential loss is 13 pence and the greatest potential gain is 17 pence.

If the bull spread had been established with puts, selling the 360 would have resulted in an in-payment of 26 and buying the 330 would have cost 7, so the net cost would have been 19. Surprisingly, the position established with calls would have cost 13 and the same position via puts would have cost 19. The difference reflects the imminent payment of a dividend of 5.2 pence and the early-exercise value of the puts.[3]

2.3.1.2   A mildly bearish strategy: the bear spread

Selling a bull spread results, not surprisingly, in a *bear spread*. This is a position of low risk taken in the expectation of a fall in the share price. It requires the sale of a low-exercise-price call and the purchase of a higher-exercise-price call, or the equivalent in puts, as shown in Fig. 2.9.

Table 2.4 gives the data for net pay-offs to a bear spread using the 330 and 360 April BP puts and the spread is plotted in Fig. 2.10.

2.3.1.3   Volatility strategies: straddles, strangles, butterflies and condors

Sometimes an investor has information that an asset price is likely to move, but is uncertain about the direction of movement. For example, the US stock

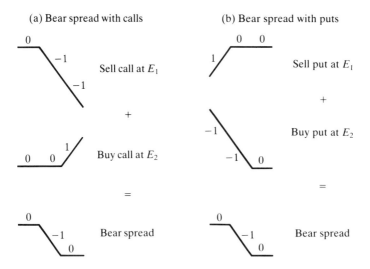

Figure 2.9   Constructing a bear spread

Table 2.4 Profit at maturity from 330/360 bear spread in BP

Buy 360 put for 26, sell 330 put for 7, net cost = 19

Stock price at maturity	Pay-out on 330	Pay-out on 360	Initial cost	Profit
300	− 30	60	− 19	11
330	0	30	− 19	11
341	0	19	− 19	0
360	0	0	− 19	− 19
390	0	0	− 19	− 19

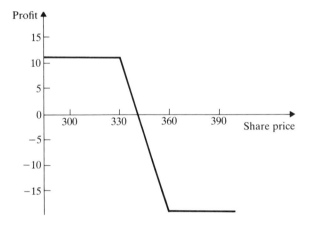

Figure 2.10 Pay-off to bear spread in BP

market tends to rise after a Republican victory in the presidential elections and to fall if a Democrat wins. Prior to the election result a move can be anticipated, but which way will it be? Another example would be the price of oil, which is likely to move after an OPEC meeting or even at the onset of a Gulf war, but the direction in which it will go is not necessarily clear. The ideal strategy in these circumstances would pay off if there were a large price movement, but have a limited loss should the movement be smaller than expected.

Since calls pay off if prices rise and puts pay off if prices fall, a simple strategy is to combine the purchase of a call and a put. This is known as *buying a straddle* (see Fig. 2.11). As an example, Table 2.5 lists the prices of the London FTSE 100 Index options on 3 June 1987, when the spot index was 2223. An election was due on 11 June. Most observers thought that if the Conservatives won the market would rise, but if Labour won there would be a large fall.

Suppose an investor bought a 2200 straddle, i.e. a call at 95 and a put at 53, a total cost of 148 points.[4] In order to make a net profit, the investor would require either (i) the index to rise above 2200 + 148 = 2348, for the call to pay

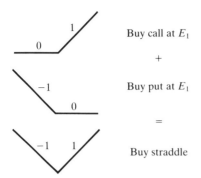

Figure 2.11   Buying a straddle

Table 2.5   FTSE 100 index options on 3 June 1987

Spot price = 2223

Exercise price	June calls	June puts
2050	215	18
2100	170	25
2150	130	35
2200	95	53
2250	68	75
2300	47	110

Source: Financial Times.

out more than 148, or (ii) the index to fall below 2200 − 148 = 2052, for the put to pay out more than 148. This is illustrated in Fig. 2.12(a).

What actually happened was that, after the Conservatives won the election on 11 June, the index hardly moved at all. If the investor had waited until expiry on 29 June, the index then stood at 2288, so the 2200 call would have paid back 88, giving a net loss of 148 − 88 = 60 points to the strategy.

If buying the straddle resulted in a loss of 60 points (before transactions costs), then *selling the straddle* would have resulted in a gain of 60 points. The diagram for the sold straddle is the mirror image of that for the purchased straddle, as shown in Fig. 2.12(b).

A potentially less expensive and less risky strategy than a straddle is a *strangle*. This is the same as a straddle except that the put and call are at different exercise prices. Continuing the FTSE index example of Table 2.5, on 3 June an investor could have bought a June 2150 put for 35 and a June 2250 call for 68, giving a total cost of 103 points. The profit diagram for this strategy looks like a flower pot (see Fig. 2.13). If the index finished between the two exercise prices, the full 103 points would have been lost. At index levels less than 2150 − 103 = 2047 or more than 2250 + 103 = 2353 it would have been

(a) Purchased FTSE straddle

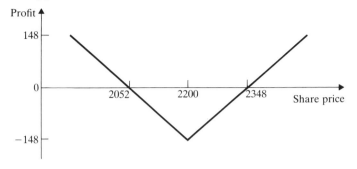

(b) Sold FTSE straddle

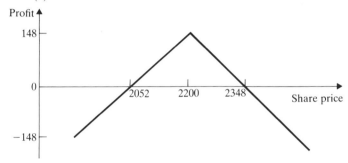

Figure 2.12   Pay-offs to index straddles

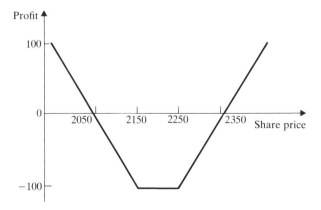

Figure 2.13   A long strangle in the FTSE Index

(a) Butterfly with calls   (b) Butterfly with puts

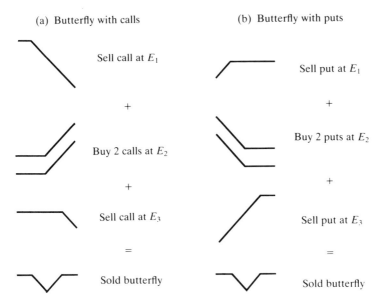

Figure 2.14 Constructing a short butterfly spread

profitable. At the final index level of 2288 on 29 June, the loss would have been 103 − 38 = 65 points. Conversely, a short strangle would have made a profit of 65 points.

An even less risky strategy, which still depends on volatility rather than direction of movement, is the *butterfly*. It is like a straddle but with 'bent wings'. As Fig. 2.14 indicates, when sold this is a $\{0, -1, +1, 0\}$ strategy and can be produced in two ways, either with calls or, equivalently, with puts. It requires the sale of each of two outer-exercise-price options and the purchase of two inner-exercise-price options.

Taking the FTSE 100 options on 3 June 1987 as an example, the investor might have sold one 2150 call for 130, bought two 2200 calls for $2 \times 95 = 190$ and sold one 2250 call for 68. The total cost would have been $-130 + 190 - 68 = -8$. In other words, there would have been an initial net inflow of 8 points. Assuming that the position was held to maturity on 29 June, when the index was 2288, the final cash flows would have been -138 on the 2150 call, $+88$ on each of the two 2200 calls and -38 on the 2250 call, i.e. a total of $-138 + 176 - 38 = 0$. The net profit (before transactions costs) would therefore have been just the initial inflow of 8 points.

Table 2.6 lists the profits that would have been made with the short butterfly had the index been at various levels at maturity. They are also plotted in Fig. 2.15. The maximum potential gain was the premium taken in at the beginning, i.e. 8 points. The maximum loss of 42 points would have arisen if the index had finished at the middle exercise price of 2200.

Table 2.6 Profits at maturity from short FTSE butterfly at different index levels

Index at maturity	Pay-out on 2150	Pay-out on 2 × 2200	Pay-out on 2250	Initial gain	Profit
2100	0	0	0	8	8
2150	0	0	0	8	8
2200	− 50	0	0	8	− 42
2250	− 100	100	0	8	8
2300	− 150	200	− 50	8	8

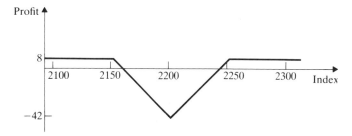

Figure 2.15 Pay-offs to a short FTSE butterfly

Buying a butterfly is the mirror image of selling one, e.g. buy one 2150 call, sell two 2200 calls and buy one 2250 call. It is profitable if the market does not move much.

Comparing the FTSE 100 butterflies and straddles in June 1987, selling a butterfly or buying a straddle were both predicated on the view that the market would move. They also both had limited risk. However, the short butterfly had less risk and a smaller potential profit: in the event, it was profitable (+ 8 points) whereas the more risky straddle was not (− 60 points).

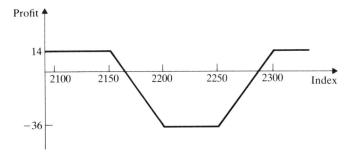

Figure 2.16 Pay-offs to a short FTSE condor

A butterfly looks like a straddle with bent-down wings. Similarly, a *condor* looks like a strangle with such wings. Instead of having two central options at a single exercise price, it has options in the middle at two separate exercise prices in order to widen the body. Thus a short condor in the FTSE 100 options on 3 June 1987 might have involved: selling a call at 2150, buying a call at 2200, buying a call at 2250 and selling a call at 2300 (see Fig. 2.16). The initial in-payment would have been $130 - 95 - 68 + 47 = 14$ points, which was also the greatest potential profit. The greatest potential loss would have occurred at final index levels between 2200 and 2250, for which the final pay-out would have been $- 50$, leading to a net loss of 36. At 2288 it would have made a profit of 2.

2.3.2   HORIZONTAL SPREADS: MAKING USE OF TIME DECAY

All of the above have been vertical spreads at a single maturity. We shall now discuss briefly *horizontal, or time spreads*. The profit diagrams for these are more difficult to draw and the building-block approach does not help, for the reason that, if options at two maturities are used, the distant leg will still have time value when the nearby leg matures. Assessing the expected pay-off to a time spread therefore requires the estimation of the value of an unexpired option.

A *short horizontal (time) spread* will be illustrated with the BP option data for 21 February 1990, which are repeated in Table 2.7.

An investor who did not expect the BP price to move very much could sell the April 330 call for 19 and buy the July 330 call for 27. The investor would be hoping that the April call would dwindle to a value of zero at maturity, as the BP price dipped below 330 pence, while the July call would keep some of its time value. Assuming a constant volatility, the expected profits for 21 April might have been as in Table 2.8.

The resulting profile, which is plotted in Fig. 2.17, is rather similar to that of a short straddle, but it is not symmetric. The loss if the share price falls cannot exceed the net cost of the position, i.e. 8 in this example. The table shows that, with a constant volatility, a minimum of 3 pence on the upside is realistic. As

Table 2.7   Market prices for BP options on 21 February 1990

Spot price = 339

Exercise price	Calls		Puts	
	April	July	April	July
300	43	46	2	5
330	19	27	7	14
360	6	14	26	29

Table 2.8 Profit on short 330 April/July time spread BP

Sell April 330 call for 19, buy July 330 call for 27

Stock price on 21 April	Pay-out on April 330	Pay-out on July 330	Initial cost	Profit
270	0	1	− 8	− 7
300	0	3	− 8	− 5
330	0	16	− 8	8
360	− 30	42	− 8	4
390	− 60	71	− 8	3
420	− 90	101	− 8	3

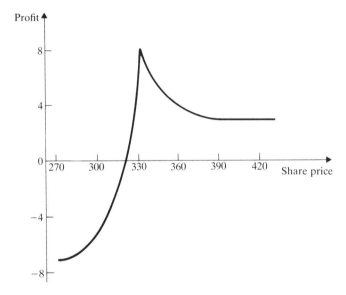

Figure 2.17 Pay-offs to short 330 April/July time spread in BP

with the short straddle, the greatest profit is made at an intermediate share price (e.g. 8 pence at share price of 360 pence in the example).

Buying the time spread would, of course, produce the mirror image of the profit shown in Fig. 2.17.

☆ 2.4 A 'guaranteed' gold deal†

Put and call options are implicit in many kinds of deal that are offered to investors. The extract from the *Financial Times* of March 1984 (Fig. 2.18)

† This section may be omitted without loss of continuity.

A costly way of squeezing out risks

STEFAN WAGSTYL explains a new scheme which allows you to sell back your gold at a guaranteed price

RISK-FREE investment in gold sounds like a contradiction in terms. From the Klondike to Krugerrands, gold has always attracted the brave, but the more timid remember that the dangers can easily outweigh the rewards.

This week, however, Mocatta and Goldsmid, bullion broker for 300 years, announced a scheme offering investors the chance to invest in gold, and in silver, without risk of a capital loss.

Its guaranteed value bullion units come with a 100 per cent money-back guarantee against falling prices for an agreed one, two or three years.

Such protection, of course comes at a price. In return for the guarantee, Mocatta claims the right to buy a percentage of the investor's holding at a previously agreed price.

So if the price soars the profits are shared between broker and investor.

The scheme is not quite open to all—the investor must have about £30,000 to spare since the minimum purchase is either 100 oz of gold or 5,000 oz of silver. Mocatta will, however, lend up to half the purchase price to help, as it says, "the smaller investor."

The deal works like this. The investor buys gold at the prevailing market price, say $400 an ounce.

The units, sold in multiples of 100 oz, then carry a guarantee from Mocatta to buy the gold back at $400 an ounce on an agreed anniversary date, in one, two or three years' time.

The buyer will of course only resort to the guarantee if the price of gold on that date is below $400.

In return for the protection Mocatta has the right to buy back an agreed proportion of the investor's gold at a pre-agreed price on the guarantee date.

Mocatta will exercise its buy-back right only if the market price of gold on the guarantee date is above the buy-back level. So if the buy-back level is set at $450 and the price rises to $470 Mocatta will buy back its share at $450.

If the price goes only to $449, Mocatta is not entitled to anything, and the investor takes all the profits.

It is the investor who picks the buy-back price and Mocatta then determines the proportion it will claim if prices are in its favour. These figures are calculated so that the higher the agreed buy-back price, the bigger the share the company can buy back at that level.

Mocatta has done its sums carefully to make sure that whatever happens to the price of gold and silver the company will not lose money on the scheme.

It has been able to do this by integrating the offer into its worldwide bullion dealing. It has made the necessary adjustments to its forward buying and selling operations to take account of the new risks and the money-back guarantee.

For the investor, the big attraction is to put money into gold without the risk of capital losses if the price shoots down.

It is a way of playing a highly volatile market while avoiding the biggest potential danger. The investor does however forgo the return he might otherwise earn if the money were on deposit.

But, the biggest potential gains of betting on gold are also diluted since Mocatta takes a share of the profit if the price goes up. The company says it has a claim to "a modest percentage" of the gold, but typically this percentage can be anything from 20 to 60 per cent depending on the terms chosen by the investor.

It is a division of risk and reward. The investor is offered a safe play in one of the world's trickiest games. But Mocatta has set the rules so that it too does not leave empty-handed.

THE TABLE SHOWS WHAT SHARES THE BROKERS MAY CLAIM ON AN INVESTMENT STARTED WITH GOLD AT $400

Guarantee time:	Price at which Mocatta may purchase gold from unit holder and percentage it may buy at that price			
One year	36% at $400	47% at $420	55% at $432	60% at $440
Two years	25% at $400	33% at $441	40% at $467	45% at $484
Three years	20% at $400	25% at $463	3(1% at $504	35% at $532

Figure 2.18 Guaranteed deal in gold

Source: Financial Times, 25 March 1984. Reproduced with permission

describes such a guaranteed deal in gold and reaches the conclusion that it is expensive. What do you think?

The deal involved the purchase by the investor of gold from Mocatta at the going price of $400 per ounce. Mocatta agreed to refund the investor if the price did not rise above a chosen level ($400, $420, $432 or $440) by a chosen date (one, two or three years ahead). In return, the investor agreed to give up some of the gain if the price of gold rose above the chosen level. Interest rates were 10% at this time. The reader should be in a position to unravel this deal's components and form an approximate view of whether it was worth while. An answer at the $400 target for one year ahead is given in the appendix to this chapter.

2.5 Summary

There is a minimum price below which an American option cannot go: either nothing, or what could be obtained from immediate exercise. This is the intrinsic value. What is left over is known as the time value.

Time values depend on: how long an option still has to run; the level of interest rates; and the distribution of possible asset prices. That may sound complicated, but options were traded for centuries before the advent of the computer: it is not difficult for almost anyone to make a reasonable guess at what an option is worth.

There are many spread strategies in options, both vertical and horizontal. Within the class of vertical spreads, almost any pay-off profile can be synthesized by using calls, puts and forward positions. It is the asymmetry of pay-offs to options that makes them so interesting in this regard. Strategies differ with respect to risk and potential return: the lower the risk, the lower the return. Some strategies are directional, depending for their profit on which way the asset price moves, but others are non-directional or 'volatility' trades.

Finally, the investor should be somewhat cautious about using strategies that require the buying and selling of many options. While these have the potential to produce almost any desired pay-off profile, the more options used, the higher the transactions costs. Brokers offer concessions on commission for multiple positions, but there is still the implicit bid/ask spread to be paid on each option.

Notes

1. The approach is based upon Smithson (1988).
2. Since the same goal is achieved either way, it must be the case that the forward price today is the same as the spot price compounded by the cost of interest to the maturity date, i.e. $F = S(1 + r)^t$, where F is the forward price, S is the spot price, r is the rate of interest and t is the time to maturity in years. In equilibrium the pay-off to buying today or making a forward contract is therefore the same.
3. A dividend of 5.2 pence was due to shareholders registered on 26 February. Ignoring the dividend effect, a trading strategy would now be to *sell* the overpriced put-bull-spread for 26 and *buy* the underpriced call-bull-spread for 19. Marketmakers do this frequently, but it is unlikely that an outside investor would find it worth while, given transactions costs. The resulting

aggregate position is known as a *box conversion*. Checking that its value is zero is a simple way of verifying the consistency of call and put prices. In this case its value, 26 − 19 = 7, is close to the forthcoming dividend of 5.2.

4. At £10 per point the total cost would have been £1480 per contract.

Reference

Smithson, C. (1988), 'A LEGO approach to financial engineering: an introduction to forwards, futures, swaps and options', *Midland Bank Corporate Finance Journal*, **4**, 16–28.

APPENDIX

A2.1   An answer to the Mocatta gold offer

Mocatta offers to sell you gold at the current price of $400 per ounce, agreeing to buy it back in one year's time at the same price, if you so choose. However, if the price in one year is above $400 per ounce, Mocatta has the right to buy 36% of your gold at $400 per ounce.

There are two one-year options implicit in this deal. Mocatta gives the investor a put option at an exercise price of $400. At the same time, the investor gives Mocatta a call option on 36% of the gold at an exercise price of $400. These options, together with the spot gold, are depicted in Fig. 2A.1. Because the call is on 36% of the gold, its pay-off is less steep than that of the put, which is on 100% of the gold.

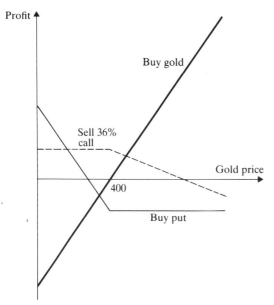

Figure 2.A1   Mocatta gold deal unravelled

Whether this is a good deal depends on the value of call and put options on gold. The deal implies that a put for exercise at $400 is worth the same as 0.36 calls at the same exercise price. From gold options traded on that day, a fair premium was about $49 for a call and $11 for a put. Hence Mocatta was giving the investor a put worth $11 and receiving 0.36 calls worth $0.36 \times 49 = \$17.64$. The company was making a net $6.64 at the outset, i.e. a fee of 1.66% to cover its costs. The deal might not therefore have been a particularly 'expensive way of squeezing out risks' after all.

PART TWO

Valuation of stock options

This part of the book is essential to an understanding of the later chapters on various applications. It is concerned with the theory of option pricing and its application to stock options. It begins in Chapter 3 with arbitrage bounds. These are the limits within which the price of an option should stay, because outside of these bounds a risk-free arbitrage would be possible. They allow us to constrain an option price to a limited range and do not require any assumptions about whether the asset price is normally or otherwise distributed. In Chapter 4 we explain the simple binomial, or two-state, method of valuing options, developed by Cox, Ross and Rubinstein in 1979. This method is accurate and easily adapted to different situations. It assumes that time is discrete, i.e. divided into chunks. If the chunks are very short, then an approximation to so-called 'continuous' time is achieved. In Chapter 5 the famous Black/Scholes equation is developed as the continuous limit of the binomial approach. We then use the equation to investigate the sensitivity of option prices to changes in the share price, time, interest rates and volatility. In Chapter 6 some problems in applying the Black/Scholes and binomial methods to stock options are discussed: how to estimate the volatility; what adjustments to make for dividends; and how to value American puts that have early-exercise value. The final chapter of this part of the book, Chapter 7, examines whether it is satisfactory to assume, as the Black/Scholes model does, that returns on assets are normally distributed with constant variance and that there are no transactions costs.

3

Arbitrage bounds on valuation

Arbitrage bounds are really just organized common sense. Any reasonably numerate person, after a little thought, would know that if these bounds are exceeded then a profit can be made without taking any risk. Not surprisingly, such arbitrages do not exist for very long and the price is forced back within the bound. This chapter organizes such common sense in relation to calls and puts on shares.[1]

3.1 Arbitrage bounds on call prices

The first bound is that an option (either call or put) cannot be worth less than zero. Suppose the option is a call on something unpleasant, such as a tanker-load of sewage. Would it have a negative value? Clearly not, because the option (and sewage) could be abandoned. Having the right to do something is either worth zero or some positive amount. This means that for a European call with price c, we have:

$$c \geq 0. \tag{3.1}$$

The second bound is that the call price cannot exceed the asset price (S):

$$c \leq S. \tag{3.2}$$

The reason is that the right to buy an asset cannot be worth more than the asset. After all, if the right is exercised it just gives the asset and no more. Utilizing a diagram (Fig. 3.1) of the call price against the asset price, this bound is a line running from the origin at 45 degrees. The shaded area to the left of the $c = S$ line is excluded by the bound.

The third bound is similarly straightforward. It applies only to American call options, i.e. those that can be immediately exercised. We already saw in Chapter 2 that the minimum value for such a call is the asset price (S) minus the exercise price (E). Otherwise the purchase of the call and its immediate exercise

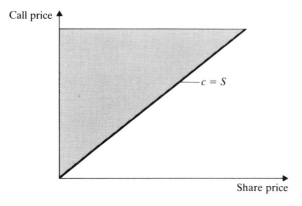

Figure 3.1   Call price cannot exceed asset price

would give a net profit, at no risk. This is the intrinsic-value bound. Hence, we have for an American call (denoted in capitals as C):

$$C \geq S - E \tag{3.3}$$

The result is that prices are excluded from the shaded area to the right of the $S - E$ line in Fig. 3.2.

The fourth bound is a little more subtle, but has already been illustrated for the option to buy an apartment at the end of Chapter 1. Suppose I want to guarantee the purchase of a share in one year's time. Let the unknown share price in one year be S^*. Two possible ways to effect the purchase would be:

(a) buy the share today at a price of S; or
(b) buy a one-year call on the share at a price of c and, at the same time, deposit enough money at the risk-free rate to give me the exercise cost, E, in one year's time. That will allow me to exercise the option if I so choose. The sum to deposit now is the present value of E, or PV(E).

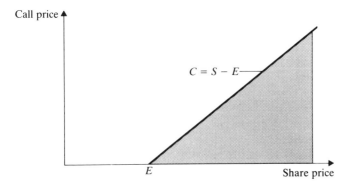

Figure 3.2   American call is worth at least its intrinsic value

Table 3.1 Pay-offs to alternative strategies for the deferred purchase of a share

	Pay-off at maturity	
Strategy	$S^* < E$	$S^* \geq E$
(a) Buy share	S^*	S^*
(b) Buy call	0	$S^* - E$
Make deposit	E	E
Total	E	S^*

Although both approaches guarantee that I obtain the share in one year's time, if the share price finishes below the exercise price then strategy (b) pays more: it will pay E, whereas the first strategy will only pay the share price S^*. The four final pay-offs that are possible (two strategies and two possible share price levels) are summarized in Table 3.1.

If $S^* \geq E$, both strategies pay S^*, but if $S^* < E$, strategy (b) pays E. Because strategy (b) pays more in some 'state of nature' than strategy (a), and always pays at least as much, it follows that the cost today of (a) must exceed the cost today of (b). This gives us:

$$c + PV(E) \geq S,$$

or, rearranging,

$$c \geq S - PV(E). \tag{3.4}$$

Relationship (3.4) is plotted in Fig. 3.3.

Notice how this bound lies above the intrinsic-value $(S - E)$ bound, so the latter is, in practice, redundant. This is because $[S - PV(E)] \geq (S - E)$. If immediate exercise pays $S - E$, but the minimum value of the call today is

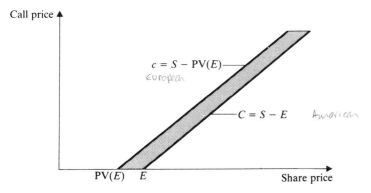

Figure 3.3 Lower bound to a European call price

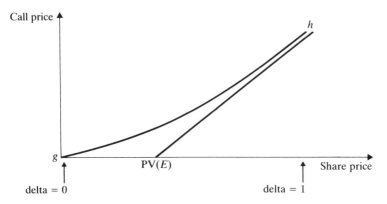

Figure 3.4 Line denoting the call price

$S - PV(E)$, it follows that being able to exercise early confers no extra value. As Merton (1973) expressed it, call options are worth more alive than dead, so there is no point in killing them early. This means that European calls and American calls are, in the absence of dividends, equal in value. (What happens when there are dividends will be discussed in Chapter 6.)

Two more limits to a call price may be readily appreciated. The first is that if the asset price, S, is zero then the call price must also be zero. An option on a worthless asset is itself worthless. The second is that if the asset price, S, is very high relative to the exercise price, E, then the call price approaches its lower bound of $S - PV(E)$. The reason is that the probability of eventual exercise of the call reaches 100%, so it has no extra uncertainty value remaining.

These two limits allow us to place two points on the call/share-price graph. The first (g) is at the origin and the second (h) is infinitesimally above the $S - PV(E)$ line at a high value of S. In Fig. 3.4, g and h are joined by a line denoting the actual behaviour of the call price in relation to the share price. The call-price line in Fig. 3.4 has been drawn with a slope that starts near the origin (g) at approximately zero, i.e. $\partial c/\partial S \approx 0$ (where ∂ is the calculus notation for a small change in one variable). The reason is that the option is so far out-of-the-money that a one-unit increase in the share price has hardly any impact on the probability of profitability exercising the option at maturity. Conversely, the slope of the line at high share prices (such as at point h) must be almost unity, because eventual exercise has a probability of 1, i.e. $\partial c/\partial S \approx 1$.

The slope of this line is called *delta* and is very important in terms of hedging an option position. For example, if a marketmaker sold an option that had a delta of 0.5, than that person would know that for every one unit change in share price the call price would change by 0.5. If the call was on 100 shares (as it would be in Chicago), the marketmaker would need to buy $0.5 \times 100 = 50$ shares in order to hedge the option position against a change in the share price.

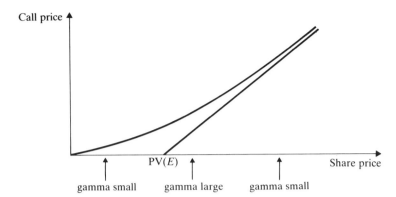

Figure 3.5   Gamma: the rate of change of delta

As delta is not constant, ranging between 0 and 1, a hedge of the kind just outlined would only be effective for small changes in the share price. For larger changes in the share price there would be a windfall gain or loss. For example, the marketmaker above might initially buy 50 shares to hedge his or her option. If, on the next day, the share price rose, then the delta would also rise, for example to 0.6. The marketmaker would suffer a small loss because too few shares were held to be completely balanced all the time and he or she would now want to revise the hedged position to 60 shares.

The rate of change of delta is known as *gamma*. Informally, it is the extent to which the call-price line in Fig. 3.5 is not linear. Formally it is the second partial derivative of c with respect to S, i.e. $\partial^2 c/\partial S^2$. It is common for traders to talk about 'gamma risk', meaning that the hedge will need to be revised and that small profits or losses will have to be sustained. Gamma risk is largest for options that are at-the-money, as Fig. 3.5 indicates.

3.2   Arbitrage bounds on put prices

It might be thought that puts are the converse of calls, and therefore the bounds are just transposed. That is almost, but not entirely, correct. Equivalent to the first three call bounds we have:

$$p \geq 0, \tag{3.5}$$

$$p \leq E, \tag{3.6}$$

and

$$P \geq E - S, \tag{3.7}$$

where p is the European put value and P is the American put value. Respectively, the bounds imply that: a put cannot have a negative value (3.5);

Table 3.2 Pay-offs to alternative strategies for the deferred purchase of a share

	Pay-off at maturity	
Strategy	$S^* < E$	$S^* \geq E$
(a) Buy share	S^*	S^*
(b) Sell put	$-(E - S^*)$	0
Make deposit	$+ E$	E
Total	S^*	E

the price of a put cannot exceed the exercise price, because that is what it would pay at maturity if S was zero (3.6); and an American put has an intrinsic value of $E - S$ (3.7).

Just as we had $c \geq S - PV(E)$, so we have,

$$p \geq PV(E) - S. \tag{3.8}$$

The arbitrage argument to prove (3.8) is analogous to that used for a call. Once again, we can consider two portfolios, as shown in Table 3.2. Either: (a) I buy a share today and hold it; or (b) I sell a put today and invest the present value of its exercise price. If the share price falls below the exercise price, then the put is exercised against me but I have a deposit of E to offset that. If the share price is above E, then the put will not be exercised and I keep E.

If $S^* \leq E$, the pay-off to (a) is the same as for (b). But if $S^* > E$, the pay-off to (a) exceeds that to (b). Therefore, the cost of (a) must exceed the cost of (b). Hence we have

$$S \geq -p + PV(E),$$

which, rearranged, is

$$p \geq PV(E) - S.$$

However, in contrast to the American call, which we found to be worth more alive than dead, the American put may be worth more dead than alive. The 'live' bound (3.8) is less than the intrinsic ('dead') value prior to maturity, i.e.

$$PV(E) - S \leq E - S,$$

so that

$$p \leq P. \tag{3.9}$$

This can be seen clearly in Fig. 3.6, in which the American bound to the put price lies above the European bound. This difference between European and

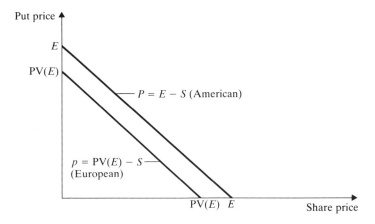

Figure 3.6   Lower bounds for European and American puts

American puts is rather important, since it means that different models are required for the two kinds of option. We can also locate the price-line for an American put at low and high share prices. At a low share price its value will approach $E - S$, since it then has no uncertainty value. At a high share price it has almost no chance of being profitably exercised, so its value will approach zero. These two conditions allow us to place points j and k in Fig. 3.7.

Figure 3.7 also indicates how the delta for a put, defined as $\partial P/\partial S$, changes from -1 at the lowest share price to 0 at the highest share price.

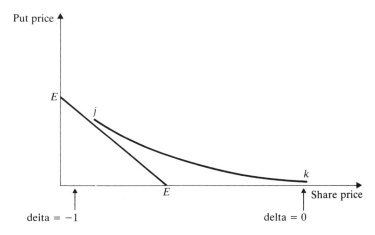

Figure 3.7   American put price line

3.3 The relationship between European put and call prices: put/call parity

In Chapter 2 it was shown, somewhat informally, that any two of the three instruments—calls, puts and forwards—could be used to replicate the third. We also noted that this only worked precisely if the put and call were written at the forward price. To replicate a call {0, 1} we had:

Buy forward	1,	1
+ Buy put	− 1,	0
= Buy call	0,	1

Buying forward is equivalent to buying spot and borrowing to finance the transaction. We can therefore anticipate the result that a call may be replicated by buying spot, borrowing, and buying a put.

To show this precisely, let us set up two portfolios. If they pay the same amount under all conditions at maturity, then they must cost the same today. Portfolio (a) consists simply of a purchased call. Portfolio (b) comprises: a share purchased at price S; a European put purchased at price p; and a borrowing of $PV(E)$. The pay-offs at maturity are given in Table 3.3.

The two portfolios pay the same amount, so they must initially cost the same amount. Hence we have

$$c = S + p - PV(E),$$

and so

$$p = c - S + PV(E). \tag{3.10}$$

Equation (3.10) indicates that buying a European put may be replicated by buying a call, selling the share and depositing the present value of the exercise price. This form of parity is only valid for European puts. We already know that an American put may be worth more than a European put (Eq. (3.9)), so the relationship between an American put and the other instruments can only

Table 3.3 Pay-offs to alternative portfolios to demonstrate put/call parity

		Pay-off at maturity	
Strategy		$S^* < E$	$S^* \geq E$
(a)	Buy call	0	$S^* - E$
(b)	Buy share	S^*	S^*
	Buy put	$E - S^*$	0
	Borrow	$- E$	$- E$
	Total	0	$S^* - E$

be expressed as a one-sided bound rather than an equality. Adapting Eq. (3.10), we have

$$P \geq c - S + PV(E). \tag{3.11}$$

3.4 Put/call parity example and the impact of dividends

An example may help to illustrate put/call parity and also to check if it holds. On 16 January 1991 mid-prices[2] for options on Glaxo in London were as shown in Table 3.4 at the close of trading. The mid-share price at the same time was 825. The sterling interest rate was 14% per annum. The March options were 69 days from maturity; the June options were 161 days from maturity; and the September options were 252 days from maturity.

Let us begin with the March 800 options and ignore transactions costs. The put cost 20 pence. To replicate a European put (Eq. (3.10)) required the purchase of a March call costing 56 pence, the sale of a share for 825 pence and the deposit for 69 days of the present value of the exercise price of 800 pence. Hence,

$$p = c - S + PV(E),$$

Put replicating
portfolio cost
(800, March) $= 56 - 825 + \dfrac{800}{1.14^{(69/365)}}$

$= 11.4.$

It appears that the replicating portfolio would have cost only 11.4 pence, but the put in the market cost 21 pence.

Now try the March 850, for which the put cost 45:

Put replicating
portfolio cost
(850, March) $= 28 - 825 + \dfrac{850}{1.14^{(69/365)}}$

$= 32.2.$

Again the market price of the American put exceeds its replicated European value, this time by $45 - 32.2 = 12.8$ pence.

Table 3.4 Glaxo option prices in London on 16 January 1991

	Calls			Puts		
Exercise price	Mar.	June	Sept.	Mar.	June	Sept.
800	56	86	110	21	31	41
850	28	57	82	45	56	65

Now try the June 800 and 850 options. The calculations are:

Put replicating
portfolio cost
(800, June) $= 86 - 825 + \dfrac{800}{1.14^{(161/365)}}$

                $= 16.1.$

(850, June) $= 57 - 825 + \dfrac{850}{1.14^{(161/365)}}$

                $= 34.3.$

Both of these are much less than the market prices of the American puts, which were 33 and 58 respectively.

What is wrong? One factor is that the market trades American puts, so the observed prices will be higher than their European equivalents. A second factor is that a dividend of about 8 pence was expected to be paid in 54 days' time.

We assume that, when a dividend is paid, the share price will fall by the full amount of the dividend. The present value of the fall is $PV(\hat{D})$, where $\hat{D}$ is the dividend in pence. The put/call parity equations can then be rewritten, (i) with $[S - PV(\hat{D})]$ substituted for S, and (ii) as a lower bound for an American put (P):

$$P \geq c - [S - PV(\hat{D})] + PV(E)$$

or

$$P \geq c - S + PV(\hat{D}) + PV(E). \tag{3.12}$$

For Glaxo, $PV(\hat{D}) = 8/[1.14^{(54/365)}] = 7.8$ pence. Hence the replicating European put portfolios will cost an extra 7.8 pence each. The March replicating put prices are now 19.2 pence (800 series) and 40 pence (850 series), much closer to the market values of 21 and 45 pence respectively. Similarly the June replicating put prices are now 23.9 pence (800 series) and 42.1 pence (850 series), cf market values of 31 and 56 pence respectively. Note how the early-exercise differential is larger for the in-the-money 850 series (5 pence March, 14 pence June), than for the out-of-the-money 800 series (2 pence March, 7 pence June).

Readers might like to check for themselves the put/call parity for the September options in Table 3.4, taking account not only of the dividend of 8 pence in 54 days but also of another dividend of 20 pence in 240 days.

3.5 Summary

In this chapter we discovered some important bounds to the prices of calls and puts. Neither option can have a negative value. For calls, the effective lower bound is not the intrinsic value, but the share price (S) less the present value of the exercise price [$PV(E)$]. It follows that calls are worth more alive than dead, so American calls that allow early exercise will be no more valuable than European calls. However, this result depends on the absence of dividends, as will be seen in Chapter 6. Deltas for calls range from 0 to 1.

The lower (intrinsic-value) bound for an American put $(E - S)$ is higher than the equivalent bound for a European put $[PV(E) - S]$. This means that American puts are likely to be worth more than European puts. They may be worth more dead than alive. Hedge ratios for puts range from -1 to 0.

There is a put/call parity relationship, which holds exactly for European puts but only provides a lower bound for American puts. This relationship can be easily modified to take account of expected dividends.

Notes

1. This presentation largely follows that given by Richard Bookstaber (1981).
2. These have been derived from the asking prices, by deducting 2 pence per option.

References

Bookstaber, R. (1981), *Option Pricing and Strategies in Investing*, Addison Wesley, Reading, Mass.

Merton, R. (1973), 'Theory of rational option pricing', *Bell Journal of Economics and Management Science*, **4**, 141–83.

4
Valuing options with the binomial method

In this chapter the binomial, or two-state, method of valuation will be developed, which was first demonstrated by Cox *et al.* (1979). This method is flexible enough to be used for almost any kind of option. As it will be used frequently in the remainder of the book, it is important that the reader follows and understands the argument. Fortunately, the approach uses only the simplest of mathematics and is intuitively straightforward.

Throughout this chapter we shall assume that we want to find 'fair' values for options on shares. Initially we assume that there are no dividends, but later we shall generalize to take account of them.

4.1 The binomial method for one period

Suppose that a share has a price of 100 today, but that in the next period it will either rise to 115 or fall to 95. We do not know the probabilities of these moves, but merely the resulting prices. Now suppose that there is a one-period call option on the share at an exercise price of 100. If the share rises to 115 then the option will pay 15, but if the share falls to 95 then the option will pay zero, as shown in Fig. 4.1.

If we buy the share and sell the call, then the total portfolio will have a rather stable end value. The reason is that we would gain 15 if the share price rose, but in those circumstances we would also lose 15 on the pay-out to the sold call. On

Figure 4.1 Share prices and call values

the other hand, if the share price fell, we would lose 5 on the share but nothing on the pay-out to the sold call. Buying one share and selling one call would therefore give final pay-outs of

$$115 - 15 = 100 \quad \text{if share price rises}$$
$$95 - 0 = 95 \quad \text{if share price falls.}$$

From what we already know, it seems likely that there exists some ratio of bought shares to sold calls that would give the same total pay-off regardless of whether the share price rises or falls. This would be the delta for the call, as discussed in Chapter 3.

We appeared to have too many shares in the trial above, so now suppose that we only bought 0.5 shares and sold 1 call. The pay-offs would be

$$0.5(115) - 15 = 42.5 \quad \text{if share price rises}$$
$$0.5(95) - 0 = 47.5 \quad \text{if share price falls.}$$

The portfolio pay-off to a price rise is now 42.5 and is exceeded by the pay-off to a price fall, which is 47.5. We now appear to be buying too few shares relative to the sale of the call.

Suppose we buy 0.75 of a share per sale of 1 call. The pay-offs would be

$$0.75(115) - 15 = 71.25 \quad \text{if share price rises}$$
$$0.75(95) - 0 = 71.25 \quad \text{if share price falls.}$$

As the pay-offs to rising and falling share prices are the same, i.e. 71.25, we have found the delta or hedge-ratio for the call. It is three-quarters.

We have succeeded in creating a *risk-free portfolio*. So what? The answer is that we know something special about such a portfolio: it must pay the risk-free rate of interest. We have the relationship

$$\frac{\text{Gross pay-off}}{\text{Investment}} = 1 + r, \qquad (4.1)$$

where r is the risk-free rate of interest per period.

The gross pay-off to our portfolio is the guaranteed sum of 71.25. The investment is the cost of the shares, i.e. 0.75(100), less the inflow from the sale of the call, i.e. a call price of c. If the interest rate per period is 5%, then we have for our example:

$$\frac{71.25}{0.75(100) - c} = 1 + 0.05.$$

Solving for c we obtain

$$c = 7.143.$$

What we have achieved is remarkable. We have found that this particular call option must be worth 7.143. To do this all we had to assume was that we knew the possible share-price moves and the risk-free rate of interest. The key to

Share price moves   Call option values

Figure 4.2   Share prices and call values

solving for the option value was to set up a hedged position, with the call and the share, which must pay the risk-free rate.

The thoughtful reader will now ask what would happen if the call option cost 9 in the market, as compared with the 7.14 that we know to be 'fair'? The answer is that it would be possible to capture the 1.86 of mis-pricing as a risk-free profit. The way to do this would be to sell the overpriced option and buy three-quarters of a share, just as above. The final pay-off to the portfolio would be the same as before, 71.25, but it would have cost $9 - 7.14 = 1.86$ less to establish than before. The 1.86 would be pocketed as a risk-free, arbitrage gain.

Having derived the hedge ratio by trial and error, we may now derive it in a more efficient manner. Let S be the initial share price, which in the next period will either rise by an upward factor U to SU or fall by a downward factor D to SD. The corresponding pay-offs to a call will be denoted as c_u and c_d respectively, as shown in Fig. 4.2. If the exercise price is E, then $c_u = SU - E$ and $c_d = SD - E$.

Let the hedge ratio be denoted by h, then if we buy h shares and sell 1 call, the pay-offs will be

$$hSU - c_u \quad \text{if share price rises}$$
$$hSD - c_d \quad \text{if share price falls.}$$

However, we know that the two pay-offs must be the same, so we can write

$$hSU - c_u = hSD - c_d.$$

Solving for h, we find

$$h = \frac{c_u - c_d}{S(U - D)}. \tag{4.2}$$

As a check on Eq. (4.2), for the example we would have

$$h = \frac{15 - 0}{100(1.15 - 0.95)} = 0.750$$

i.e. the hedge ratio is three-quarters.

In addition, the return to this risk-free investment must be the risk-free rate of interest, r. Choosing the pay-off to the higher share price (which is the same in value as the pay-off to the lower share price), we may repeat Eq. (4.1) and apply it:

$$\frac{\text{Gross pay-off}}{\text{Investment}} = 1 + r.$$

Hence,

$$\frac{hSU - c_u}{hS - c} = 1 + r.$$

Rearranging, we have

$$hSU - c_u = hS(1 + r) - c(1 + r);$$

hence

$$c(1 + r) = hS(1 + r - U) + c_u. \tag{4.3}$$

The unknowns in Eq. (4.3) are h and c, but we derived a formula for h above at Eq. (4.2). Substituting for h, we have

$$c(1 + r) = \frac{c_u - c_d}{S(U - D)} S(1 + r - U) + c_u.$$

A few more lines of algebra eventually reveal that

$$c = \frac{mc_u + (1 - m)c_d}{1 + r} \tag{4.4}$$

where

$$m = \frac{1 + r - D}{U - D}.$$

Equation (4.4) is the binomial options-pricing equation. To check that it solves our example, we have

$$m = \frac{1 + 0.05 - 0.95}{1.15 - 0.95} = 0.50.$$

Then,

$$c = \frac{0.5(15) + 0.5(0)}{1.05}$$

$$= 7.143.$$

Examining Eq. (4.4) more closely, we see that the denominator is just the present value factor, $(1 + r)$. The numerator is a weighted average of the pay-offs to higher (c_u) and to lower (c_d) share prices, where the weights are m

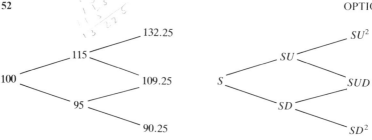

Figure 4.3   Share-price outcomes after two periods

and $(1 - m)$ respectively. If we interpret m and $(1 - m)$ as implicit probabilities, then:

> **The fair call price (c) is just the present value of the probability-weighted pay-offs.**

This is an important result.

4.2   The binomial method for many periods

If the share price in each period either rises by a factor of U or falls by a factor of D, then after two periods there will be three possible outcomes, as shown in Fig. 4.3.

Similarly, after two periods there will be three possible pay-offs to a call option: one for each possible share price, i.e. $SU^2 - E$, $SUD - E$ and $SD^2 - E$. For our example, in which the exercise price is 100, we therefore have $c_{uu} = 32.25$, $c_{ud} = 9.25$ and $c_{dd} = 0$. The call-price tree is shown in Fig. 4.4.

If we now take the top two branches of the tree, we can apply our binomial formula (4.4) as:

$$c_u = \frac{mc_{uu} + (1 - m)c_{ud}}{1 + r,}$$

which, in the example, yields

$$c_u = \frac{(0.5)(32.25) + (0.5)(9.25)}{1.05} = 19.762.$$

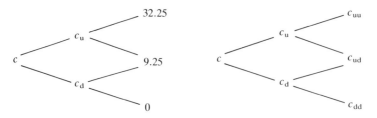

Figure 4.4   Call-price outcomes after two periods

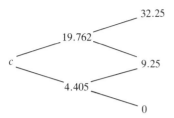

Figure 4.5 Two-period call-price tree with one period left to solve

Similarly, taking the bottom two branches we have

$$c_d = \frac{(0.5)(9.25) + (0.5)(0)}{1.05} = 4.405.$$

We now have a tree that looks like Fig. 4.5.

This can be solved for c, as it has only the two pay-offs, 19.762 and 4.405:

$$c = \frac{(0.5)(19.762) + (0.5)(4.405)}{1.05} = 11.508.$$

We therefore find that, for our example, a two-period call option would be worth 11.51.

Let us summarize the method of solution. The entire tree comprises successive two-branch segments. Valuation begins with the known final pay-off and works backwards, one step at a time, until the present time is reached. This procedure is sometimes known as 'backward induction' or 'recursive programming'. As can be seen, it is extremely simple, if a little tedious when there are many periods.

In order to obtain realistic option prices, we need to choose U and D carefully and divide the time to maturity into many small steps. The choice of U and D will be discussed at the beginning of the next chapter. The method can be extended to options that have any number of discrete periods to maturity, so that each period can be made arbitrarily short. As the 'chunks' of time become shorter and shorter, discrete time will tend to continuous time and the jumps of the share-price in each period will become infinitesimally small. For reasonably accurate results, the time to maturity should be divided into at least 50 steps.

4.3 Hedge ratios, early exercise/puts and dividends in the binomial model

4.3.1 HEDGE RATIOS

The two-period example may be utilized to show how the hedge ratio changes at each node of the tree. At the c_u node (of Fig. 4.4) it is equal to

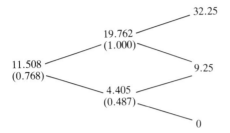

Figure 4.6   Two-period call tree with hedge ratios

$$h = \frac{c_{uu} - c_{ud}}{S(U - D)}$$

$$= \frac{32.25 - 9.25}{115(1.15 - 0.95)}$$

$$= \frac{23}{23}$$

$$= 1.0.$$

At the c_d node it is equal to

$$h = \frac{9.25 - 0}{95(1.15 - 0.95)} = 0.487.$$

Finally, at the initial c node it is equal to

$$h = \frac{19.762 - 4.405}{100(1.15 - 0.95)} = 0.768.$$

Redrawing the possible call values, together with their associated hedge ratios (in brackets), we have Fig. 4.6. The hedge ratio starts at 0.768, If the upper branch is taken, it then rises to 1.000 because the call is now so far in-the-money that it has a positive pay-off in all circumstances, i.e. either 32.25 or 9.25. The holder of the call knows that final exercise is certain at this point. By contrast, if the lower branch is taken from the root of the tree, then the hedge ratio falls from the initial 0.768 to 0.487.

A two-period example with such large jumps in share price is not very realistic. However, it does indicate the need to revise the hedge ratio as time passes. If time to maturity is divided into a large number of short periods, then the hedge ratio from Eq. (4.2) may be used to determine the exposure quite accurately.

4.3.2   EARLY EXERCISE AND PUT PRICES

In Chapter 3 it was shown that the right to exercise an option early did not have value for calls, but it did have value for puts. These results were derived in the

Share price moves   Put option values

Figure 4.7   One-period share and put trees

absence of any dividend payments. The binomial prices derived above did not allow for early exercise at intermediate nodes.

Making such an allowance for early exercise is very simple. At each node the unexercised price is calculated in the normal way with Eq. (4.4). At the same time, the exercised value is calculated, i.e. $(S - E)$ for a call or $(E - S)$ for a put. The larger of the two values is then assumed to be the option value at that node, and this value is used in all further calculations within the tree.

To demonstrate this procedure realistically, we first need to know how to adapt the binomial formula for a put rather than a call. The one-period put tree is shown in Fig. 4.7.

We know that a hedged position may be obtained by simultaneously selling some shares and one put. However, to be totally consistent with the call-price derivation, let us assume that h_p shares are to be bought, where h_p is the put hedge ratio and will be negative. The pay-offs to rising and falling share prices will be

$$h_p SU - p_u \quad \text{if share price rises}$$
$$h_p SD - p_d \quad \text{if share price falls.}$$

The two pay-offs may be equated to give the hedge ratio,

$$h_p = \frac{p_u - p_d}{S(U - D)}, \tag{4.5}$$

that is, $-5/20 = -0.25$. As expected, the hedge ratio is negative for the put, implying the sale of 0.25 shares per sale of one put. Equating the return on the hedged position to the risk-free rate, we have

$$\frac{h_p SU - p_u}{h_p S - p} = 1 + r. \tag{4.6}$$

Substituting for h_p and solving for p, we obtain

$$p = \frac{mp_u + (1 - m)p_d}{1 + r}, \tag{4.7}$$

where m is exactly as before, i.e. $m = (1 + r - D)/(U - D)$.

The put formula, (4.7), is therefore the same as the call formula, (4.4), except that the put pay-offs p_u and p_d are substituted for the call pay-offs c_u and c_d. Hence, the put price in our example is equal to[1]

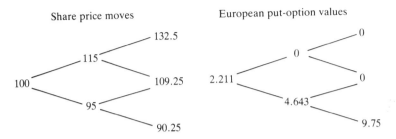

Figure 4.8   Two-period trees for share and European put

$$p = \frac{(0.5)(0) + (0.5)(5)}{1.05}$$

$$= 2.381.$$

Let us now return to the question of early exercise and the value of American puts. If we take the two-period example, the European put values are as shown in Fig. 4.8.

The European put would be worth 2.211 today. It would have no value along the upper branches, but with one period remaining it would be worth 4.643 along the lower branch. However, the share price along the lower branch, with one period remaining, would be 95 and exercise of the put at that time would pay 5. Hence the American put would be worth more (5) than the European put (4.643), so that a value of 5 should be carried back when assessing American options. The revised tree of American put-option values is given in Fig. 4.9. The two-period American put is worth 2.381, whereas the equivalent European put is worth 2.211.

4.3.3   DIVIDENDS IN THE BINOMIAL MODEL

As mentioned in Chapter 3, when a dividend is paid the price of a share will fall by the amount of the dividend. If it fell by less than the dividend, then a trader could buy the share just prior to the ex-dividend date, capture the dividend and sell the share immediately it had fallen in price. Tax consideration may complicate the situation, but we shall assume that a fall in price of the full dividend occurs.[2]

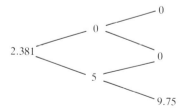

Figure 4.9   Two-period tree for American put

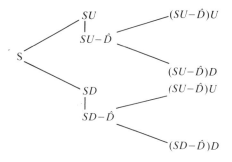

Figure 4.10   Two-period share-price tree with a dividend after one period

The significance of dividends for the binomial method is that the share-price tree will be knocked sideways at the ex-dividend date. If a given dividend in pence is assumed to be paid, the tree will start to have branches that no longer 'join-up' in the middle. This is illustrated in Fig. 4.10 for a dividend of size $\hat{D}$, and results in a new, separately developing tree being formed for each node that existed at the time of the dividend payment. The computational burden is greatly increased.

This problem arose because the dividend was assumed to be a fixed sum in pence. Instead, we may assume that it is some proportion δ of the share price at that point in the tree. The share price after payment will then be, for example, $SU(1 - \delta)$ after one up-step rather than $SU - \hat{D}$. For the whole tree the geometric (multiplicative) process can be maintained and the nodes continue to recombine, as shown in Fig. 4.11.

How accurate is the assumption that the dividend is a certain proportion δ of the share price, rather than a fixed payment in pence? The dividend is likely to be small relative to the share price (maximally 2–3%, and probably much less). It may also be a forecast rather than a known sum. Consequently, it makes very little difference whether one takes the proportional or the fixed-sum approach. Indeed, for options with long lives it may be more accurate to assume a particular dividend yield than to assume a particular dividend, as yields tend to

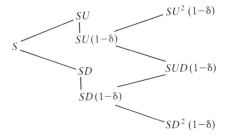

Figure 4.11   Two-period share-price tree with multiplicative dividend after one period

be more stable. The binomial tree can therefore be easily adapted for proportional dividends, leading to no increase in the number of nodes in the tree.

4.4   The binomial formula for many periods

We said earlier that many periods are necessary before the binomial model can give accurate results. If we consider our two-period tree in Fig. 4.4, we had

$$c_u = \frac{mc_{uu} + (1 - m)c_{ud}}{1 + r}$$

and

$$c_d = \frac{mc_{ud} + (1 - m)c_{dd}}{1 + r}.$$

But for one period ahead we know that

$$c = \frac{mc_u + (1 - m)c_d}{1 + r}.$$

Hence, substituting for c_u and c_d we may write

$$c = \frac{m[mc_{uu} + (1 - m)c_{ud}] + (1 - m)[mc_{ud} + (1 - m)c_{dd}]}{(1 + r)^2}$$

$$= \frac{(1)m^2[c_{uu} + (2)m(1 - m)c_{ud} + (1)(1 - m)^2 c_{dd}}{(1 + r)^2} \tag{4.8}$$

The (1), (2), (1) sequence in Eq. (4.8) is the well-known binomial expansion. The terms of the expansion can be found from Pascal's triangle, in which an element in the succeeding row is the sum of the adjacent elements above it:

$$
\begin{array}{ccccccccc}
& & & & 1 & & & & \\
& & & 1 & & 2 & & 1 & \\
& & 1 & & 3 & & 3 & & 1 \\
& 1 & & 4 & & 6 & & 4 & & 1 \\
1 & & 5 & & 10 & & 10 & & 5 & & 1
\end{array}
$$

More formally, when there have been n periods, the kth element of the binomial expansion may be expressed as

$$\binom{n}{k} = \frac{n!}{(n - k)!\, k!} \tag{4.9}$$

where $n! = n(n - 1)(n - 2) \ldots$ For example, for a three-period tree the four binomial weights are

$$
\begin{array}{lll}
k = 0: & 3!/(3!)(0!) = 1 & \text{(noting that } 0! = 1) \\
k = 1: & 3!/(2!)(1!) = 6/2 = 3 & \\
k = 2: & 3!/(1!)(2!) = 6/2 = 3 & \\
k = 3: & 3!/(0!)(3!) = 1 &
\end{array}
$$

Using the above notation for the binomial expansion, we can write the many-period binomial options-pricing formula as

$$c = \frac{1}{(1 + r)^n} \sum_{k=0}^{n} \left[\binom{n}{k} m^k (1 - m)^{n-k} \max\{(SU^k D^{n-k} - E), 0\} \right]. \quad (4.10)$$

This a European formula, as it takes no account of any value from early exercise. It considers the option to be worth simply the present value of the expected final pay-off in a binomial tree with n steps. We shall see in the next chapter that Eq. (4.10) is the discrete-time analogue of the continuous-time Black/Scholes formula.

4.5 What assumptions were made to derive the formula?

It is useful to summarize what had to be assumed in this chapter in order to derive formula (4.10). What was necessary for the construction and solution of the binomial trees? The assumptions were:

1. The distribution of share prices was a multiplicative binomial.
2. The U and D multipliers (and hence the variances of returns) were the same in all periods.
3. There were no transactions costs, so that a riskless hedge could be established for each period between the option and the asset at no sunk cost.
4. Interest rates were constant.

In addition, Eq. (4.10) assumed that

5. Early exercise was not possible (options were European).
6. There were no dividends.

Assumptions 5 and 6 can be relaxed, as discussed earlier, when the tree is solved sequentially rather than just for the final period via Eq. (4.10).

It is important to note that it was not necessary to assume that investors had a particular attitude to risk. All investors should place the same value on an option, regardless of whether they are millionaires or paupers. The option has a 'fair value'. If it deviates from that value, then a riskless profit may be made.

4.6 Summary

In this chapter an exact pricing formula for European call and put options has been derived. It depends on the asset price moving in jumps, but, as those jumps can be made arbitrarily small, in the limit the method approximates a continuous-time solution. This formula relies on the insight that a correct combination of the asset and the option would form a risk-free portfolio. The return on such a portfolio must be the risk-free rate. Although the formula is derived from arbitrage arguments, it implies that an option is only worth the present value of its expected pay-off.

We have also seen how the hedge ratio is an automatic by-product of the calculations. The approach allows early-exercise values to be imposed, thus facilitating the numerical calculation of values for American put options. Dividends can be incorporated under the assumption that a certain dividend yield is paid at a given future date.

Notes

1. We can check this result by put/call parity. We have

$p = c - S + \text{PV}(E)$
$= 7.143 - 100 + (100/1.05)$
$= 2.381.$

2. There is some dispute about whether the share price should fall by the tax-adjusted dividend (e.g. 70% of the dividend if the tax rate is effectively 30%), or by the full amount of the dividend. American evidence (e.g. Heath and Jarrow, 1988) suggests the full amount of the dividend, but in Britain the fall is net of tax.

References

Cox, J., Ross, S. and Rubinstein, M. (1979), 'Option pricing: a simplified approach', *Journal of Financial Economics*, **7**, 229–63.

Heath, D. and Jarrow, R. (1988), 'Ex-dividend stock price behaviour and arbitrage opportunities', *Journal of Business*, **61**, 95–108.

5

From discrete to continuous time: the Black/Scholes equation

The Black/Scholes (B/S) equation for the price of an option (Black and Scholes, 1973) is of great importance in modern finance. It demonstrates the power of arbitrage pricing. Yet the binomial approach is also based on arbitrage and is theoretically correct, so why is the B/S equation so famous? One reason is that it is an analytical, one-step, solution that is more elegant than the multi-step binomial solution. Another reason is that it is computationally much more efficient than the binomial approach—up to 100 times faster. A third reason is that it assumes that returns on assets are normally distributed, which is widely accepted to be a reasonable premise.

This chapter begins by showing graphically how, after several periods, the asset prices in a binomial tree develop a lognormal shape. That implies that the returns in the tree tend to a normal distribution. The B/S equation is then introduced and explained. An informal proof is given (which may be omitted without loss of continuity) in which the call value is equated to the present value of its expected pay-off. Then the B/S equation is utilized to show how the price of a call is affected by changes in share prices, time to maturity, interest rates and volatility.

5.1 Share prices and returns: from binomial trees to lognormal distributions

The binomial model of the last chapter was based upon a multiplicative process for the share price. This kind of 'geometric' process is rather plausible for the prices of many assets, including shares. In particular, if the down (D) multiplier in the binomial model is chosen as the inverse of the up (U) multiplier, i.e. $D = 1/U$, then returns to holding the asset will be symmetric.

Before this is demonstrated, we need to be clear about the way in which returns are measured. This is not as obvious as the reader might think. Let us assume that the share price follows the sequence through time of 100, 110, 100. If we naively measure returns as the gain (loss) divided by the original share price, we obtain a sequence of two returns, which are equal to $(10/100) = +10\%$ and $-(10/110) = -9.909\%$. The negative return in the second period would appear to be smaller than the positive return in the first period, yet we finished with the share at its original level. Something is wrong!

The problem is that the base for measurement changed from 100 to 110. If, however, we measure returns as the log of each successive price divided by its predecessor, then we obtain $\log(110/100) = 0.0953$ or 9.53% and $\log(100/110) = -0.0953$ or -9.53%. Returns are now symmetric. For this reason returns are conventionally measured by taking the logs of successive prices, i.e.

$$R_t = \log\left(\frac{S_t}{S_{t-1}}\right),\tag{5.1}$$

where R is the return, S is the asset price and t denotes time.

Prices that are lognormally distributed lead to returns that are distributed according to the well-known normal distribution.

Suppose we start with a share price S, which may rise to SU or fall to S/U $(= SD)$. The returns will be $\log[(SU)/S]$ for a rise and $\log[(S/U)/S]$ for a fall. Dividing by S, they will be $\log(U)$ and $\log(1/U)$ respectively. Since $\log(1/U) = -\log(U)$, the returns may be very simply stated as $+\log(U)$ for a price rise and $-\log(U)$ for a price fall. Hence the returns will be symmetric in such a geometric process.

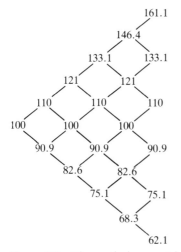

Figure 5.1   Five-period geometric tree

An example of a binomial tree with $U = 1.1$ and $D = (1/U)$ is given in Fig. 5.1. It starts at a share price of 100 and continues for five periods. There are two interesting features of such a geometric process: (i) the rising branches rise at an accelerating rate; and (ii) the falling branches decline at a decreasing rate and never reach zero. The latter condition makes the process suitable for most assets, which cannot have negative prices.[1]

The width of a binomial tree is related to the size of U (per step) and the number of steps that have occurred. The equivalent assumption for an asset that has normally distributed returns is that the variance of returns is constant per period. Then, if the variance per year is expressed as σ^2, the variance for some period of t years may be expressed as $\sigma^2 t$. Taking the square root, the standard deviation of returns over t years would be equal to $\sigma \sqrt{t}$. This standard deviation per year is often referred to as the *volatility* of the asset. For example, if the standard deviation of returns were 20% per annum, then the standard deviation of returns over 0.5 year would be $20\sqrt{0.5} = 14.14\%$.

We are now ready to discuss the actual values to use for the up and down multipliers in a binomial tree in order to make it consistent with normally distributed returns. If we let σ be the annual standard deviation of returns, t the number of years to maturity and n the number of periods into which t is divided, the binomial process for the asset price gives normally distributed returns in the limit if

$$U = e^{\sigma \sqrt{t/n}} \tag{5.2}$$

and

$$D = \frac{1}{U} = e^{-\sigma \sqrt{t/n}}. \tag{5.3}$$

It is shown in the notes to this chapter that after a large number of steps this choice of U and D leads to a variance of $\sigma^2 t/n$.[2]

Suppose we choose $S = 100$, $\sigma = 0.3$, $t = 0.5$ and $r = 0.08$ per instant of time, with $n = 10$ iterations. Then the time step is 0.05 year and

$$U = 1.0694, \quad D = 0.9351.$$

From the binomial call-price equation of the last chapter (Eq. (4.4)), the up-probability will be

$$m = \frac{1 + (0.05)(0.08) - 0.9351}{1.0694 - 0.9351} = 0.5130$$

and the down-probability will be

$$(1 - m) = 0.4870.$$

The resulting distributions of final prices and returns after ten periods are given in Figs 5.2 and 5.3. The asymmetry of the price distribution in Fig. 5.2 is clearly

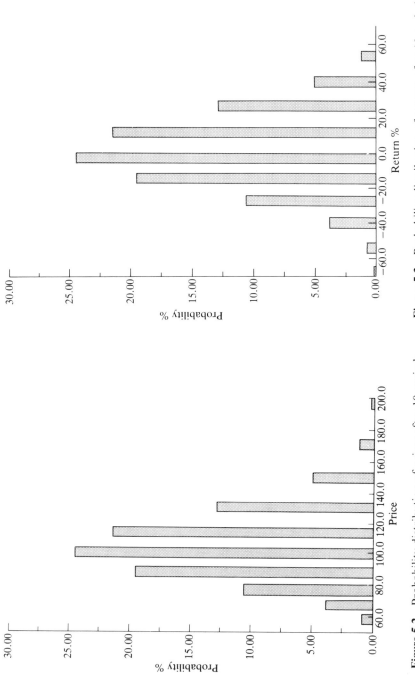

Figure 5.3 Probability distribution of returns after 10 periods

Figure 5.2 Probability distribution of prices after 10 periods

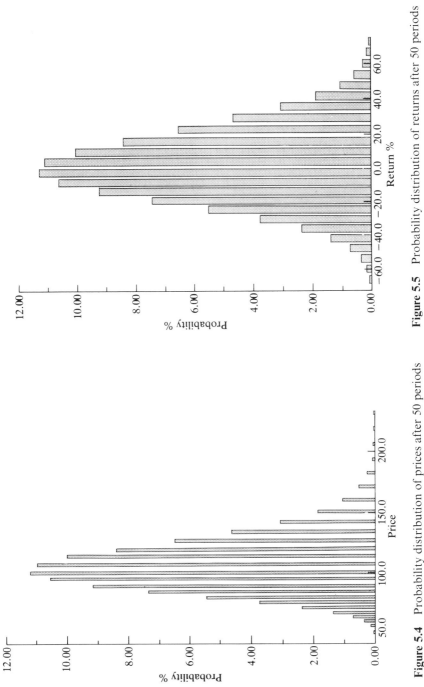

Figure 5.4 Probability distribution of prices after 50 periods

Figure 5.5 Probability distribution of returns after 50 periods

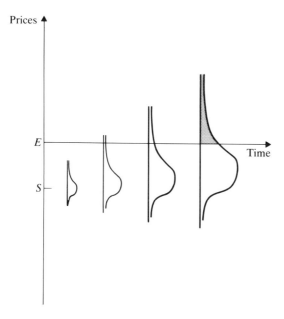

Figure 5.6   Call value rising as the price distribution widens over time

apparent, while the return distribution of Fig. 5.3 is symmetric and already looks almost 'normal' in shape, despite only ten iterations.

The same process, divided into 50 subperiods rather than just 10, is shown in Figs 5.4 and 5.5. The price distribution is clearly tending to the lognormal, with a steep left-hand tail and a stretched right-hand tail. The return distribution has the bell-shaped character of the normal distribution.

If we assume that prices are lognormal, we can imagine the distribution widening as time goes by, just as the binomial tree widened at successive branches. Figure 5.6 takes snapshots of such a distribution through time, in relation to the valuation of an out-of-the-money call option. Beginning at a price S at time zero, the distribution widens until, eventually, part of it exceeds the exercise price E. At maturity, the pay-off to the option is the shaded area above E. The Black/Scholes value of the option today is simply the present value of this shaded area.

5.2   The Black/Scholes equation

The Black/Scholes equation makes exactly the same assumptions as the binomial approach, but with one exception: the asset price is assumed to follow a lognormal distribution for which the variance is proportional to time. To be precise, the assumptions are:

1. The asset price follows a lognormal distribution, so that returns are normally distributed.
2. The value of returns is known and is directly proportional to the passage of time.
3. There are no transactions costs, so that a riskless hedge may continuously be established between the option and the asset at no sunk cost.
4. Interest rates are known and constant.
5. There is no early exercise (options are European).
6. There are no dividends.

The B/S equation for a call is

$$c = SN(d_1) - E\,e^{-rt}N(d_2), \tag{5.4}$$

where c is the call price, S the asset price, $N(x)$ a normal distribution probability, E the exercise price, r the interest rate in continuous form, and t is years to maturity.

The $N(d_1)$ and $N(d_2)$ values, which are probabilities from the normal distribution, have values for d_1 and d_2 calculated as follows:

$$d_1 = \frac{\log(S/E) + rt + 0.5\sigma^2 t}{\sigma\sqrt{t}} \tag{5.5}$$

and

$$d_2 = d_1 - \sigma\sqrt{t}, \tag{5.6}$$

where σ is the standard deviation of returns on the asset for a one-year period. To find the European put price, we may invoke put/call parity:

$$p = c - S + PV(E).$$

Substituting from the B/S equation (5.4) for c, we have

$$\begin{aligned} p &= [SN(d_1) - E\,e^{-rt}N(d_2)] - S + E\,e^{-rt} \\ &= S[N(d_1) - 1] - E\,e^{-rt}[N(d_2) - 1]. \end{aligned} \tag{5.7}$$

The basic call formula (5.4) is simple—but the $N(d_1)$ and $N(d_2)$ terms are rather puzzling. If there is no volatility ($\sigma = 0$), these probabilities will both be equal to 1. The equation will then give the result:

$$c = S - E\,e^{-rt}. \tag{5.8}$$

Now e^{-rt} is simply the continuous-time discount factor, so that Eq. (5.8) is just the continuous-time form of the lower bound to a European call price, $c \geq S - PV(E)$ (i.e. Eq. (3.4) of Chapter 3).

Given some degree of volatility ($\sigma > 0$), the B/S equation applies a weight $N(d_1)$ to S and a weight $N(d_2)$ to $E\,e^{-rt}$. If the equation is to give values above the bound, $N(d_1)$ must exceed $N(d_2)$.

Here is an example of a B/S calculation. Let $S = 100$, $E = 110$, $t = 0.5$, $\sigma = 0.3$ and $r = 0.08$ (continuous). Then,

$$d_1 = \frac{\log(100/110) + 0.08(0.5) + 0.5(0.3)^2(0.5)}{0.3\sqrt{0.5}}$$

$$= -0.1547.$$

$$d_2 = d_1 - 0.3\sqrt{0.5}$$

$$= -0.3668.$$

We now need to use the normal distribution table (given on page 268, together with a numerical approximation), to find the probabilities of observing these d_1 and d_2 values. From the table we find that the probabilities are

$$N(d_1) = 0.4384 \quad \text{and} \quad N(d_2) = 0.3568.$$

The resulting call price is therefore,

$$c = 100(0.4384) - 110 \, e^{-0.08(0.5)}(0.3568)$$

$$= 43.84 - 37.71$$

$$= 6.13.$$

Using put/call parity, the European put price is then

$$p = c - S + PV(E)$$

$$= 6.13 - 100 + 110 \, e^{-0.08(0.5)}$$

$$= 11.82.$$

The put is worth more than the call because it is in-the-money by 10 ($S = 100$, $E = 110$). It should, however, be remembered that as this formula is for a European put, an American put might be worth more.

☆ 5.3 Informal derivation of the Black/Scholes equation†

From our binomial considerations, we know that the value of the call is just the present value of its expected pay-off. One vitally important discovery was that the discount rate for finding the present value was simply the risk-free rate. *There was no risk-premium in the calculation.* As that was the case, we are at liberty to assume that an option would have exactly the same price in a risk-averse as in a risk-neutral world. Hence we shall, conveniently, choose to value it under the assumption of risk neutrality, discounting its final pay-off at the risk-free rate.

How can we calculate the expected value of the pay-off, given a lognormal distribution, in order to derive the Black/Scholes equation? Without imposing any distribution, we may write the final call value equal to its expected pay-off as

$$c_T = \epsilon[\max(S_T - E), 0], \tag{5.9}$$

† This section may be omitted without loss of continuity.

where ϵ denotes an expected value for the items in brackets and the subscript T denotes the maturity date.

This equation encompasses two distinct possibilities:

(i) the option finishes worthless (at- or out-of-the-money) ($S_T \le E$); or
(ii) the option finishes in-the-money ($S_T > E$).

Let Φ be the probability that $S_T > E$. Then the call value at maturity may be expressed as a probability $(1 - \Phi)$ of zero, plus a probability Φ of the expected pay-off should it finish in-the-money. The latter is known as a *conditional expectation* and we shall denote it by $\tilde{\epsilon}$. The expected pay-off at maturity may then be written as,

$$c_T = (1 - \Phi)0 + \Phi\tilde{\epsilon}[S_T - E]$$
$$= \Phi\tilde{\epsilon}[S_T - E]. \tag{5.10}$$

Now let us rewrite the Black/Scholes equation, (5.4), in a way that is consistent with (5.10). By doing this, we shall know what is to be proved. First, because we are considering values at maturity rather than today, we may multiply the Black/Scholes equation by a compounding term, e^{rt}, to give

$$c_T = \{S\,e^{rt}N(d_1) - EN(d_2)\}.$$

If $N(d_2)$ is taken outside the bracket, we obtain

$$c_T = N(d_2)\left\{S\,e^{rt}\left[\frac{N(d_1)}{N(d_2)}\right] - E\right\}. \tag{5.11}$$

In order to prove that Eq. (5.10) is the same as the rewritten B/S formula (5.11), it is therefore sufficient to show that

$$\Phi = N(d_2) \tag{5.12}$$

and

$$\tilde{\epsilon}[S_T - E] = \left\{S\,e^{rt}\left[\frac{N(d_1)}{N(d_2)}\right] - E\right\}. \tag{5.13}$$

In other words, we need to show that $N(d_2)$ is just the probability (Φ) that the call finishes in-the-money, (5.12); and the expected in-the-money pay-off would be equal to $\{S\,e^{rt}[N(d_1)/N(d_2)] - E\}$. These two steps will occupy Sections 5.3.1 and 5.3.2 respectively. Readers who prefer to by-pass the mathematics, may go to Section 5.4 without loss of continuity.

☆ 5.3.1 THE PROBABILITY THAT THE CALL IS IN-THE-MONEY, $\Phi = N(d_2)$

We know that returns on the asset are (by assumption) normally distributed. To bring the call option into the money requires a price move of the asset from S_0 to E, which is a required return of $\log(E/S_0)$. For example, if $S_0 = 100$

and $E = 110$, then the required return to bring the call into the money is $\log(110/100) = 0.0953$, or 9.53%.

For assets that follow normal distributions we can write the standardized variable

$$Z = \frac{f - \mu}{\sigma^*}, \tag{5.14}$$

where f is a critical value of the variable, μ is its mean and σ^* is its standard deviation. The resulting Z variable has a mean of 0 and a variance of 1.

In our example f has the value of 9.53%, but what are μ and σ^*? Let us begin with σ^*. One of the Black/Scholes assumptions was that the variance of returns was proportional to time, so we may immediately write

$$\sigma^* = \sigma \sqrt{t}, \tag{5.15}$$

where σ is the annual standard deviation of returns and t is the time to maturity in years.

Now we must find an expression for μ. This is the expected return to buying and holding the share until the maturity of the option. The return is $\log(S_T/S_0)$, so we may write μ as

$$\mu = \epsilon \left[\log \left(\frac{S_T}{S_0} \right) \right]. \tag{5.16}$$

There is a well-known relationship between the expected value of a log and the log of an expectation.[3] For a variable y it is

$$\epsilon[\log(y)] = \log(\epsilon[y]) - 0.5\sigma_y^2. \tag{5.17}$$

Hence, we know that

$$\epsilon \left[\log \left(\frac{S_T}{S_0} \right) \right] = \log \left(\epsilon \left[\frac{S_T}{S_0} \right] \right) - 0.5\sigma^2 t. \tag{5.18}$$

It remains to determine the value of $\epsilon[S_T]$ in this equation. In a risk-neutral world the expected return on all assets is the risk-free rate, so that

$$\epsilon[S_T] = S_0 \, e^{rt}. \tag{5.19}$$

Substituting (5.18) and (5.19) into (5.16) we find that

$$\mu = \epsilon \left[\log \left(\frac{S_T}{S_0} \right) \right]$$

$$= \log \left(S_0 \, \frac{e^{rt}}{S_0} \right) - 0.5\sigma^2 t$$

$$= rt + \log \left(\frac{S_0}{S_0} \right) - 0.5\sigma^2 t$$

$$= rt - 0.5\sigma^2 t. \tag{5.20}$$

We can now form the standard normal variable Z:

$$Z = \frac{f - \mu}{\sigma^*}$$

$$= \frac{\log(E/S_0) - (rt - 0.5\sigma^2 t)}{\sigma\sqrt{t}}$$

However, this is the Z value required for calculating the size of the *left-hand* tail of the distribution. Because the distribution is symmetric, $-Z$ is the value required for calculating the size of the *right-hand* tail. Hence

$$-Z = \frac{\log(S_0/E) + rt - 0.5\sigma^2 t}{\sigma\sqrt{t}} \tag{5.21}$$

But $-Z$ in (5.21) is exactly the same as d_2 in the B/S equation (5.6), and $\Phi = N(-Z)$. Hence we have shown that $\Phi = N(d_2)$. The proof is complete.

Looking back to the example of Sec. 5.2, we see that $N(d_2)$ equalled 0.3568. We can therefore also now say that the probability of the call being in-the-money at maturity was 35.68%.

☆ **5.3.2   THE EXPECTED PAY-OFF, GIVEN THAT THE OPTION IS IN-THE-MONEY**

The expected pay-off, given that the option finishes in the money, is just the weighted average S_T value in the shaded portion of Fig. 5.7 less the cost of exercising, which is E.

We need to integrate the normal distribution to find this weighted average.

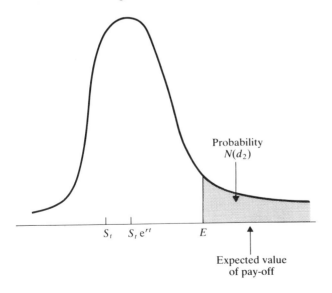

Figure 5.7   Call-option pay-off from a lognormal distribution

This is beyond the simple mathematics of this presentation, so we shall just give the result (see Jarrow and Rudd, p. 94):

$$\tilde{\epsilon}[S_T] = \epsilon[S_T \text{ for } S_T > E]$$

$$= S_0 \ e^{rt} \left[\frac{N(d_1)}{N(d_2)} \right], \tag{5.22}$$

where d_1 and d_2 are as defined above. Hence,

$$\tilde{\epsilon}[S_T - E] = \left\{ S \ e^{rt} \left[\frac{N(d_1)}{N(d_2)} \right] - E \right\},$$

which completes the proof.

We know for the example of Sec. 5.2 that $N(d_1)$ was equal to 0.4348 and $N(d_2)$ was equal to 0.3568. We therefore also now know that the conditionally expected share price in that example was equal to

$$\tilde{\epsilon}[S_T] = S_0 \ e^{rt} \left[\frac{N(d_1)}{N(d_2)} \right]$$

$$= 100 \ e^{0.08(0.5)} \left[\frac{0.4384}{0.3568} \right]$$

$$= 127.8844.$$

The corresponding conditional pay-off was $127.88 - 110 = 17.88$. This pay-off had a probability of 0.3568, so was unconditionally expected to be $0.3568 \times 17.88 = 6.38$. Its present value was therefore equal to $6.38 \ e^{-(0.08)(0.5)} = 6.13$. The value of the call was 6.13.

5.4 Sensitivity of option prices to inputs

Now that we have a formula for the call price, it is possible to demonstrate more clearly how the price is affected by the various inputs.

5.4.1 DELTA AND ELASTICITY

The sensitivity of the call price to the share price, i.e. the call delta, is very easily found from the B/S equation. Taking the first (partial) derivative, it is

$$\Delta_c = \frac{\partial c}{\partial S} = N(d_1).$$

In our previous example, the delta was therefore equal to 0.4384. For a one unit rise or fall in the share price, the call would rise or fall by 0.4384 units.

The sensitivity of the put price to the share price, i.e. the put delta, is

$$\Delta_p = \frac{\partial p}{\partial S} = N(d_1) - 1.$$

In our example it was therefore equal to $(0.4384 - 1) = -0.5616$.

These deltas, or hedge ratios, are very useful. They indicate the 'share-equivalence' of an option position. For example, a marketmaker in options will end the day with a particular 'book' of options—calls and puts, bought and sold, at a variety of different exercise prices and maturities. If the deltas are known, they may be summed for the whole book to give the aggregate exposure in share-equivalents. Using the data from our previous example, if options are on 100 shares and the marketmaker sells one call and sells one put, then the net exposure is equivalent to $100(-0.4384(-)-0.5616) = 12.32$ shares.

Table 5.1 uses the B/S model with a particular example to demonstrate how delta approaches zero at low share prices and rises to unity at high share prices. (See also Fig. 5.8.) The table also gives each call's elasticity with respect to the share price, defined as:

$$\text{Elasticity} = \left(\frac{\partial c}{\partial S}\right)\left(\frac{S}{c}\right).$$

The elasticity is a measure of the leverage obtained with an option; it is the percentage change in the call price for a 1% change in the share price. The table and Fig. 5.9 indicate that it ranges from a very large number (such as 20) out-of-the-money to a much smaller number (such as 4) in-the-money. In the limit the range is from infinity to 0.

Another useful concept, which is related to the elasticity, is an option beta. A share beta is a linear measure of its sensitivity to changes in the return on an index of all shares. For example, if a share has a beta of 1, then its return will on average move up and down exactly in line with the return on the index of shares. An option beta is simply equal to the share beta times the option elasticity, i.e.

$$\text{Option beta} = \text{Option elasticity} \times \text{Share beta}.$$

Option betas are therefore several times as large as share betas, indicating once again the riskiness of options.

Table 5.1 Sensitivity of call price to S

$E = 100$, $t = 0.25$, $r = 0.08$, $\sigma = 0.30$

S	c	Delta	Elasticity	Gamma
70	0.0530	0.0150	19.8534	0.00361
80	0.5371	0.1004	14.9534	0.01467
90	2.4945	0.3106	11.2076	0.02615
100	6.9615	0.5825	8.3677	0.02603
110	13.9553	0.8006	6.3105	0.01694
120	22.6458	0.9228	4.8897	0.00804
130	32.1750	0.9748	3.9338	0.00301

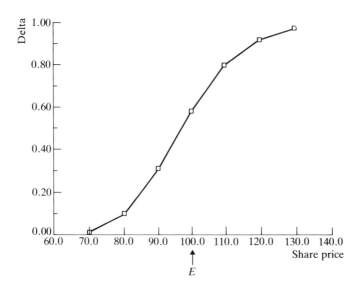

Figure 5.8   Call delta as a function of share price

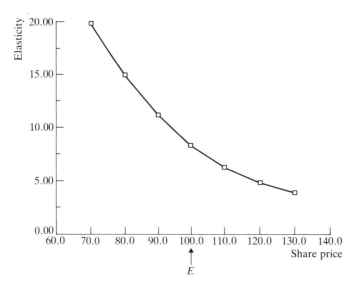

Figure 5.9   Call elasticity as a function of share price

5.4.2 SENSITIVITY OF DELTA TO S: GAMMA

As discussed in Chapter 3, delta changes continuously as the share price changes, and the rate of change is known as gamma. It is defined as the second derivative of the option price with respect to the share price. For a Black/Scholes call it is

$$\gamma_c = \frac{\partial^2 c}{\partial S^2}$$

$$= \frac{N'(d_1)}{S\sigma\sqrt{t}},$$

where

$$N'(d_1) = \frac{1}{\sqrt{2\pi}}e^{-(0.5\,d_1^2)}.$$

Gamma is seldom calculated but often discussed. Traders are just aware that they are exposed to a 'gamma risk'. For our example call ($S = 100$, $E = 110$, $t = 0.5$, $r = 0.08$, $\sigma = 0.3$), it would be

$$\gamma_c = \frac{(1/\sqrt{2\pi})e^{-(0.5)(-0.1547)^2}}{100(0.3)\sqrt{0.5}} = \frac{0.3942}{21.2132}$$

$$= 0.0186.$$

This means that the delta, initially 0.4384, will increase by 0.0186 to 0.4570 if the share price rises from 100 to 101. The analogous put gamma may be found by substituting $(1 - d_1)$ for d_1 in the above formula. Call gammas are always positive, while put gammas are always negative. Gammas were listed in Table 5.1 for a range of share prices, and the relationship of gamma to share prices in that example is plotted in Fig. 5.10.

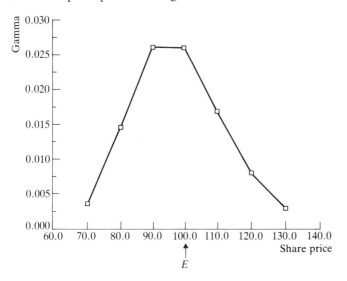

Figure 5.10   Call gamma as a function of share price

5.4.3 SENSITIVITY OF OPTION PRICE TO t: THETA

Theta is the sensitivity of the option price to time to expiry. For the Black/Scholes equation it is,

$$\theta_c = \frac{\partial C}{\partial t}$$

$$= \left[\frac{S\sigma}{2\sqrt{t}}\right] N'(d_1) + E\, e^{-rt} r N(d_2),$$

where $N'(d_1)$ is as defined above. This is always positive, i.e. the longer the call has to run, the higher its price.

Traders seldom calculate theta. They prefer to recalculate the B/S value with one day less to run to maturity, as that is intuitively (and financially!) more meaningful. Continuing our long-running example, we calculated above that $N'(d_1)$ was equal to 0.3942, so the theta of the call would be

$$\theta_c = \left[\frac{100(0.3)}{2\sqrt{0.5}}\right] [0.3942] + 110\, e^{-(0.08)(0.5)}(0.08)(0.3568)$$

$$= [21.2132][0.3942] + 3.0167$$
$$= 11.3789.$$

This means that the call price will fall by 11.379 for each reduction of one year in its time to maturity. Hence, per one day (linearly interpolating) it will fall by approximately $11.379/365 = 0.0312$.

It is easier just to recalculate the value of the call after one day, i.e. with $t = (181.5/365)$ days. The call price would be 6.1034 (compared with 6.1346 initially)—a fall of 0.0312, which is the same answer.

Table 5.2 and Fig. 5.11 indicate the general way in which a call price responds to time to maturity. They show that for an in-the-money option the time decay is almost linear. For an at-the-money option the rate of decay

Table 5.2 Sensitivity of call price to t

$E = 100, r = 0.08, \sigma = 0.30$

	Call price with		
t	$S = 90$	$S = 100$	$S = 110$
0.25	2.4945	6.9615	13.9533
0.20	1.9081	6.1371	13.1779
0.15	1.3082	5.2261	12.3570
0.10	0.7101	4.1803	11.4916
0.05	0.1813	2.8752	10.6141
0.01	0.0020	1.2372	10.0805

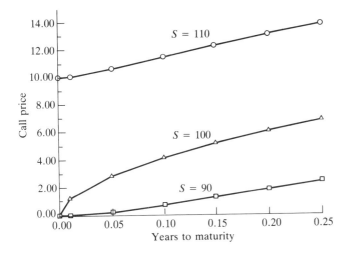

Figure 5.11   Call price as a function of time to maturity

accelerates, while for an out-of-the-money option it decelerates. This behaviour is simple to explain. The in-the-money option will probably remain in-the-money—it has little time value. The at-the-money option may 'flip' on the last day to finish in or out of the money: it is very time-sensitive in the last few days. The out-of-the-money option has some chance of 'coming good' prior to the last few days, but if it is out-of-the-money in those last days it has little chance of any pay-off—it has little time value left to erode and so has a flat profile.

Large traders are sometimes accused of trying to manipulate the share price on the last day, in order to flip their otherwise out-of-the-money options into-the-money (or the converse). This will be discussed in Chapter 15.

5.4.4   SENSITIVITY OF CALL PRICE TO INTEREST RATES: RHO

This is the least important of the sensitivities. While it is positive for options on shares, it is negative for some other assets, such as options on futures:

$$\rho_c = \frac{\partial c}{\partial r} = tE\, e^{-rt} N(d_2).$$

Table 5.3   Call price sensitivity to interest rate

$S = 100,\ E = 100,\ t = 0.25,\ \sigma = 0.30$

r	Call price	r	Call price
0.00	5.9803	0.12	7.4841
0.04	6.4605	0.16	8.0274
0.08	6.9615	0.20	8.5906

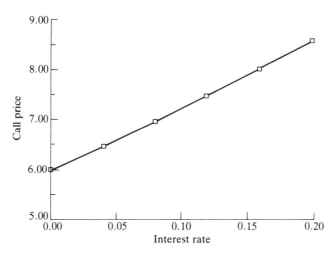

Figure 5.12 Call price as a function of interest rate

Its value, for our example, would be

$$p_c = (0.5)(110) \, e^{-(0.08)(0.50)}(0.3568) = 18.85.$$

Table 5.3 and Fig. 5.12 demonstrate that the call price is only modestly changed by relatively large changes in the interest rate.

5.4.5 SENSITIVITY OF CALL PRICE TO VOLATILITY: LAMBDA

The sensitivity of the call price to volatility is large and almost constant. The derivative is sometimes known as lambda, but also as kappa and vega. Most often it is simply called volatility risk. Formally, it is

$$\lambda_c = \frac{\partial C}{\partial \sigma} = S\sqrt{t} \, N'(d_1),$$

where $N'(d_1)$ is as defined above. For our example, the value of lambda would be

$$\lambda_c = (100)\sqrt{0.5} \, [0.3942] = 27.874.$$

Table 5.4 and Figure 5.13 indicate the approximately linear relationship between volatility and call price, using the example inputs. The sensitivity is

Table 5.4 Call price sensitivity to σ

$S = 100, \ E = 100, \ t = 0.25, \ r = 0.08$

σ	Call price	r	Call price
0.00	1.9801	0.30	6.9615
0.10	3.1204	0.40	8.9167
0.20	5.0163	0.50	10.8717

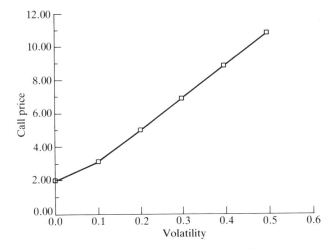

Figure 5.13   Call price as a function of volatility

extremely high, as expected, which confirms the great importance of forecasting σ in options pricing.

5.5   Summary

This chapter introduced and informally derived the Black/Scholes equation. The call value in the equation was shown to be equal to the present value of the expected pay-off. Because of the possibility of establishing a riskless hedge, that pay-off could be discounted to the present at the risk-free rate.

The formula was used to indicate, with examples, some important freatures of options that had already been introduced in Chapter 3. Call prices were found to be very sensitive to volatility, quite sensitive to share prices and to time remaining to maturity, but not very sensitive to interest rates.

Notes

1. Readers may think of exceptions. One 'asset' that may have a negative price is a futures-market spread between adjacent months. Another would be a spread between classes of oil, such as Brent and West Texas Intermediate.

2. The expected return per period is

$$\begin{aligned} \epsilon(R) &= m \log U + (1 - m)\log D \\ &= m \log U + (1 - m)(-\log U) \\ &= (2m - 1)\log U. \end{aligned}$$

The variance per period is

$$\begin{aligned} V(R) &= \epsilon(R^2) - (\epsilon(R))^2 \\ &= m(\log U)^2 + (1 - m)\log(D)^2 - (2m - 1)^2(\log U)^2 \\ &= m(\log U)^2 + (1 - m)(-\log U)^2 - (2m - 1)^2(\log U)^2 \\ &= (\log U)^2 - (2m - 1)^2(\log U)^2. \end{aligned}$$

The larger is n, the closer is m to 0.5 and the smaller the second term in the above expression for the variance. Hence we have

$$V(R) \approx (\log U)^2.$$

We assume that the variance increases linearly with time, so may be written in continuous form as

$$V(R) = \sigma^2 t/n.$$

Equating the discrete and continuous forms we have,

$$(\log U)^2 \approx \sigma^2 t/n.$$

Hence,

$$U \approx e^{\sigma \sqrt{t/n}}.$$

A more formal proof is given by Cox and Rubinstein (1985), pp. 196–201. Jarrow and Rudd (1983) show that a better approximation to the correct variance is given by

$$U = e^{\sigma \sqrt{t/n} + (r - 0.5\sigma^2)(t/n)},$$

where r is the continuously compounded rate of interest. This approximation is better because it has the correct first and second moments for finite n.

3. This is the relationship between geometric and arithmetic means, i.e. between $V[\log(x)]$ and $\log(V[x])$. If there is any variance at all, then the geometric mean is smaller. Here is an example:

y value	$\log(y)$
100	4.605
110	4.700
115	4.745
120	4.605
mean 106.25	4.664

Hence the geometric mean is $\exp(4.664) = 106.06$, which is smaller than the arithmetic mean of 106.25.

References

Black, F. and Scholes, M. (1973), 'The pricing of options and corporate liabilities', *Journal of Political Economy*, **81**, 637–59.

Cox. J. and Rubinstein, M. (1985), *Options Markets*, Prentice-Hall, Englewood Cliffs, New Jersey.

Jarrow, R. and Rudd, A. (1983), *Options Pricing*, Irwin, Homewood, Illinois.

APPENDIX

A5.1   Derivation of the Black/Scholes equation in continuous time

We derived the equation in the main text by finding the expected pay-off and then discounting it at the risk-free rate. Black and Scholes use an approach that is much closer to the one we used for the binomial model in Chapter 4, except that continuous time replaces discrete time: a continuously hedged position is set up and the model is solved by equating the hedge return to the risk-free rate.

Let the hedge portfolio consist of h shares each at a price of S and one sold call at a price of c. The value of the hedge portfolio is Q, and may be expressed as

$$Q = hS - c. \tag{A5.1}$$

The first derivative of Q with respect to S is

$$\frac{dQ}{dS} = h - \frac{dc}{dS}.$$

Rearranging, we have the instantaneous change in the value of the hedge portfolio as S changes, which is

$$dQ = h\,dS - dc. \tag{A5.2}$$

We assume that the stock price follows a random walk with drift. This is sometimes called a generalized Wiener process, and is denoted by

$$\frac{dS}{S} = \mu\,dt + \sigma\,dz, \tag{A5.3}$$

where μ is the drift per instant of time, dt is a small increment of time, σ is the standard deviation of returns and dz is a Wiener process.

Equation (A5.3) states that the proportional change in price of the stock (dS/S) is equal to a constant per period of time ($\mu\,dt$) plus a random term ($\sigma\,dz$).

The Wiener process is sometimes called *geometric Brownian motion*, which may be written as

$$dz = \Omega\sqrt{dt},$$

where Ω is a random drawing from a standard normal (zero mean, unit variance) distribution.

Denoting a variance by V, we may write the variance of (dS/S) as

$$V\left(\frac{dS}{S}\right) = V(\mu\,dt + \sigma\,dz). \tag{A5.4}$$

Since $\mu\,dt$ is constant, the variance simplifies to

$$V\left(\frac{dS}{S}\right) = V(\sigma\,dz) = \sigma^2\epsilon(dz^2),$$

where ϵ denotes an expectation of the bracketed terms.
But

$$\epsilon(dz^2) = \epsilon(\Omega\sqrt{dt})^2 = dt;$$

hence,

$$V\left(\frac{dS}{S}\right) = \sigma^2\,dt. \tag{A5.5}$$

We find that the variance of (dS/S) is simply $\sigma^2 dt$; i.e. the variance of proportional price changes is linearly related to time—the assumption that was expressed less formally in Chapters 4 and 5.

The next question is, given that the stock price follows the generalized Wiener process (A5.3), how does the call price change as the stock price changes? Clearly the call price depends on the stock price. Black and Scholes used a famous relationship known as Ito's lemma to solve this. If c depends on S as in Eq. (A5.3), then the lemma states that

$$dc = \frac{\partial c}{\partial S}\, dS + \frac{\partial c}{\partial t}\, dt + \frac{1}{2}\frac{\partial^2 C}{\partial S^2}\, \sigma^2 S^2 dt. \tag{A5.6}$$

Substituting (A5.6) into (A5.2) we have

$$dQ = h\, dS - \frac{\partial c}{\partial S}\, dS - \frac{\partial c}{\partial t}\, dt - \frac{1}{2}\frac{\partial^2 c}{\partial S^2}\, \sigma^2 S^2 dt. \tag{A5.7}$$

We know that, for small changes in S, the hedge ratio is just

$$h = \frac{\partial c}{\partial S}. \tag{A5.8}$$

Substituting (A5.8) into (A5.7) we therefore have

$$dQ = \frac{\partial c}{\partial S}\, dS - \frac{\partial c}{\partial S}\, dS - \frac{\partial c}{\partial t}\, dt - \frac{1}{2}\frac{\partial^2 c}{\partial S^2}\, \sigma^2 S^2 dt$$

$$= -\frac{\partial c}{\partial t}\, dt - \frac{1}{2}\frac{\partial^2 c}{\partial S^2}\, \sigma^2 S^2 dt. \tag{A5.9}$$

The change in the value of the hedge portfolio is now expressed in terms of the time increment, dt, changes in S and changes in c. But the latter depend in an explicit way on changes in S, so the only stochastic variable is S.

But the proportional change in the value of the hedge portfolio must equal the risk-free rate, hence:

$$\frac{dQ}{Q} = r\, dt$$

or

$$dQ = Qr\, dt, \tag{A5.10}$$

where r is the instantaneous risk-free rate. Hence,

$$Qr\, dt = -\frac{\partial c}{\partial t}\, dt - \frac{1}{2}\frac{\partial^2 c}{\partial S^2}\, \sigma^2 S^2 dt.$$

Substituting for Q from (A5.1) and using (A5.8) we find

$$\left(\frac{\partial c}{\partial S}\, S - c\right) r\, dt = -\frac{\partial c}{\partial t}\, dt - \frac{1}{2}\frac{\partial^2 c}{\partial S^2}\, \sigma^2 S^2 dt$$

which, after rearranging, is

$$\frac{\partial c}{\partial t} = rc - rS\frac{\partial c}{\partial S} - \frac{1}{2}\frac{\partial^2 c}{\partial S^2}\sigma^2 S^2. \tag{A5.11}$$

Equation (A5.11) is the Black/Scholes differential equation for a European call. We also know that at maturity a call option has the boundary value

$$c = \max(0, S - E). \tag{A5.12}$$

Black and Scholes use the heat-exchange equation from physics to solve for the price of the call, c, in (A5.11), subject to the boundary condition (A5.12). This gives the final Black/Scholes equation,

$$c = SN(d_1) - E\,e^{-rt}N(d_2), \tag{A5.13}$$

where $N(x)$ is a normal distribution probability,

$$d_1 = \frac{\log(S/E) + rt + 0.5\sigma^2 t}{\sigma\sqrt{t}} \tag{A5.14}$$

and

$$d_2 = d_1 - \sigma\sqrt{t}. \tag{A5.15}$$

6
Using models to price stock options

The previous two chapters were concerned with the development of binomial and Black/Scholes models. In this chapter we consider how to apply the models to stock options. There are three problems in doing so, which will be discussed in turn. They are:

(i) how to estimate volatility;
(ii) what to do about dividends; and
(iii) how to allow for the early-exercise value of American puts.

These matters may appear rather technical, but they are essential for valuing stock options.

6.1 Estimation of volatility

In the previous chapter it was shown that the option price was extremely sensitive to the level of volatility, which was defined as the standard deviation of returns. That is probably a familiar, statistical concept to many readers, but be warned: it is a *forecast* of volatility over the life of the option that we require, and not just an estimate of past volatility. To emphasize the difference, consider the outbreak of the Gulf War on 15 January 1991. In December 1990 this was already an event that could be predicted with some confidence. Stock prices had not been especially volatile in 1990, but could be expected to be more volatile in 1991. Forecasts of volatility based on the recent past were likely to be far too low.

There are basically two approaches to forecasting volatility. The first is to use the history of past returns to develop a forecast. Despite its limitations, the behaviour of volatility in the past may give some guidance to its future evolution. We shall name such forecasts *historic*. The second is to simply make a judgement of whether volatility will be relatively high or low, based upon likely future events, such as wars, elections, meetings of the G7 nations, etc. We shall name these forecasts *subjective*. Most practitioners combine these two

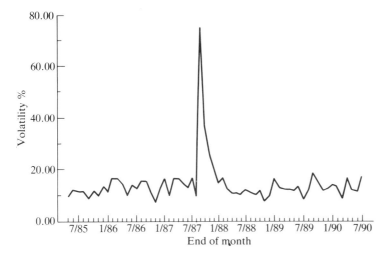

Figure 6.1 Volatility of the London FTSE Index (based upon 30 working days of data)

approaches: the historic forecast is used as a base, which is then subjectively adjusted for anticipated future events.

The prices of options, as observed in the marketplace, reflect a consensus view about the level of future volatility. As we shall see below, this consensus forecast may be revealed with an options pricing model and is known as the *implied volatility*. Because it is set by practitioners, it reflects both their historic and their subjective forecasts.

Before examining the alternative approaches, it is unfortunately necessary to recognize an inconsistency of logic. The options-pricing models of the previous chapters assumed that volatility was constant. If that were the case, there would be no forecasting problem! Everyone would know, for example, that the volatility for BP is 0.21, for IBM is 0.25, etc., for all times. Figure 6.1 gives the historic volatility for London's FTSE 100 Index over the 1985–90 period, based upon 30-day data. Clearly, it is not constant. Nevertheless, as we shall discuss in the next chapter, the assumption that it is constant over the life of an option may not lead to a large bias.

6.1.1 ESTIMATING VOLATILITY FROM PAST DATA

6.1.1.1 *Unweighted estimates*

The simplest approach is to take a sequence of past prices and dividends, calculate returns, calculate their standard deviation and annualize it. For example, Table 6.1 gives a sequence of 20 end-of-week prices and dividends for the British oil company BP. Returns are then calculated as $\log(\text{price}_t + \text{dividend}_t/\text{price}_{t-1})$. Note that the relevant date for the dividend is

Table 6.1   Weekly prices and returns for BP (23 August to 3 January 1992)

Week	Price	Dividend	Return r_i (%)	$(r_i - R)^2$
1	347.0			
2	352.5		1.5726	5.8456
3	346.0		− 1.8612	1.0323
4	337.0		− 2.6356	3.2055
5	331.0		− 1.7965	0.9049
6	336.5		1.6480	6.2159
7	339.0		0.7402	2.5134
8	341.0		0.5882	2.0547
9	352.0		3.1749	16.1608
10	331.0		− 6.1513	28.1547
11	328.0		− 0.9105	0.0043
12	332.5		1.3626	4.8744
13	324.0	5.6	− 0.8760	0.0010
14	311.0		− 4.0951	10.5617
15	302.0		− 2.9366	4.3740
16	291.0		− 3.7104	8.2093
17	297.5		2.2091	9.3286
18	279.0		− 6.4202	31.0813
19	277.0		− 0.7194	0.0158
20	290.5		4.7586	31.4025
Sum			− 16.0584	165.9406

$$\text{Mean return } (R) = (1/n)\Sigma_i r_i$$
$$= (1/19)(- 16.0584)$$
$$= - 0.8452\%$$

$$\text{Weekly s.d.* } (\sigma_w) = \sqrt{[1/(n - 1)]\Sigma_i (r_i - R)^2}$$
$$= \sqrt{[1/18](165.9406)}$$
$$= 3.0363\%$$

* s.d. = standard deviation.

that on which shareholders have to be registered in order to receive it, the so-called ex-dividend date. The mean return (R) for the series is $- 0.8452\%$ per week and the standard deviation (σ_w) is 3.0363% per week.

We shall continue to assume, as we did in Chapters 4 and 5, that the variance of returns increases in direct proportion to the passage of time. This means that the annual variance (σ^2) may be estimated as 52 times the weekly variance and the annual standard deviation (σ) as $\sqrt{52}$ times the weekly standard deviation (σ_w):

$$\sigma = \sigma_w \sqrt{52}.$$

Hence, for our example of BP,

$$\sigma = 3.0363 \sqrt{52} = 21.8951\%.$$

Our estimate of the historic volatility for BP is therefore about 22%. This could then be used with the Black/Scholes or binomial models as the forecast of future volatility.[1]

There is no consensus on how many weeks or months of data are required for estimation. The most common approach is to use about 20 weeks of data, with each week given an equal weight. However, it could be argued that more recent observations should be given a higher weight, as will now be discussed.

6.1.1.2 *Weighted estimates*

Suppose we have a set of weights, $g_1, g_2, \ldots, g_i, \ldots, g_n$, which together sum to unity; i.e.

$$\sum_i g_i = 1.$$

Then the estimated variance using these weights will be

$$\sigma^2 = \left(\frac{1}{n-1}\right) \sum_i (n g_i r_i - R)^2. \tag{6.1}$$

For example, with only three observations the g_i weights might be $(1/6)$, $(2/6)$ and $(3/6)$. That would be a linearly increasing set of weights. A more sophisticated set of weights would be an exponentially increasing sequence. If the most recent weight is set to a, the one prior to that is set to $a(1 - a)$, the one prior to that to $a(1 - a)^2$, etc., then the weights are exponential. a is required to be between 0 and 1. For example, suppose $a = 0.1$, then the sequence would be 0.1, 0.09, 0.081, . . .

These weights will only sum to unity if the series is infinitely long; i.e.

$$a + a(1 - a) + a(1 - a)^2 + a(1 - a)^3 + \cdots = 1, \tag{6.2}$$

where $0 < a \leq 1$.

Table 6.2 indicates the result of applying an exponential weighting scheme to the data on BP with $a = 0.1$. The sum of the 19 weights is equal to 0.8649 (see column 4), so they have each been divided by this to make them sum to unity in column 5 (which is headed 'Adjusted weight g_i').

In Table 6.2 the exponentially weighted standard deviation of 31.1% is much larger than the equally weighted estimate of 21.9%. This reflects the large deviation from the mean of two recent weekly returns.

More sophisticated time-series methods may be used to estimate the parameters underlying the evolution of the volatility, and an introduction to the time-series approach is given in the appendix to this chapter. Exponential weighting is just a very simple (and rather crude) example of such methods. One

Table 6.2   Weekly returns for BP with exponential weights for variance ($a = 0.1$)

Week	Return r_i (%)	i	Weight	Adjusted weight g_i	$(ng_i r_i - R)^2$
2	1.5726	18.00	0.0150	0.0174	1.8597
3	− 1.8612	17.00	0.0167	0.0193	0.0267
4	− 2.6356	16.00	0.0185	0.0214	0.0518
5	− 1.7965	15.00	0.0206	0.0238	0.0011
6	1.6480	14.00	0.0229	0.0264	2.8002
7	0.7402	13.00	0.0254	0.0294	1.5838
8	0.5882	12.00	0.0282	0.0327	1.4644
9	3.1749	11.00	0.0314	0.0363	9.2041
10	− 6.1513	10.00	0.0349	0.0403	14.9494
11	− 0.9105	9.00	0.0387	0.0448	0.0049
12	1.3626	8.00	0.0430	0.0498	4.5528
13	− 0.8760	7.00	0.0478	0.0553	0.0057
14	− 4.0951	6.00	0.0531	0.0614	15.4886
15	− 2.9366	5.00	0.0590	0.0683	8.7855
16	− 3.7104	4.00	0.0656	0.0759	20.2728
17	2.2091	3.00	0.0729	0.0843	19.2098
18	− 6.4202	2.00	0.0810	0.0937	111.9106
19	− 0.7194	1.00	0.0900	0.1041	0.3331
20	4.7586	0.00	0.1000	0.1156	127.6594

$R = -0.8452$ Sum $= 0.8649$ 1.0000   340.1643

Weighted weekly s.d.* $(\sigma_w) = \sqrt{[1/(n-1)]\Sigma_i(ng_i r_i - R)^2}$

$$= \sqrt{[1/18](340.1643)}$$
$$= 4.3472\%$$

Annual s.d. $= 4.3472\sqrt{52}$
$$= 31.3480\%$$

* s.d. = standard deviation.

useful, commonsense observation is worth mentioning now, however. If volatility is high, then it is likely to fall. If volatility is low, it is likely to rise. By 'high' and 'low' we mean relative to the long-term average. In other words, there is a tendency for the volatility to come back to its normal level, a phenomenon known as 'reversion to the mean'. This suggests the following approach. The last few days or weeks of data are used to give a short-term value for the standard deviation, denoted by σ_{short}. The last year or more of data are used to give a long-term value for the standard deviation, denoted σ_{long}. Then if the short-term reverts to the long-term at a proportion Φ per period, the forecast (σ^*) of the next period's volatility would be:

$$\sigma^* = \sigma_{short} + \Phi(\sigma_{short} - \sigma_{long}). \tag{6.3}$$

Note that for use in option pricing the period should coincide with the time to maturity of the option.

An example of mean-reverting volatility is given by the period after the Crash of October 1987: volatilities for shares reached 70%, as compared with long-term values of about 15%. It could be expected that the 70% would revert to 15% at some relatively smooth rate. Figure 6.1 shows that volatilities in the London market (as elsewhere) fell back to the mean quite rapidly. A logarithmic formulation of Eq. (6.3) is estimated in the appendix, which indicates that there was about 70% reversion to the mean over one month.

6.1.1.3 *Estimates based upon high/low range*

A third approach to estimating volatilities from past data is to use the daily high/low range of prices (see Garman and Klass, 1980; Beckers, 1983). Although the closing prices from day to day or week to week may be rather stable, the daily high/low range may be quite wide. Chartists are well aware that a high/low graph conveys much more information than a simple graph of closing prices. As an example, Fig. 6.2a indicates the daily high/low range for BP for 100 working days at the end of 1991 and the beginning of 1992. Tall bars, such as those occurring at the end of the series, are an indication of an increase in volatility.

The relevant high/low estimator for the variance of returns is

$$\sigma^2 = \frac{1}{n} \sum_t \left\{ 0.5 \left[\log\left(\frac{h_t}{l_t}\right) \right]^2 + 0.39 \left[\log\left(\frac{c_t}{c_{t-1}}\right) \right]^2 \right\}, \qquad (6.4)$$

where h denotes a high price, l denotes a low price and c denotes a closing price.

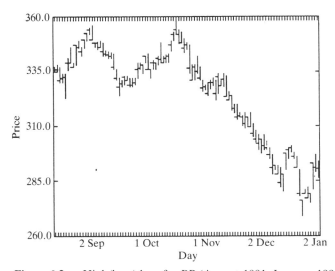

Figure 6.2a   High/low/close for BP (August 1991–January 1992)

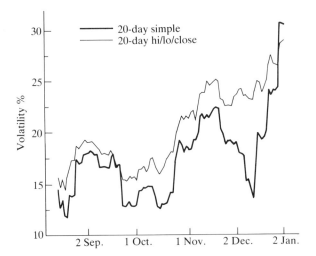

Figure 6.2b   Volatitlity of BP: comparison of high/low/close and simple estimates

This is an equally weighted estimator, but other weightings are possible. The choice of *n* periods is subjective and could be optimized from past data. Simple estimates of volatility may require at least 50 days of data, but the high/low estimator should work well with 20 days of data as long as the share is regularly traded (see Wiggins, 1991). Figure 6.2b compares the simple and high/low estimates for BP, using 20 days of data for each. The high/low estimates are larger for this sequence, which is just by chance. More importantly, they are less prone to sudden movements because they utilize more information than the simple estimates.

6.1.2   ESTIMATING THE IMPLIED VOLATILITY

Volatility is the only unknown input to the pricing equation. If it is assumed that the market price of an option is 'fair', then that price may be plugged into the model and the model solved for the *implied* volatility. The solution has to be accomplished iteratively, i.e. by trial and error. A first guess of the correct σ is made and the model solved for the option price. If that price is too high, the σ estimate is reduced and the option price found again. This process is repeated until model and market prices are the same.[2] Assuming the model to be correct, the implied volatility thus found is a market consensus forecast of the actual volatility.

We may use the BP data again to demonstrate this procedure. BP options in London on 3 January 1992 (the last day of our price series) had market prices as shown in Table 6.3. The table also gives (in brackets) Black/Scholes prices for the options, based upon a volatility of 0.22. The model overvalues all the calls by a large margin, except those expiring in January, and it undervalues all the puts.

Table 6.3 Market and model prices for BP on 3 January 1992

Expiry price	Calls						Puts					
	Jan.		Apr.		July		Jan.		Apr.		July	
280	13	(14)	20	(26)	26	(34)	4	(1)	9	(6)	12	(8)
300	3	(3)	10	(14)	16	(23)	13	(10)	20	(14)	24	(15)

Notes:
1. $S = 291$, $r = 0.11$ per annum (0.1044 continuous), $\sigma = 0.21$, expiry in days: Jan. 19, Apr. 110, July 201.
2. B/S model prices in brackets.

The April 300 call will be treated as the 'marker' for all the other prices, since it was nearest to the money and had just over three months remaining to expiration. We shall therefore search for the volatility that would have equated the model and market prices for this option. The trial-and-error values are given in Table 6.4. Our first guess is $\sigma = 0.21$, for which the model price of 13.5 pence is too high. So, for our second guess we choose the lower value of $\sigma = 0.18$, leading to a price of 11.6 pence, which is still 1.6 pence above the market price of 10 pence. If a change of 0.03 in σ leads to a change of 1.9 pence in the call price, then to reduce the call price by a further 1.6 pence might require (by simple proportions) a further change of $(1.6/1.9) \times 0.03 = 0.025$ in σ. Hence, the next guess for σ is $0.180 - 0.025 = 0.155$

Setting σ to 0.155, the model price is 10.0, which is exactly equal to the market price. The implied volatility is therefore about 0.16. That is surprisingly different from the historic estimate of 0.22. The implied volatilities presented in Table 6.5 for all the BP options show a remarkably wide range from 0 to 0.32, with the call values much smaller than the put values. The zero volatility for the July 280 call indicates that its market price was less than the lower bound of $S - PV(E)$.

Clearly something is wrong. There are two reasons why the calls have such low volatilities and the puts have such high ones. The first is that dividends of 5.6 pence were due to shareholders on 24 February and 11 May. These reduce the value of April and July call options and increase the value of the corresponding puts. The second is that these options are American: we know that

Table 6.4 Finding the implied volatility for April 300 call (market price = 10)

Guess of volatility	Model price
0.210	13.5
0.180	11.6
0.155	10.0

Table 6.5 Implied volatilities for BP options on 3 January 1992

	Calls			Puts		
Expiry price	Jan.	Apr.	July	Jan.	Apr.	July
280	0.15	0.08	0	0.34	0.28	0.28
300	0.22	0.16	0.14	0.33	0.32	0.33

American puts are worth more than the European puts assumed by the Black/Scholes model. Hence the model will give unreasonably large implied volatilities for puts.

These two issues are addressed in the other two sections of this chapter, but for the moment, let us ignore these problems. A knowledge of the implied volatility may be extremely useful for several reasons:

1. If the analysis of BP were correct, then the calls would be undervalued and the puts overvalued relative to the 0.22 estimate for historic volatility. A trading strategy would be indicated—buy calls, sell puts, or do both.
2. All options of a given maturity should have the same implied volatility, because they all reflect pay-offs to the same distribution of share prices at maturity. Looking at the January calls, which are unaffected by dividends so should be correctly priced by the model, it appears that the 280 option ($\sigma = 0.15$) is undervalued relative to the 300 option ($\sigma = 0.22$). A low-risk strategy would be to sell the 300 and buy the 280. The risk could be made. even lower if the spread were made delta-neutral, i.e. with value unaffected by changes in the share price. To find the deltas, we need to know the 'true' volatility. An average of the 300 and 280 options would give $\sigma = 0.185$. The deltas from the Black/Scholes model with this volatility would be 0.28 for the 300 call and 0.86 for the 280 call.

Let x and y be the numbers of each option to be bought, and let Δ_x and Δ_y be their respective deltas. Then, for delta neutrality in the combined position we require

$$x \Delta_x + y \Delta_y = 0.$$

Hence,

$$-\frac{x}{y} = \frac{\Delta_y}{\Delta_x}.$$

The ratio of the numbers of the two options (one bought, the other sold) is equal to the inverse ratio of their deltas. The relation of x to y is

$$y = -x \frac{\Delta x}{\Delta y}.$$

In our example, let x be the 280 call and let y be the 300 call. If one 280 call is purchased ($x = 1$), then

$$y = -1\left(\frac{0.86}{0.28}\right) = 3.07.$$

For every 280 call purchased we therefore should sell three 300 calls in order to obtain delta neutrality. The 280 call is more sensitive to movements in the share price, so we must have less of it relative to the position in the 300 call.[3]

3. A knowledge of the implied volatility is useful to financial institutions and intermediaries when hedging. For example, a marketmaker's back office may use the implied volatility to compute the hedge ratio for each option and derive the aggregate exposure in terms of underlying shares.

6.1.3 SUMMARY ON VOLATILITY

Volatility is difficult to forecast but is the key input to option pricing. Almost every practitioner uses the implied volatility to reveal the consensus forecast, but the quality of that consensus will depend on the information used by each participant. If all participants just used implied volatility, then no one would be doing any forecasting and the consensus would become useless. The most widespread approach therefore has the following steps:

(i) estimate a historic volatility, possibly using some weighting scheme;
(ii) adjust the forecast according to events (such as elections) which had an abnormal impact on the estimation period or which may have such an impact in the next period;
(iii) adjust more distant volatilities to be nearer to the long-term mean (if necessary);
(iv) further adjust them if they are widely different from the consensus indicated by the implied volatilities.

6.2   Adjusting for dividends

Dividends have a large impact on option prices. When a dividend is paid, the share price falls. In the absence of any tax effects, the fall should be exactly equal to the dividend. A dividend is a pay-out to a shareholder which the holder of a call option does not get, yet suffers the fall in share price. Conversely, the holder of a put option will benefit from the fall in share price that follows a dividend. Dividends that will be paid over the lives of options therefore reduce call prices and raise put prices.

If a dividend is sufficiently large, it will be profitable to exercise a call just before the dividend is due. In most countries, shares go ex-dividend before the actual payment is made, so the fall in share price occurs on the 'xd' date. Exercising a call at that time yields an extra dividend, but results in the loss of time-value on the call.

Suppose that there is no volatility ($\sigma = 0$). Let S be the share price, let E be the exercise price and let a dividend of $\hat{D}$ be due for payment. The share will fall to $(S - \hat{D})$ on the xd date. We assume that the call is in-the-money ($S > E$). Then:

(i) exercising just before the xd date gives a pay-off after dividend payment equal to $(S - \hat{D}) - E + D = S - E$;
(ii) not exercising, but waiting to maturity, results in a value today (when there is no volatility) equal to the lower bound of $(S - \hat{D}) - \text{PV}(E)$.

With zero volatility, exercise will therefore be worth while if

$$S - E > S - \hat{D} - \text{PV}(E).$$

Hence, it requires that

$$\hat{D} > E - \text{PV}(E). \tag{6.5}$$

This implies that early exercise is more likely if: (i) the dividend ($\hat{D}$) is large relative to the exercise price (E); and (ii) the option does not have long to run, so that $\text{PV}(E) \approx E$. We also know that exercise is more likely if (iii) volatility is low, so that the time value given up by exercise is low.

As an example, suppose we have $S = 102$, $E = 100$, $t = 0.1$, $r = 0.1$. We can now find that particular dividend (D^*) that would result in early exercise if volatility were zero. It would be

$$D^* > E - \text{PV}(E)$$
$$> 100 - 100\, e^{-0.1(0.1)}$$
$$> 1.00.$$

For this extreme case of zero volatility, a dividend exceeding 1% would result in early exercise. The evidence from the markets is that early exercise does occur for those calls that are in-the-money and have only a short time to maturity.

We already saw in Chapter 4 that the binomial model could easily be adjusted to take account of dividends. We shall therefore only be concerned here with adjusting the Black/Scholes model. There are two approaches: the first is to assume that the dividend is paid continuously, and the second is to evaluate the options at the ex-dividend date to see if exercise would be valuable. We will consider each in turn.[4]

6.2.1 MERTON'S CONTINUOUS DIVIDEND ADJUSTMENT

If the dividend is paid continuously, then the share price will not rise at the investors' required rate of return, but at that rate *less* the dividend rate. This does not worry the holders of shares because they are compensated by the dividend. It does worry the holders of call options on the shares, because they do not get the dividend. The share price, as viewed by an option player, has now to be discounted by the rate of dividend. The Black/Scholes model becomes

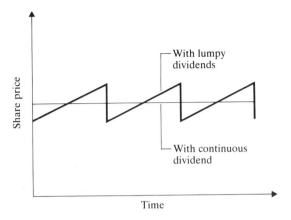

Figure 6.3 Behaviour of actual share price and behaviour assumed by Merton's model

$$c = S\,e^{-\delta t}N(d_1) - E\,e^{-rt}N(d_2), \qquad (6.6)$$

where δ is the continuous dividend rate and d_1, d_2 are as before, except that $S\,e^{-\delta t}$ replaces S everywhere.

The continuous dividend rate (yield) can easily be derived from actual dividends. For example, if a dividend of 4% is paid once per year, the continuous equivalent is $\delta = \log(1.04) = 0.039$.

Equation (6.6) was discovered by Merton (1973). It has very wide application to all dividend-paying assets, such as currencies (which pay the short-term foreign interest rate) and bonds (which pay the long-term domestic interest rate).

The equation's performance for stock options depends on the frequency of dividend payments. If they are frequent, such as those on stock indices with many shares (e.g. the S&P 500), then the equation performs quite well. If, however, dividends are infrequent and relatively large, such as the twice annual dividends on most British shares, then the equation is a relatively poor approximation. Figure 6.3 contrasts, in outline, the share price assumed by the Merton model with an actual share price. The Merton model is liable to underprice calls in some periods and overprice them in others. In general, it will be better to make an adjustment which allows for the lumpiness of dividends, a subject to which we turn in the next section.

6.2.2 PSEUDO-AMERICAN ADJUSTMENT FOR DIVIDENDS

The pseudo-American approach,[5] first outlined by Black (1975), compares the value of an option that is 'killed' just before the xd date with one that is allowed to run to maturity. The correct value of the call will be the higher of the two.

We assume, at first, that there is only one xd date over the life of the option. Figure 6.4 indicates how the share price will fall after time interval t_1, when the

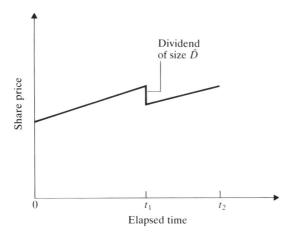

Figure 6.4   Share price behaviour for pseudo-American calls

share goes ex-dividend, but that the option potentially continues for a whole period of time t_2.

The buyer of an American call is now considered to have effectively two European options. The first call, worth c_{short}, expires at t_1, immediately after which the stock pays a dividend of $\hat{D}$. The call price equation may be written in outline as

$$c_{\text{short}} = f(S - D\,e^{-rt_1}, t_1, r, \sigma, E - \hat{D}), \qquad (6.7)$$

where $f(\ldots)$ denotes a functional relationship.

The stock price is discounted by the present value of the dividend, but this is offset as the exercise price is reduced by the payment of the dividend.

The second call, worth c_{long}, expires at t_2 and pays no dividend. It may be written in outline as

$$c_{\text{long}} = f(S - D\,e^{-rt_1}, t_2, r, \sigma, E). \qquad (6.8)$$

As before, the stock price is discounted by the present value of the dividend, but this time there is no receipt of the dividend to reduce the exercise price.

As the holder of the American call option has effectively two mutually exclusive European call options, the call will be valued today at the higher of the two, i.e.

$$C = \max(c_{\text{short}}, c_{\text{long}}). \qquad (6.9)$$

Two Black/Scholes evaluations are made and the larger value is chosen as the correct call value.

This approach may be extended to situations where more than one dividend will be paid over the life of the option. Suppose that there are two such dividends, paying $\hat{D}_1$ and $\hat{D}_2$ at times t_1 and t_2 respectively. There is now a need to evaluate three alternatives: exercise at the first xd date, giving a value of c_{short} today; exercise at the second xd date, giving a value of c_{medium} today; and exercises at maturity, giving a value of c_{long} today.

The share price in the Black/Scholes model must now be discounted by the two dividends, so it becomes

$$S - \hat{D}_1 e^{-rt_1} - \hat{D}_2 e^{-rt_2}.$$

The three options are then as follows. Firstly, the short option is

$$c_{short} = f(S - \hat{D}_1 e^{-rt_1} - \hat{D}_2 e^{-rt_2}, t_1, r, \sigma, E - \hat{D}_1 - \hat{D}_2 e^{-r(t_2 - t_1)}). \quad (6.10)$$

In this case the early exercise results in a benefit of the dividend $\hat{D}_1$, which is immediately paid, and also of the present value at that time of $\hat{D}_2$. Hence, the exercise price is adjusted to become

$$E - \hat{D}_1 - \hat{D}_2 e^{-r(t_2 - t_1)}.$$

Secondly, the medium option is

$$c_{medium} = f(S - \hat{D}_1 e^{-rt_1} - \hat{D}_2 e^{-rt_2}, t_2, r, \sigma, E - \hat{D}_2). \quad (6.11)$$

In this case there is only the benefit of one dividend $\hat{D}_2$, which is immediately paid on exercise, so the exercise price becomes $E - \hat{D}_2$.

Thirdly, the long option is

$$c_{long} = f(S - \hat{D}_1 e^{-rt_1} - \hat{D}_2 e^{-rt_2}, t_3, r, \sigma, E). \quad (6.12)$$

In this case, no adjustment of the exercise price is necessary, as the option runs to maturity.

Finally, the American call is valued as the largest of all three call values:

$$C = \max(c_{short}, c_{medium}, c_{long}). \quad (6.13)$$

The pseudo-American adjustment is very widely used and relatively accurate. It will, however, undervalue the call slightly. The reason is that it *assumes* that the holder has to decide today when the call will be exercised (if at all). In fact, that choice remains open until just before each of the xd dates.

6.2.3 COMPARATIVE EXAMPLE ON DIVIDEND ADJUSTMENTS

The following example demonstrates the alternative dividend adjustments and shows that quite different estimated call values may result. Suppose we have a share with a price of $S = 100$, which will pay a single dividend of 2 in 0.1 year ($t_1 = 0.1$). A call is written at an exercise price of $E = 100$, which expires in $t_2 = 0.2$ years. The continuous interest rate is 10% ($r = 0.1$) and the volatility is 20% ($\sigma = 0.2$).

1. If the dividend is ignored entirely, the value of the call is estimated to be

$$c = SN(d_1) - Ee^{-rt_2}N(d_2) = 4.61.$$

2. Let us assume that Merton's correction is used. If the dividend of 2 is the only one paid annually, then the estimated dividend yield in continuous form is log(1.02) = 0.0198. The equation is

$$c = S\,e^{-\delta t_2}N(d_1) - E\,e^{-r t_2}N(d_2)$$

where $\delta = 0.0198$. Hence, we find that

$$c = 4.37.$$

3. Suppose we find c_{short} and c_{long} for the pseudo-American value, then we have

$$
\begin{aligned}
c_{short} &= f(S - \hat{D}\,e^{-r t_1}, t_1, r, \sigma, E - \hat{D}) \\
&= f(100 - 2\,e^{-0.1(0.1)}, 0.1, 0.1, 0.2, 100 - 2) \\
&= 2.99.
\end{aligned}
$$

$$
\begin{aligned}
c_{long} &= f(S - \hat{D}\,e^{-r t_1}, t_2, r, \sigma, E) \\
&= f(100 - 2\,e^{-0.1(0.1)}, 0.2, 0.1, 0.2, 100) \\
&= 3.50.
\end{aligned}
$$

Hence

$$
\begin{aligned}
C &= \max(2.99, 3.50) \\
&= 3.50.
\end{aligned}
$$

4. Finally, suppose we use the binomial model under the assumption that a dividend of 2 will be 1.98% of the share price at the xd date.[6] The result is

$$C = 3.66.$$

If we take the binomial as the correct answer, then the pseudo-American value is about 4% low, the Merton value is 19% high and the non-adjusted value is 26% high.

6.2.6 CONCLUSION ON DIVIDEND ADJUSTMENT

We conclude that ignoring dividends can be dangerous: a pseudo-American or binomial correction will be necessary for American calls if dividends are large. By contrast, dividends will reduce the value of early exercise for puts, so only the share price need be adjusted in their evaluation. However, American puts have other problems, which form the subject of the next section.

6.3 Corrections for American puts

In most texts, a discussion of American puts is left until a late chapter. Unfortunately, the Black/Scholes model is highly inadequate with respect to their valuation and the user of the model is forced to make some adjustment. Naturally, the simpler the adjustment the better.

To recapitulate, the problem is that early exercise may be profitable for a put,

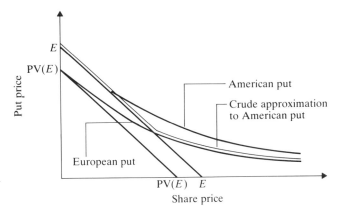

Figure 6.5 Comparison of European and American put price lines

especially in the absence of dividends. There is no analytic equivalent of the B/S equation that allows for this, because in principle exercise could occur at almost any date between today and the maturity of the option. One approach would simply be to abandon the B/S model and use the binomial model. The latter is accurate because the exercised value can be considered at each node of the tree. However, that is slow. Some approximation based upon the B/S equation may be tolerably accurate, and much faster.

Figure 6.5 contrasts the European (i.e. B/S) price line for a put with the American price line. The displacement of the European to the American line appears to be a relatively smooth function of how far the put is into the money. A first approximation would be to impose the higher of the B/S value or $(E - S)$, the exercise value of the put. That would at least give the thin line in Fig. 6.5. Further adjustments may be based upon adding some factor to the B/S model; i.e.

$$P_A = P_E + FA, \tag{6.14}$$

where P_A is the American put price, P_E is the European put price, and FA is the difference in value between European and American puts.

There are two ways in which FA can be calculated. The simplest, published by Hull and White in 1988 but widely used before then, is the so-called control-variate approach. Two binomial estimates of the value of the put are computed, one estimate being European and other American. The difference between the two estimates is FA. Surprisingly, although about 50 iterations are required for convergence of the binomial to the B/S model, an acceptable estimate of FA can be obtained with only 10–20 iterations. Hull and White suggest 25 iterations, but my experiments suggest that 10 are sufficient for options with a few weeks to run, and 15 for longer options.

The second way to calculate FA is from an equation based upon the same variables as the B/S equation. Johnson (1983) gave one such equation, which is too complicated to report here but is very fast, although it does not work well for long-term options. Geske and Johnson (1984) showed how considering exercise at three or four intermediate times could be used for the projection of a limit price that was accurate. That approach is slow and rather complicated to program. Macmillan (1986), publicized by Barone-Adesi and Whaley (1987), gave a relatively simple (if messy) equation for FA. The intuition is that FA is itself the value of an option: it is the option to exercise early and may be analysed along B/S lines as follows.[7]

Early exercise will occur if the stock price, S, falls below some critical level S^{**}, as shown in Fig. 6.6. Below S^{**} the put is therefore simply given its intrinsic value, i.e.

$$P_A = E - S \quad \text{for } S \leq S^{**}. \tag{6.15}$$

Above the critical stock price, the put value is computed as

$$P_A = P_E + FA \quad \text{for } S > S^{**}. \tag{6.16}$$

The correction factor (FA) depends on how far the stock price (S) is above the critical level (S^{**}). It is

$$FA = A_1 \left(\frac{S}{S^{**}} \right)^{q_1}, \tag{6.17}$$

where

$$q_1 = 0.5 \left[-(M - 1) - \sqrt{(M - 1)2 + 4\left(\frac{M}{W}\right)} \right]$$

$$A_1 = -\left(\frac{S^{**}}{q_1} \right) N(d_1^{**})$$

in which d_1^{**} is the Black/Scholes d_1 value at $S = S^{**}$

$$M = \frac{2r}{\sigma^2}$$

$$W = 1 - e^{-rt}.$$

The critical stock price (S^{**}) is found by an iterative procedure as follows:

(a) Calculate q_1 from the equation above, which is a constant.
(b) Guess a value for S^{**}, the critical stock price, and calculate A_1 from the equation above.
(c) See whether the exercised value, $E - S$, exactly equals the approximated un-exercised value; i.e. whether

$$E - S = P_E + A_1 \left(\frac{S}{S^{**}} \right)^{q_1}.$$

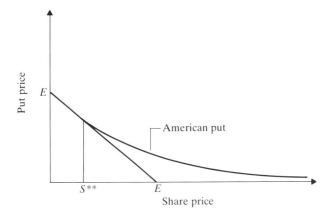

Figure 6.6 Demonstration of critical stock price S^{**}

This may be simplified for $S = S^{**}$ to whether

$$E - S = P_E + A_1.$$

If this equality holds, then the critical stock price S^{**} has been found. If the equality does not hold, choose a new S^{**} and try again at step (b). New S^{**} values may be chosen by simple proportions (as for implied volatilities).

This approach may be clarified with an example.[8] Suppose we have $S = E = 100$, $t = 0.25$, $r = 0.12$ and $\sigma = 0.20$. Then we have

$$q_1 = 0.5\left[-(M-1) - \sqrt{(M-1)2 + 4\left(\frac{M}{W}\right)} \right]$$

$$= 0.5\left[-(6-1) - \sqrt{(6-1)2 + 4\left(\frac{6}{1 - e^{-0.12(0.25)}}\right)} \right]$$

$$= -16.966.$$

From the standard B/S model we have (in the first row of Table 6.6),

$$P_E = 2.626.$$

Now we must choose a starting value for the critical stock price, S^{**}. We know that it needs to be an in-the-money value, so we begin with $S^{**} = 92$. The result is shown in the second row of Table 6.6. The approximated value of the American put (P_A^*) is 8.497, but the exercised value would be $100 - 92 = 8$. The chosen S^{**} is therefore too high, so we try $S^{**} = 90$ in the third row of the table. The result is $P_A^* = 9.536$, which is too small. By simple proportions from the first two attempts, we next choose $S^{**} = 90.97$ and the result is that

Table 6.6   Iterative values in finding S^{**}, the critical stock price

$S = E = 100; t = 0.25; r = 0.12; \sigma = 0.20$

S^{**}	P_E	$N(d_1)$	A_1	P_A^*	$E - S^{**}$
100	2.626	0.36			0
92	6.816	0.69	1.681	8.497	8
90	8.263	0.76	1.273	9.536	10
90.97	7.543	0.72	1.501	9.044	9.03

Note: $P_A^* = P_E + A_1$ in this table, because A_1 is exactly equal to the correction factor (FA) at the critical stock price S^{**}.

$P_A^* = 9.04$. This is very close to the exercised value of 9.03. We therefore have found the critical stock price to be about 90.97.

Having found the critical stock price, we can now use it to calculate FA for the actual stock price of $S = 100$. We have

$$FA = A_1 \left(\frac{S}{S^{**}}\right)^{q_1} = 1.501 \left(\frac{100}{90.97}\right)^{-16.966}$$

$$= 0.301.$$

Hence, the approximated value of the American put is

$$P_A = P_E + FA = 2.626 + 0.301$$
$$= 2.927.$$

6.3.1   SUMMARY ON AMERICAN PUTS

If speed is not vital, the binomial or another numerical approach is to be recommended. The binomial method is simple, accurate and can easily be adapted for dividends. If speed is important, then the Macmillan method works well. The control-variate approach is a little slower, but easier to understand than the Macmillan method. It involves the estimation with a small number of iterations of two binomial put values, one European and the other American. The difference is then added to the Black/Scholes put value.

6.4   Summary

This chapter showed that a knowledge of the Black/Scholes model is not enough to go and trade options. The trader must be able to forecast volatility. To make such a forecast, the trader is likely to use a historic estimate, modified by a personal view of the future and taking into account the market's consensus as revealed by the implied volatility. The trader must also adjust any model for dividends that will be paid over the life of the option. The adjustments needed

Table 6.7 Implied volatilities for BP options corrected for dividends and early exercise

	Calls			Puts		
Expiry price	Jan.	Apr.	July	Jan.	Apr.	July
280	0.15	0.19	0.20	0.30	0.24	0.22
300	0.21	0.20	0.21	0.30	0.25	0.25

Note: Forecast dividends of 5.6 pence to be paid to holders of the share on 24 February (52 days) and 11 May (129 days).

for discrete dividends are relatively simple and quite accurate. Finally, most puts are American, allowing early exercise. The B/S model requires a further correction for this, but the binomial method does not.

6.4.1 A FINAL EXAMPLE

Now that the issues of dividends and American puts have been clarified, we may close this chapter by recalculating in a more appropriate way the implied volatilities of the BP options. Table 6.7 gives the implied volatilities for the BP example, with dividends of 5.6 pence on 24 February and 11 May and with early exercise allowed for the puts. The computation is with the binomial method.

The implied volatilities now range from 0.15 to 0.30, with the January puts and calls being somewhat inconsistent and the puts in other months still having larger volatilities than the calls. Nevertheless, the implied volatilities are 'better behaved' than they were before we made adjustments for dividends and early exercise.

Notes

1. Note that if daily data had been used, the procedure to annualize the daily variance would require a multiple of 250, since there are about 250 working days in a year.
2. The procedure may be speeded-up by making a good initial guess. Brenner and Subramanyam (1988) suggest that a good approximation is
$$\sigma \approx (C/S)(1/0.398\sqrt{t}).$$
3. The degree of mispricing in this example is very small, because the options are only 19 days from maturity. The potential gain from the delta-neutral spread is only 1p per 280 option, which would not be sufficient to cover transactions costs. However, the principles of this example are correct.
4. There are other approaches. In particular, Roll (1977) noted that the option to exercise a call early in order to obtain the dividend is 'an option on an option'. Evaluation of this involves a bivariate normal distribution. See Chapter 10 of Jarrow and Rudd (1983).
5. This section follows Jarrow and Rudd (1983).
6. In a risk-neutral world with an interest rate of 0.1, the share price will have risen to 101.005 after 0.1 year. A dividend of 2 at that time is therefore equivalent to $2*100/101.005 = 1.98\%$ of the risk-neutral share price.
7. Barone-Adesi and Whaley (1987) give a generalization which allows for the price of a futures

contract to exceed the spot price by less than the interest rate. Such a complication is not helpful at this stage of our analysis.
8. The Barone-Adesi and Whaley (1987) paper is presented in a rather complicated way.

References

Barone-Adesi, G. and Whaley, R. (1987), 'Efficient analytical approximation of American option values', *Journal of Finance*, **42**, 301–20.

Beckers, S. (1983), 'Variances of security price returns based on high, low and closing prices', *Journal of Business*, **56**, 97–112.

Black, F. (1975), 'Fact and fantasy in the use of options', *Financial Analysts Journal* (July/August), 36–72.

Brenner, M. and Subramanyam, M. (1988), 'A simple formula to compute the ISD', *Financial Analysts Journal*, **44**, 80–3.

Garman, M. and Klass, M. (1980), 'On the estimation of security price volatilities from historical data', *Journal of Business*, **53**, 67–78.

Geske, R. and Johnson, H. (1984), 'The American put valued analytically', *Journal of Finance*, **39**, 1511–24.

Hull, J. and White, A. (1988), 'The use of the control variate technique in option pricing', *Journal of Financial and Quantitative Analysis*, **23**, 237–51.

Jarrow, R. and Rudd, A. (1983), *Option Pricing*, Irwin, Homewood, Illinois.

Johnson, H. (1983), 'An analytical approximation for the American put price', *Journal of Financial and Quantitative Analysis*, **18**, 141–8.

Macmillan, L. (1986), 'An analytical approximation for the American put price', *Advances in Futures and Options Research*, **1**, 119–39.

Merton, R. (1973), 'The theory of rational option pricing', *Bell Journal of Economics and Management Science*, **4**, 141–83.

Roll, R. (1977), 'An analytic valuation formula for unprotected American call options on stocks with known dividends', *Journal of Financial Economics*, **5**, 3–51.

Wiggins, J. (1991), 'Empirical tests of the bias and efficiency of the extreme-value variance estimator for common stocks', *Journal of Business*, **64**, 417–32.

APPENDIX

A6.1   Time-series models and volatility

In this appendix we shall outline two time-series models and estimate the parameters of one, using British stockmarket data. We then also examine the way in which the implied volatility changes over time and compare its forecasting performance with that of the estimated time-series model.

A6.1.1   TIME-SERIES

Theory tells us little about the appropriate kind of time-series model. The basic presumption is that this period's volatility is a function of past volatility and that it is mean-reverting. In his review, Taylor (1991) divides the models that have been used into two main kinds: autoregressive random variance (ARV) models, mainly found in the finance literature; and generalized autoregressive conditionally heteroscedastic (GARCH) models, mainly found in the econometric literature. A typical ARV formulation is:

$$\log(\sigma_t) = \log(a) + \Phi[\log(\sigma_{t-1}) - \log(a)] + \eta_t, \tag{A6.1}$$

where a, Φ and Ω are constants and η_t is a normally distributed disturbance term (with mean zero and constant variance). a in this model is the long-term median volatility, to which the short-run value (σ_t) reverts with an elasticity of Φ. If the coefficient Ω differs from unity, then there is autoregression.

GARCH models are basically just weighted-average variance models, which also allow for autoregression:

$$\sigma_t^2 = a_0 + \sum_{i=1}^{q} a_i(X_{t-i} - \mu)^2 + \sum_{j=1}^{p} b_j\sigma_{t-j}^2, \tag{A6.2}$$

where a_i, b_j are constants, X_t is a return on the asset and μ is the mean of X_t.

A GARCH(1, 1) model would set both p and q to 1. There are many variations on this theme. In particular, X_t may be given a t-distribution or other fat-tailed distribution (Baillie and Bollerslev, 1989). The variance may also be made asymmetric (Nelson, 1991), e.g. rising more in a falling market than it falls in a rising market.

Taylor (1991) discusses the similarity of these two approaches. We adopt the ARV approach for two reasons: firstly, it is intuitively more appealing, given the simple interpretation of its mean reversion; secondly, it is widely used in the options-pricing literature (see, for example, Wiggins, 1987; Chesney and Scott, 1989). On the other hand, the estimation of GARCH parameters is by maximum-likelihood methods and is well documented, whereas that is not the case for ARV parameters. In the interests of simplicity, we shall use ordinary least squares for estimation.

For purposes of estimation, the ARV model (A6.1) may be rewritten as,

$$\log\left(\frac{\sigma_t}{\sigma_{t-1}}\right) = (1 - \Phi)\log a - (1 - \Phi)\log \sigma_{t-1} + \eta_t. \tag{A6.3}$$

Estimates of parameters will be illustrated with data from London's FTSE 100 Index and index options for the period 1985–90. Using a 30-day, equally weighted estimate of σ, which we denote as $\hat{\sigma}$ to indicate that it is an estimate of the true value, and the 63 separate months of non-overlapping data, ordinary least squares gave the result:

$$\log\left(\frac{\hat{\sigma}_t}{\hat{\sigma}_{t-1}}\right) = \underset{(1.73)}{0.6797} - \underset{(1.76)}{0.2535} \log \hat{\sigma}_{t-1}. \tag{A6.4}$$

with

$$R^2 = 0.049$$
$$F = 3.09$$
$$DW = 2.44$$
$$N = 62$$

t-values in brackets.

These coefficients only reach 10% significance, using a traditional t-test. However, that test is biased, given the lagged dependent variable on the right-hand side. The correct Dickey–Fuller test indicates even lower significance. However, the estimate of the long-term volatility (a) is 14.6%, which is feasible. The estimated elasticity of mean reversion, Φ, is 0.7465. This is significantly different from zero and indicates that there is 75% reversion to the mean in each month.

Suppose that traders form their expectations of long-term volatility from the past year's events. Let us call this LTSIG_t and substitute it into Eq. (A6.3) in place of a. Allowing for a drift term τ, we obtain:

$$\log\left(\frac{\sigma_t}{\sigma_{t-1}}\right) = \tau - (1 - \Phi)\log\left(\frac{\sigma_{t-1}}{\text{LTSIG}_{t-1}}\right) + \eta_t. \qquad \text{(A6.5)}$$

Estimating (A6.5), with an extra year of data to give the initial LTSIG, leads to

$$\log\left(\frac{\hat{\sigma}_t}{\hat{\sigma}_{t-1}}\right) = -0.0038 - 0.2966 \log\left(\frac{\hat{\sigma}_{t-1}}{\text{LTSIG}_{t-1}}\right) \qquad \text{(A6.6)}$$
$$\phantom{\log\left(\frac{\hat{\sigma}_t}{\hat{\sigma}_{t-1}}\right) = }(0.84) \quad (2.45)$$

with

$$R^2 = 0.091$$
$$F = 6.02$$
$$DW = 2.08$$
$$N = 62.$$

This is a significant relationship, even if only 9% of the variance has been explained. The estimate of Φ is $(1 - 0.2966) = 0.7034$, indicating an elasticity of mean reversion of 70% per month.

We therefore conclude that volatility is mean reverting, but that a time-series (ARV) model has only modest explanatory power for this sample of monthly data.[1]

A6.1.2 TIME-SERIES BEHAVIOUR OF IMPLIED VOLATILITY

Data on 63 one-month options were used to calculate the implied volatility, an average of at-the-money puts and calls which we will denote by ATISD.[2] Assuming that this follows the same mean-reverting (ARV) process as the historic volatility (Eq. (A6.3)), we estimated:

$$\log\left(\frac{\text{ATISD}_t}{\text{ATISD}_{t-1}}\right) = 1.0055 - 0.3404 \log(\text{ATISD}_t) \qquad \text{(A6.7)}$$
$$\phantom{\log\left(\frac{\text{ATISD}_t}{\text{ATISD}_{t-1}}\right) = }(3.50) \quad (3.52)$$

with

$$R^2 = 0.171$$
$$F = 12.40$$
$$N = 62$$
$$DW = 2.08.$$

This indicates an elasticity of mean reversion of $1 - 0.3404 = 0.6596$ or 66% and the long-run value to which it reverts is $\exp(1.0055/0.3404) = 19.18\%$. This result is similar to that of Franks and Schwartz (1991), who found that only 3% of any shock was left after 13 weeks. Our equation implies that only 4% remains after such a period.[3]

We conclude that the time-series behaviour of the implied volatility is similar to that of the historic volatility: both revert to the mean quite rapidly.

A6.1.3 FORECASTING PERFORMANCE COMPARED

Figure A6.1 compares the time-series forecast of volatility (Eq. (A6.6)) with the contemporaneous implied volatility. The behaviour is similar: the correlation of the two series is 0.90. However, the implied volatility has a mean of 20.22%, which is significantly larger than the time-series mean of 14.20%. The reason

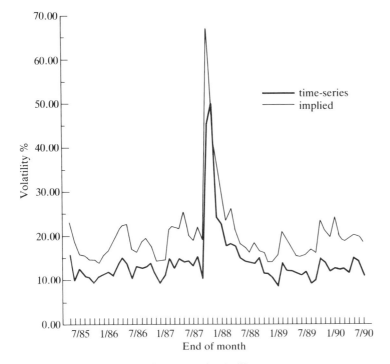

Figure A6.1 Alternative forecasts of volatility

for this difference is not clear. One possibility is that marketmakers base their prices on FTSE futures rather than on the spot index, and the futures are about 20% more volatile (see Yadav and Pope, 1990).[4]

In order to compare the forecasting ability of the two alternatives, a regression was run in which subsequent volatility was made a function of both ATISD (and at-the-money implied volatility) and TSF (the time-series forecast of volatility). The result was

$$\hat{\sigma}_t = 5.6610 + 0.7073 \text{ ATISD}_{t-1} - 0.3698 \text{ TSF}_{t-1} \qquad (A6.8)$$
$$\quad (1.88) \quad (2.26) \qquad\qquad (1.02)$$

with

$$R^2 = 0.149$$
$$F = 5.24$$
$$N = 63$$
$$DW = 2.16.$$

The F-test for exclusion confirms that the time-series forecast, TSF, made no significant contribution. This is even more surprising when one considers that TSF was estimated *within* this sample period, so it should have had an 'unfair' advantage. Dropping that variable, we obtained

$$\hat{\sigma}_t = 6.2294 + 0.4195 \text{ ATISD}_{t-1} \qquad (A6.9)$$
$$\quad (2.10) \quad (3.07)$$

with

$$R^2 = 0.134$$
$$F = 9.24$$
$$N = 63$$
$$DW = 2.09.$$

The at-the-money implied volatility can explain 13% of subsequent volatility over the option's life. The relationship is significant at the 1% level.

Figure A6.2 plots the ATISD and the subsequent outcome. The spike associated with the Crash is so large that the whole-period regressions could be merely a result of this 'outlier'. Equation (A6.9) was therefore re-estimated for the pre-Crash (February 1985 to September 1987) and post-Crash (November 1987 to July 1990) periods. The result was that, while TSF had forecasting ability in neither subperiod, ATISD had significant forecasting ability in *both* subperiods.

A6.1.4 CONCLUSION ON TIME-SERIES BEHAVIOUR OF VOLATILITY

This simple study demonstrated one time-series model for volatility. The results are similar to those found by other researchers. They confirm that past volati-

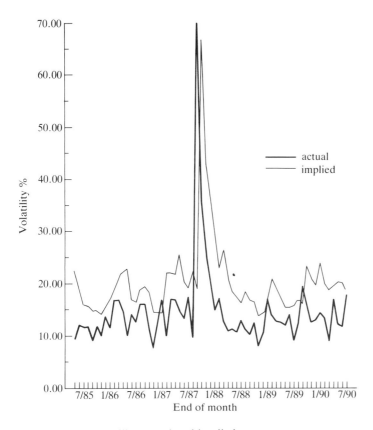

Figure A6.2 Volatility actual and implied

lity may be used to forecast future volatility, but the forecasting performance is very poor. It is also inferior, in terms of capturing changes, to the implied volatility from the options. It appears that mechanistic forecasts of volatility are of rather limited value for pricing options. Perhaps that is why most practitioners use relatively simple weighted averages of past returns, rather than more sophisticated methods, when calculating historic volatility.

Notes

1. The sample period straddles the Crash, but results were of equally low significance if the sample was divided into pre- and post-Crash periods.
2. A binomial model was used with adjustment for dividends.
3. See Merville and Pieptea (1989) for a study of the behaviour of implied volatility for US options.
4. Even after allowing for the extra volatility of futures, there would still appear to be a bias. It is not an error of calculation and it is too large to be accounted for by transactions costs. It *may* indicate a market inefficiency.

References

Baillie, R. and Bollerslev, T. (1989), 'The message in exchange rates: a conditional variance tale', *Journal of Business and Economic Statistics*, **7**, 297–305.

Chesney, M. and Scott, L. (1989), 'Pricing European currency options: a comparison of the modified Black–Scholes model and a random variance model', *Journal of Financial and Quantitative Analysis*, **24**, 267–84.

Franks, J. and Schwartz, E. (1991), 'The stochastic behaviour of market variance implied in the prices of index options', *Economic Journal*, **101**, 1460–75.

Merville, L. and Pieptea, D. (1989), 'Stock-price volatility, mean-reverting diffusion, and noise', *Journal of Financial Economics*, **24**, 193–214.

Nelson, D. (1991), 'Conditional heteroskedasticity in asset returns: a new approach', *Econometrica*, **59**, 347–70.

Taylor, S. (1991), *Modeling Stochastic Volatility*, Department of Accounting and Finance, University of Lancaster.

Wiggins, J. (1987), 'Option values under stochastic volatility: theory and empirical estimates', *Journal of Financial Economics*, **19**, 351–72.

Yadav, P. and Pope, P. (1990), 'Stock index futures pricing: international evidence', *Journal of Futures Markets*, **10**, 573–603.

7
Valuing options: is Black/Scholes robust?

In the last chapter we were concerned with procedures that were really essential if the Black/Scholes model was to be accurate in valuing options on shares. In this chapter we examine whether two particular assumptions are likely to render the model inaccurate. The first is that returns on the asset are normally distributed with constant variance; the second is that there are no transactions costs. Do these assumptions really matter?

7.1 Are returns normally distributed with constant variance?

7.1.1 THE DISTRIBUTION HAS FAT TAILS (LEPTOKURTOSIS)

We know that returns are *not* normally distributed. The observed distributions for all sorts of assets have fat tails, as shown in Fig. 7.1. Evidence of this was

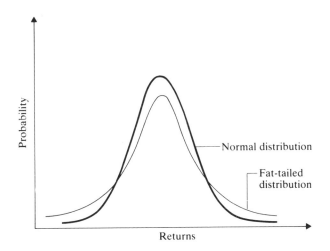

Figure 7.1 Comparison of fat-tailed and normal distributions

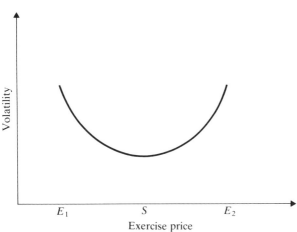

Figure 7.2 Volatility with a smile

first noted by Fama (1965) and a useful summary of later evidence may be found in Taylor (1986). It follows that the Black/Scholes model will tend to undervalue both out-of-the-money puts and out-of-the-money calls, because it will understate the chances of large positive or negative returns. Correspondingly, because of put/call parity, if out-of-the-money puts are undervalued then in-the-money calls must also be undervalued, and if out-of-the-money calls are undervalued so also will in-the-money puts.

In these circumstances, using the Black/Scholes model will result in larger implied volatilities for options at high or low exercise prices as compared with at-the-money options. For example, let us suppose that the BP share price is 320 pence and that there are options for a given maturity with exercise prices of 300, 320 and 340. We might observe the pattern of implied volatilities given in Table 7.1, in which the 300 and 340 options have higher volatilities than the 320 options. Traders talk of such an exercise-price pattern as 'volatility with a smile', as depicted in Fig. 7.2.

Table 7.1 assumes that the pattern of implied volatilities for calls and puts is exactly the same. It need not be. Transactions costs and the early-exercise value

Table 7.1 Hypothetical implied volatilities for BP

| | Implied volatilities (%) | |
Exercise price	Calls	Puts
300	33	33
320	25	25
340	30	30

of puts make put/call arbitrage somewhat imperfect, but it will prevent puts and calls from having widely different volatilities.

While there is general agreement that fat tails exist, there is no such agreement over the reasons for this. Three possible explanations are:

1. The observed distribution has a changing variance, so what is observed is actually a mixture of distributions with different variances. In effect, the observed distribution consists of a sequence of normal distributions, each with a different variance. Added together, such distributions lead to fat tails, as depicted in Fig. 7.3a.
2. It is possible that prices follow a smooth diffusion process most of the time, but occasionally there is a jump, as depicted in Fig. 7.3b. An analogy might be with a pencil that is being moved across a sheet of paper, but is occasionally lifted and then lowered at another place. The jumps result in the observed fat tails. The Crash of 1987 is an obvious candidate for such a discontinuous process.
3. It is possible that our preference for normal distributions is simply misguided and that fat-tailed distributions (such as in Fig. 7.1) are more appropriate. Prices move smoothly, but not according to a normal distribution.

The empirical evidence from options markets tends to support 'volatility with a smile' (see, for example, Rubinstein, 1985, for US options; Gemmill, 1986, for British options; Kemna, 1989, for Dutch options).

If fat tails exist, how should the B/S model be adjusted, if at all? Most practitioners are not surprised when they find 'volatility with a smile'. They do not require the theoretical nicety that volatility should be the same for all exercise prices at a given maturity. So when using models, they simply up-rate the volatility for options that are far-from-the-money. On the other hand, it is

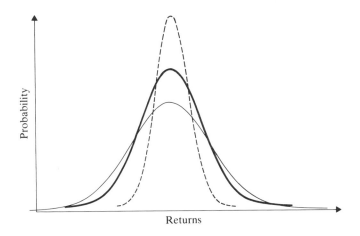

Figure 7.3a A mixture of normal distributions

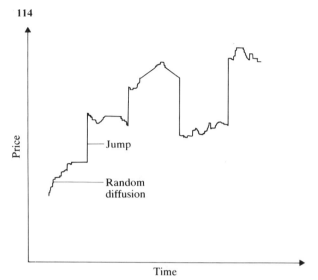

Figure 7.3b   A diffusion–jump process

relatively easy to develop models that have an increasing variance as the share price moves away from its present level. An example in the binomial framework is outlined in Fig. 7.4. The U_j multipliers are made larger at each successive step, so that the tree grows outwards at an increasing pace.

For the case of random jumps, Merton (1976) shows how the B/S model may be adjusted. The solution depends on the jumps being diversifiable in a large portfolio, so they do not earn a risk-premium. It therefore remains possible to set up a risk-free position and to value options under the assumption of risk neutrality. In a binomial context, occasional jumps would be like random dividends being paid, some of which would be positive and some negative. A tree of this kind is outlined in Fig. 7.5.

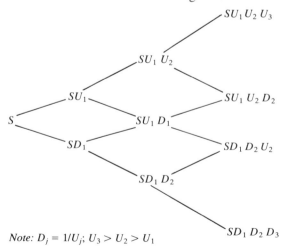

Note: $D_j = 1/U_j$; $U_3 > U_2 > U_1$

Figure 7.4   Binomial tree with variance rising away from current asset price

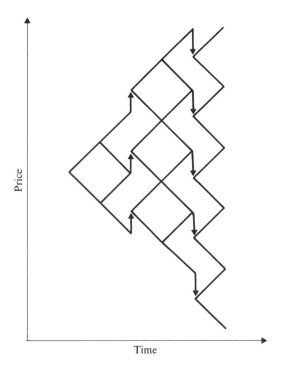

Figure 7.5   Binomial diffusion–jump tree

7.1.2   THE DISTRIBUTION IS SKEWED

The distributions in Fig. 7.1 were symmetric. However, there is some evidence for shares that the variance rises as the price falls (see Beckers, 1980, and Christie, 1982, for example). One rationale for this would be that a fall in share price increases the debt/equity ratio of a company and so makes the equity more risky. The higher variance at low prices is seen as a fatter tail on the left side of the return distribution than on the right side, as depicted in Fig. 7.6. Once again, we may actually be observing a mixture of symmetric distributions that have larger variances at lower prices.

The implication of such skewness would be that the Black/Scholes model would undervalue low-exercise-price options, but overvalue high-exercise-price options. Equivalently, the implied volatilities would differ across exercise prices. This has become known as the 'exercise-price bias'. Researchers confirm that it exists, but the bias seems to change from period to period. For example, Black (1975) found that low-exercise-price calls had low implied volatilities; however, Macbeth and Merville (1979) found the opposite, i.e. that high-exercise-price calls had low implied volatilities, which would be consistent with the skewed distribution of Fig. 7.6. The most thorough study to date was by Rubinstein (1985) who used all transactions in the 50 largest stock options on

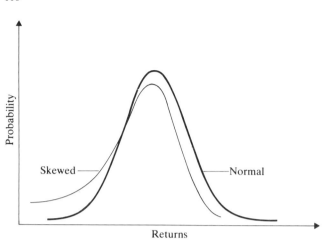

Figure 7.6   Normal and left-skewed distributions

the CBOE for 1976–78. He found that in the first part of his study the bias was in one direction (i.e. low-exercise-price options had low implied volatilities), and in the second period the bias was in the opposite direction.

Non-American studies of the bias are few. Kemna (1989) did not find one for Dutch options. In London, Gemmill (1991) found that low-exercise-price index options usually had higher implied volatilities that at-the-money options, but the degree of skewness changed from month to month.

If there is some skewness, how may it be modelled? Once again, a trader would just use a different volatility with the Black/Scholes model at each exercise price. More elegantly, the binomial model may be adjusted to give this effect and there is a generalization of the Black/Scholes model, called the constant elasticity of variance (CEV) model, which has an analytical solution in continuous time (see Cox and Rubinstein, 1985). We shall discuss the CEV model in more detail in Chapter 13, in the context of commodity options.

7.1.3   IS THE VARIANCE CONSTANT AND THE SAME AT ALL MATURITIES?

We saw in Chapter 6 that volatility does not appear to be constant. If it were, then a volatility of, say, 0.2 could always be used to price options on IBM, which is clearly nonsense. As we discussed in the appendix to Chapter 6, most of the change in volatility cannot be explained by previous changes, i.e. they are random rather than systematic. Nevertheless, there may be two systematic components to the movement of volatility, the first of which is acknowledged to exist, but the second is controversial.

The first systematic component is that, if volatility is very high or very low, it is likely to be less extreme in the next period. This characteristic, known as 'reversion to the mean', has already been introduced in Chapter 6. For example, immediately after the Crash 1-month implied volatilities on stocks were 70% or more, but 3-month and 6-month implied volatilities were much lower. There was a general expectation that a 70% volatility could not last for very long.

The second, controversial, component is that long-term volatilities may have a lower mean (to which they revert) than short-term volatilities. Thus, long-term options may be priced with lower implied volatilities than short-term options. The reason for this would be that share prices revert towards some long-term mean and thus prevent variances from expanding linearly with time. While other kinds of assets, such as interest rates and commodities, are acknowledged to show this behaviour, the evidence for shares is less clear. Studies by Fama and French (1987) and Poterba and Summers (1988) support the mean reversion of prices, but Kim *et al.* (1991) attribute these results to peculiarities of the 1926–46 period. If one looks for evidence from options that implied volatility is inversely related to maturity, it is somewhat sparse (see Rubinstein, 1985, for a very careful study).

What are the implications of changing volatility for the Black/Scholes model? If changes are random (i.e. volatility is stochastic), the impact on options prices appears to be rather small (see Hull and White, 1987; Johnson and Shanno, 1987). In other words, volatility 'moves around' but our inability to forecast its random movements is probably not very important. However, the systematic changes may be important. The volatility to use in the model should be an average of the values expected to exist over the life of the option. That average should definitely reflect mean reversion of volatility and also, possibly, mean reversion of prices.

Figure 7.7 indicates schematically the volatilities that might have been

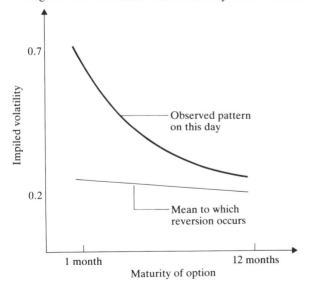

Figure 7.7 Behaviour of implied volatility soon after the Crash

appropriate for use in the Black/Scholes model immediately after the Crash. The 1-month options are given a 70% volatility and revert to an assumed mean of 25%. The one-year options are given a 30% volatility and revert to a mean of 20%.

7.1.4 SUMMARY AND IMPLICATIONS: NORMALITY OF RETURNS AND THE BEHAVIOUR OF VOLATILITY

Let us summarize.

1. There is clear evidence that the distribution of returns on shares has fat tails and options are priced to take this into account (volatilities with a smile).
2. There is less clear evidence that the distribution of returns is skewed. *A priori*, the low-exercise-price options on shares should be given higher volatilities, to reflect the influence of leverage. However, evidence from the options indicates that skewness may change from period to period.
3. There is evidence that volatility reverts to the mean, but only weak evidence (from examining both distributions and options prices) that longer term volatilities are lower than shorter term volatilities.

Do any of the above mean that the Black/Scholes model should be replaced? The answer is probably 'no'. More complicated models require the estimation of parameters that are not well defined. They may also give prices that are not greatly different (see Cox and Rubinstein, 1985, pp. 364, 371). Galai (1987) concludes from a survey of empirical work on options as follows: 'To sum up, the various simulations show that while the B-S model can give a wrong price for the option if some of the underlying assumptions . . . are violated, the deviations are small and on average insignificant' (p. 29). Likewise, Jarrow (1987) concludes that, 'When predicting market prices, the Black–Scholes model with an implicit volatility . . . will automatically adjust the model to account for these generalizations' (p. 35). In other words, practitioners use different volatilities for different exercise prices and maturities in order to take account of deviations from normality (and other factors). Further examples are given by Finucane (1989).

7.2   Transactions costs and option prices

7.2.1   DISCUSSION

The Black/Scholes and binomial models are based upon arbitrage, in which any option can be exactly replicated by a position in the underlying share plus some borrowing or lending. The existence of transactions costs means that arbitrage no longer results in a single price but in a channel of feasible prices. For example, if a call option is overvalued according to the model, it will not be worth while selling the call and buying the replicating portfolio unless the

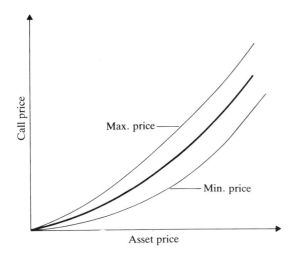

Figure 7.8   Channel of call prices resulting from transactions costs

expected profit exceeds transactions costs. Replication now imposes upper and lower bounds on options prices and a channel of prices is produced such as that indicated in Fig. 7.8.

Transactions costs arise in two slightly different ways. Firstly, if at time 0 I sell a call and buy 'delta' shares, I only receive the bid price for the call, C_{0b}, but I have to pay the asking price for the shares, S_{0a}. When the position is reversed at time 1, I receive the bid price for the shares, S_{1b}, and have to pay the asking price for the call, C_{1a}. The existence of a bid/ask spread of $(S_a - S_b)$ on the share will cause a bid/ask spread on the call option of $h(S_a - S_b)$, where h is the hedge ratio or delta.

Secondly, I will have to adjust (or 'rebalance') the hedge as the share price moves, because the delta is not constant. There will be a trade-off: the more frequent the rebalancing, the larger the transactions costs, but the smaller the hedging errors. In order to obtain a perfect hedge, transactions would have to be continuous: in the limit there would be an infinite number of transactions and so infinite transactions costs! Clearly, going to the limit would not be a good idea. Rebalancing will be done whenever the share price has moved by some predetermined amount.

The trade-off between transactions costs from rebalancing and the implied cost of hedging errors is shown schematically in Fig. 7.9. The optimal rebalancing frequency would be at the lowest point on the upper curve, which represents the sum of the two costs. In order to convert hedging errors into costs, we have to assume that their risk cannot simply be diversified away in a large portfolio. The value placed on the risk will depend on investors' attitudes: the more risk-averse an investor, the higher the hedging-error line in Fig. 7.9 and the more frequent the optimal rebalancing.

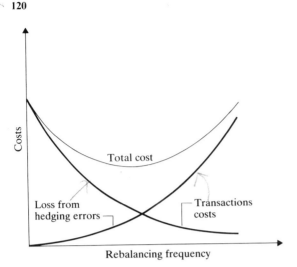

Figure 7.9   Rebalancing frequency and costs

We shall now use an extended example to demonstrate the impact of transactions costs. It will also illustrate the process of dynamic replication, which
underlies the options-pricing models. The example has two stages. In the first
we shall assume that it is possible to trade without transactions costs on either
shares or options. In the second we shall repeat the calculations with those costs
imposed.

The second column of Table 7.2 gives nine weeks of data from 1987 on the
share price of Hanson, a British company. The price starts at 157 pence and
drifts upwards to finish at 168.5 pence. The time to maturity of the call option
is, at first, 63 days (column 3). Assuming that the volatility is 0.2 and the interest
rate is 9%, the fair call price initially is 11.01 pence (column 4) and the delta is
0.78 (column 5). In the absence of transactions costs, a trader would be willing
in the first week to sell 1 call (on 1000 shares) at 11.01 pence per share and buy
780 shares at 157 pence each. The sold call would bring in £110.10 (column 8)
and the bought shares would cost £1224.60 (column 9), so the net position
would initially be − £1114.50 (column 10). This would be financed by borrowing at the assumed 9%. One week later the share price has risen to 161 pence
and the indicated delta is 0.87, so another 90 shares must be purchased to
rebalance the hedge. Similarly, in the third period there is another rise in the
share price and another 90 shares must be purchased. This process continues
until, in the last week at maturity, the call is repurchased and the shares sold. If
rebalancing had been continuous this whole process would have resulted in a
zero profit. Instead we find a very small loss in Table 7.2, of − £0.96.

We shall now repeat the example with transactions costs applied. Table 7.3 is
a repeat of Table 7.2, but with a 3 pence spread on the share (about 2%) and an
equivalent spread on the options. Shares and calls are now purchased at asking

Table 7.2 Replication example with no transactions costs

Week	Mid-price of share (pence)	Time left (days)	Mid-price of call (pence)	Delta	Call deals	Share deals	Trade values Calls £	Shares £	Total balance £
0	157	63	11.01	0.78	Sell 1	Buy 780	110.1	− 1224.6	− 1114.50
1	161	56	13.92	0.87		Buy 90		− 144.9	− 1261.32
2	168	49	20.01	0.96		Buy 90		− 151.2	− 1414.71
3	162	42	14.04	0.91		Sell 50		81.0	− 1336.16
4	166	35	17.44	0.96		Buy 50		− 83.0	− 1421.47
5	167	28	18.09	0.98		Buy 20		− 33.4	− 1457.33
6	164	21	14.84	0.98		No change		0	− 1459.85
7	167	14	17.52	1.00		Buy 20		− 33.4	− 1495.78
8	165	7	15.26	1.00		No change		0	− 1498.37
9	168.5	0	18.50	1.00	Buy 1	Sell 1000	− 185.0	1685.0	− 0.96

Notes:
1. Time left to expiry is in days.
2. Assumed $\sigma = 0.2$; $r = 0.09$.
3. Interest has been applied to the total balance from week to week.

prices and sold at bid prices. Column 2 gives share bid/ask prices. Column 5 gives call bid/ask prices, calculated as $h(S_a − S_b)$. The delta has been calculated as before from the mid-price. The initial sale of one call now only pays £98.40 (11% less than before) and the purchase of 780 shares now costs £1236.30 (1% more than before), so the total balance begins at − £1137.90 (2.1% lower than before). Each rebalancing is now more expensive. After nine weeks the call is repurchased at the asking price and the shares sold at the bid price.

The net loss is − £59.58, as compared with − £0.96 in the no-transactions-costs case. This is large relative to the initial option sale of £98.40 (at the bid price). Where did it come from? There are two sources: the 'basic' bid/ask spreads on the initial and final transactions in shares and calls; and the bid/ask spreads on the rebalancing transactions in shares. The basic bid/ask spreads account for £53.40 of the total loss, leaving £6.18 as the loss due to the rebalancing transactions on the 1000 shares. Therefore, to compensate for rebalancing alone, the price of the call would have needed to be 0.62 pence higher, i.e. 11.63 pence as compared with a no-transactions-costs mid-price of 11.01 pence.[1]

From our example, it would seem that it is possible to estimate the expected transactions costs from rebalancing and then add them to the asking price of the call. However, Leland (1985) indicates that this approach has three problems.

1. It is difficult to estimate the transactions costs because they depend on the path taken by prices. If prices are volatile, then more rebalancing will occur and so transactions costs will be higher.

Table 7.3 Replication with transactions costs

Week	Share bid/ask (pence)	Time (days)	Delta	Call bid/ask (pence)	Call deals	Share deals	Trade values		Total balance £
							Calls £	Shares £	
0	155.5/158.5	63	0.78	9.84/12.18	Sell 1	Buy 780	98.4	− 1236.30	− 1137.90
1	159.5/162.5	56	0.87	12.62/15.23		Buy 90		− 146.25	− 1286.11
2	166.5/169.5	49	0.96	18.57/21.45		Buy 90		− 152.55	− 1440.89
3	160.5/163.5	42	0.91	12.68/15.41		Sell 50		80.25	− 1363.13
4	164.5/167.5	35	0.96	16.00/18.88		Buy 50		− 83.75	− 1449.24
5	165.5/168.5	28	0.98	16.62/19.56		Buy 20		− 33.70	− 1485.45
6	162.5/165.5	21	0.98	13.37/16.31		No change			− 1488.02
7	165.5/168.5	14	1.00	16.02/19.02		Buy 20		− 33.70	− 1524.38
8	163.5/166.5	7	1.00	13.76/16.76		No change			− 1526.94
9	167.0/170.0	0	1.00	17.00/20.00	Buy 1	Sell 1000	− 200.0	1670.00	− 59.58

Notes: See Table 7.2.

2. The transactions costs will be correlated with returns on the stock and, thus, also correlated with the stockmarket as a whole. It follows that their risk will not be diversifiable, making the attempted hedge risky.
3. Transactions costs will become arbitrarily large as rebalancing is made more frequent, as already indicated in Fig. 7.9.

Leland has a solution to this problem, which is simple if not necessarily 'optimal'.[2] It transpires that if the variance is raised by some factor $(1 + g)$, then the expected return on the hedge is zero, as required, and the risk is not correlated with returns on the share. We have

$$\sigma^{*2} = \sigma^2(1 + g) \tag{7.1}$$

where

$$g = \sqrt{\frac{2}{\pi}} \left[\frac{k}{\sigma\sqrt{\Delta t}} \right] \tag{7.2}$$

k is the fractional round-trip transactions cost and Δt is the delay in rebalancing.

For example, if we continue to assume that $\sigma = 0.2$ and Δt is one week (i.e. $(1/52)$ years), if the cost of a round-trip in the share is 2% ($k = 0.02$), then we have

$$(1 + g) = 1 + \sqrt{\frac{2}{\pi}} \left[\frac{0.02}{0.2\sqrt{1/52}} \right] = 1.57536.$$

Hence $\sigma^{*2} = (0.2)^2(1.57536)$ and $\sigma^* = 0.2510$. Just to cover the cost of weekly rebalancing, the asking price for the call in our example would now be 12.05 pence (i.e. the Black/Scholes price at $\sigma = 0.25$). Similarly, the bid price required to cover rebalancing costs can found by reducing the variance by a factor of $(1 - g)$, resulting in a volatility of 0.1593 and a price of 9.85 pence.

We concluded earlier that the price of the call would have to be 0.62 pence higher to cover the cost of rebalancing. Leland's formula leads to an increase of 1.04 pence (12.05 less the mid-price of 11.01). It appears that his extra spread would more than cover the cost of rebalancing in our example. This is consistent with the results of Hodges and Neuberger (1989), that Leland overestimates the cost. Another shortcoming of this approach is that the rebalancing interval, Δt, has to be prespecified and so the options-pricing formula will still depend on risk-aversion.

The problem of rebalancing should not be overemphasized, however. Leland's calculations (and our example) assumed that an option was sold and the position was then hedged until maturity. In reality, a marketmaker in an active market will expect to reverse the position in a few days or even a few minutes. This means that observed spreads do not need to take much account of rebalancing risks, except in illiquid markets where hedges are required for long periods. Figlewski (1989) demonstrates this very clearly for US index options.

Hence one would expect to find very narrow spreads in active options markets, but spreads of Leland's magnitude in some of the over-the-counter markets.

7.2.2 CONCLUSIONS ON TRANSACTIONS COSTS

We conclude that the bid/ask spread on options will reflect: (i) the bid/ask spread on the underlying asset; and (ii) the bid/ask costs incurred in rebalancing at discrete periods rather instantaneously. The width of the spread will therefore depend on whether options marketmakers pay or receive the bid/ask spread on the asset and on the required frequency of rebalancing. Leland provides a method for calculating the rebalancing cost, assuming that its frequency has been chosen. However, in liquid markets the impact of rebalancing is likely to be minimal because options are only hedged for very short periods and not over the whole period until maturity.

The implication for investors is that bid/ask spreads on options will probably appear large relative to the options prices, but most of that will just reflect the spread on the share. It may not necessarily signal that options prices are being set inefficiently.

7.3 Summary

This chapter considered whether deviations from normality and the existence of transactions costs might invalidate the Black/Scholes model. While there are ways of allowing for different distributions and for transactions costs, neither is of particularly great importance. If appears that adjusting the volatility can allow for many of the problems that arise. In that sense, the model is robust.

Notes

1. Remember that calls are quoted per share, but one contract in this example is for 1000 shares. Hence a loss of £6.18 would be quoted as £0.00618 per share, i.e. 0.62 pence.
2. See Hodges and Neuberger for an examination of this optimal-control problem. Also Boyle and Vorst (1992) illustrate Leland's strategy in discrete time as opposed to continuous time.

References

Beckers, S. (1980), 'The constant elasticity of variance model and its implications for option pricing', *Journal of Finance*, **35**, 661–73.

Black, F. (1975), 'Fact and fantasy in the use of options', *Financial Analysts Journal* (July/August), 36–72.

Boyle, P. and Vorst, T. (1992), 'Option bounds in discrete time with transactions costs', *Journal of Finance*, **47**, 271–94.

Christie, A. (1982), 'The stochastic behaviour of common stock variances: value, leverage and interest-rate effects', *Journal of Financial Economics*, **10**, 407–32.

Cox, J. and Rubinstein, M. (1985), *Options Markets*, Prentice-Hall, Englewood Cliffs, New Jersey.

Fama, E. (1965), 'The behaviour of stock market prices', *Journal of Business*, **38**, 34–105.

Fama, E. and French, K. (1987), 'Permanent and temporary components of stock returns', *Journal of Political Economy*, **96**, 246–73.

Figlewski, S. (1989), 'Options arbitrage in imperfect markets', *Journal of Finance*, **44**, 1289–1311.

Finucane, T. (1989), 'Black–Scholes approximations of call options prices with stochastic volatilities: a note', *Journal of Financial and Quantitative Analysis*, **24**, 527–32.

Galai, D. (1987), 'Empirical tests of option-pricing models: an updated survey', paper presented at joint AMEX/SOFFEX Seminar, Zurich, October 1987.

Gemmill, G. (1986), 'The forecasting performance of options prices', *Journal of Business Finance and Accounting*, **13**, 535–46.

Gemmill, G. (1991), 'Using options prices to reveal traders' expectations', Working Paper, City University Business School, London.

Hodges, S. and Neuberger, A. (1989), 'Optimal replication of contingent claims under transactions costs', *Review of Futures Markets*, **8**, 222–39.

Hull, J. and White, A. (1987), 'The pricing of options on assets with stochastic volatilities', *Journal of Finance*, **42**, 281–300.

Jarrow, R. (1987), 'Option pricing and implicit volatilities', paper presented at joint AMEX/SOFFEX Seminar, Zurich, October 1987.

Johnson, H. and Shanno, D. (1987), 'Options pricing when variance is changing', *Journal of Financial and Quantitative Analysis*, **22**, 143–51.

Kemna, A. (1989), 'An empirical test of the option pricing model based upon transactions data of the European options exchange', in Guimares, R. *et al.* (eds), *A Re-appraisal of Market Efficiency*, Springer Verlag.

Kim, M., Nelson, C. and Startz, R. (1991), 'Mean reversion in stock prices? A reappraisal of the empirical evidence', *Review of Economic Studies*, **58**, 515–28.

Leland, H. (1985), 'Option pricing and replication with transactions costs', *Journal of Finance*, **40**, 1283–1301.

Macbeth, J. and Merville, L. (1979), 'An empirical examination of the Black/Scholes call option pricing model', *Jounal of Finance*, **34**, 1173–86.

Merton, R. (1973), 'Theory of rational option pricing', *Bell Journal of Economics and Management Science*, **4**, 141–84.

Merton, R. (1976), 'Option pricing when stock returns are discontinuous', *Journal of Financial Economics*, **3**, 125–44.

Poterba, M. and Summers, L. (1988), 'Mean reversion in stock prices: evidence and implications', *Journal of Financial Economics*, **22**, 27–60.

Rubinstein, M. (1985), 'Non-parametric tests of alternative options pricing models using all reported trades and quotes on the 30 most active CBOE option classes from August 23, 1976 through August 31, 1978', *Journal of Finance*, **40**, 455–80.

Taylor, S. (1986), *Modelling Financial Time Series*, Wiley, Chichester.

PART THREE

Valuation and use of other options

This part of the book applies the basic ideas on options pricing that were developed earlier to a wide variety of different assets. Each chapter is relatively self-contained and most have sections on contracts, markets, use and valuation. Conforming to this pattern are the chapters discussing options on currencies (Chapter 8), stock indices (Chapter 9), interest rates (Chapter 11), warrants and convertibles (Chapter 12), and commodities (Chapter 13). Exceptions to the pattern are: Chapter 10 on portfolio insurance (which logically follows that on stock indices); Chapter 14 on 'exotic' options; and Chapter 15 on the performance of options markets.

8
Currency options and hedging

We begin applications with currency options, because they are simpler than some others (such as options on bonds or stock indices). In this chapter we shall not only discuss currency options, but also use them to illustrate the various kinds of hedge that can be developed with options. The chapter begins with an overview of markets and prices. It then discusses the use of currency options in hedging. This is followed by a section on 'tailored' options, i.e. options that have been specially designed to meet the needs of particular hedgers. The fourth section of the chapter demonstrates put/call parity for currency options. The fifth, and final, section discusses valuation, which is a relatively simple variation on the Black/Scholes theme.

8.1 Introduction and markets

After the collapse of the Bretton Woods Agreement in 1973, rates between currencies were allowed to fluctuate, albeit with periodic intervention by various governments. A huge interbank market in spot and forward currencies soon developed, which continues to dwarf in turnover all other kinds of market. A survey in 1989 (Bank of England) showed that about $431 billion of currency deals were made each day in the main centres, which were London ($187 billion), New York ($129 billion) and Tokyo ($115 billion).

Currency options are complementary to these spot and forward contracts, allowing the user to 'mould' the shape of the pay-off to his or her own preferences. Over-the-counter deals in currency options began in the late 1970s and the Philadelphia Exchange listed currency options in 1983. The other important exchange is the Chicago Mercantile, where options on its currency futures contracts have been traded since 1985. The turnovers for the main contracts traded in Chicago, New York and Amsterdam are given in Table 8.1.

As the table shows, the most important contracts are in D-Marks and yen, reflecting the division of the world into D-Mark, yen and dollar zones. The size of contract varies by exchange. For example, the D-Mark contract on the

Table 8.1   Currency options turnover by exchange in 1991 (thousand contracts)

	PHX	CME	FINEX	EOE
D-Mark	7254	5643	–	–
Yen	1783	2397	–	–
Pound sterling	587	650	–	–
Swiss franc	460	–	–	–
Canadian dollar	204	–	–	–
Australian dollar	185	–	–	–
Dutch guilder	–	–	–	371
Dollar index	–	–	1418	–

Source: Adapted from data in *Futures and Options World*, February 1992.
Key: PHX is Philadelphia Exchange.
        CME is Chicago Mercantile Exchange.
        EOE is European Options Exchange (Amsterdam).
        FINEX is Financial Instruments Exchange (New York).

Philadelphia Exchange is for DM125 000 and on the Chicago Mercantile Exchange is for DM62 500. All of these markets are small relative to the spot and forward markets in currency. For example, from Table 8.1 the average turnover on the two US exchanges for D-Mark options was only 5.2 billion D-Marks per day in 1991. The really important currency options are those traded interbank. What appears on the organized exchanges is a small proportion of this 'over-the-counter' business.

Figure 8.1 gives some representative prices for currency options from the *Wall Street Journal*. It should be noted that each currency is quoted in US cents per unit. This is the usual arrangement for a 'heavy' currency such as the pound sterling, e.g. 180 cents per pound, but it is unusual for 'light' currencies such as the D-Mark, e.g. 62 cents per D-Mark, and yen, e.g. 0.73 cents per yen. This is just a convention which helps to avoid errors.

A currency option gives the right (but not the obligation) to buy (call) or sell (put) a currency on (or before, if American) a given date at a predetermined exercise price. For example, on the Philadelphia Exchange the right to buy D-Marks on 21 March 1991 at an exercise price of 61 cents on or before the end of May cost 1.11 cents per D-Mark (see Fig. 8.1). The corresponding put option cost 1.26 cents per D-Mark.

Buying one currency requires the sale of another, so a call on a currency is automatically the same as a put on the other. For example, on the CME a May *call* on the yen at an exercise price of 73 cents per 100 yen cost 1.19 cents on 21 March 1991 (see Fig. 8.1). At a spot rate of 73.05 cents per 100 yen, the call premium was $1.19/73.05 = 1.63\%$. This call on the yen was also a *put* on the dollar with a premium of 1.63%, i.e. at the exchange rate of $100/0.7305 = 136.9$ yen per dollar, it cost 2.23 yen per dollar.

FUTURES OPTIONS

JAPANESE YEN (IMM) 12,500,000 yen; cents per 100 yen

Strike Price	Calls—Settle			Puts—Settle		
	Apr-c	May-c	Jun-c	Apr-p	May-p	Jun-p
7200	1.31	1.73	2.08	0.46	0.89	1.23
7250	0.99	1.44	1.80	0.64	1.10	1.45
7300	0.72	1.19	1.54	0.87	1.34	1.69
7350	0.53	0.98	1.31	1.17	1.63	1.96
7400	0.37	0.80	1.13	1.52	1.94	2.27
7450	0.25	0.64	0.95	1.90	2.28	2.58

Est. vol. 7,917, Wed vol. 4,540 calls, 2,353 puts
Open interest Wed 49,364 calls, 37,068 puts

DEUTSCHEMARK (IMM) 125,000 marks; cents per mark

Strike Price	Calls—Settle			Puts—Settle		
	Apr-c	May-c	Jun-c	Apr-p	May-p	Jun-p
6000	1.29	1.61	1.92	0.38	0.71	1.02
6050	0.96	1.33	1.64	0.55	0.92	1.24
6100	0.69	1.06	1.38	0.78	1.15	1.47
6150	0.48	0.52	1.16	1.07	0.91	1.73
6200	0.32	0.67	0.98	1.41	1.74	2.04
6250	0.22	0.52	0.81	1.81	2.08	2.36

Est. vol. 14,925, Wed vol. 18,111 calls, 8,364 puts
Open interest Wed 95,513 calls, 81,164 puts

CANADIAN DOLLAR (IMM) 100,000 Can.$, cents per Can.$

Strike Price	Calls—Settle			Puts—Settle		
	Apr-c	May-c	Jun-c	Apr-p	May-p	Jun-p
8500	0.92	....	1.17	0.05	0.14	0.31
8550	0.48	0.66	0.85	0.12	0.28	0.49
8400	0.20	0.39	0.59	0.33	0.51	0.73
8650	0.06	0.20	0.39	0.69	....	1.02
8700	0.01	0.10	0.25	1.14	....	1.38
8750	....	0.05	0.15	....	....	....

Est. vol. 1,243, Wed vol. 514 calls, 1,018 puts
Open interest Wed 11,362 calls, 12,387 puts

BRITISH POUND (IMM) 62,500 pounds; cents per pound

Strike Price	Calls—Settle			Puts—Settle		
	Apr-c	May-c	Jun-c	Apr-p	May-p	Jun-p
1725	5.54	....	....	0.42	1.72	2.04
1750	3.60	4.62	5.48	0.96	2.00	2.86
1775	1.96	3.24	4.14	1.98	3.12	4.02
1800	1.08	2.16	3.04	3.44	4.50	5.38
1825	0.48	1.36	2.16	5.34	6.18	6.98
1850	0.24	0.82	1.50	7.58	8.12	8.76

Est. vol. 692, Wed vol. 1,430 calls, 870 puts
Open interest Wed 15,476 calls, 8,637 puts

SWISS FRANC (IMM) 125,000 francs; cents per franc

Strike Price	Calls—Settle			Puts—Settle		
	Apr-c	May-c	Jun-c	Apr-p	May-p	Jun-p
7000	1.32	1.73	2.11	0.54	0.95	1.34
7050	1.02	1.46	1.84	0.74	....	1.56
7100	0.76	1.21	1.60	0.98	1.43	1.82
7150	0.57	1.00	1.38	1.29	1.72	2.09
7200	0.40	0.81	1.17	1.62	2.01	2.38
7250	0.29	0.66	1.01	2.00	....	2.70

Est. vol. 2,938, Wed vol. 3,834 calls, 3,569 puts
Open interest Wed 28,884 calls, 25,277 puts

> FINEX—Financial Instrument Exchange, a division of the New York Cotton Exchange; IMM—International Monetary Market at CME, Chicago.

OPTIONS

PHILADELPHIA EXCHANGE

Option & Underlying	Strike Price	Calls—Last			Puts—Last		
		Apr	May	Jun	Apr	May	Jun

50,000 Australian Dollars-cents per unit.

Option & Underlying	Strike Price	Apr	May	Jun	Apr	May	Jun
ADollr	...75	r	r	2.21	r	r	r
77.17	...76	r	r	r	0.31	r	r
77.17	...77	0.56	r	r	r	r	r
77.17	...78	0.20	0.41	0.70	r	r	r

31.250 British Pounds-cents per unit.

Option & Underlying	Strike Price	Apr	May	Jun	Apr	May	Jun
BPound	170	r	r	r	0.23	r	1.55
179.94	172½	r	r	7.25	0.57	1.38	2.25
179.94	.175	r	r	r	1.05	2.00	3.40
179.94	177½	3.30	r	r	r	2.90	4.12
179.94	.180	1.72	r	2.85	r	r	r
179.94	182½	r	r	2.30	r	r	6.85
179.94	.185	0.60	1.60	r	r	r	r
179.94	187½	r	0.65	r	r	r	r

31.250 British Pounds-European Style.

Option & Underlying	Strike Price	Apr	May	Jun	Apr	May	Jun
179.94	.185	r	1.20	r	r	r	r

50,000 Canadian Dollars-cents per unit.

Option & Underlying	Strike Price	Apr	May	Jun	Apr	May	Jun
CDollr	.82½	r	r	r	r	r	0.07
86.52	.83½	r	r	r	r	r	0.14
86.52	...86	0.46	r	r	r	r	0.81
86.52	.86½	r	0.22	r	0.40	r	r

62.500 German Marks-cents per unit.

Option & Underlying	Strike Price	Apr	May	Jun	Apr	May	Jun
DMark	...57	s	s	r	s	s	0.34
61.33	...58	r	r	r	0.10	0.29	0.54
61.33	...59	r	r	r	0.20	0.48	0.79
61.33	...60	1.55	r	r	0.42	0.80	1.08
61.33	...61	0.94	1.11	1.44	0.80	1.26	1.58
61.33	...62	0.48	0.80	1.03	r	r	2.07
61.33	.62½	0.37	0.60	s	1.67	r	s
61.33	...63	0.23	0.42	0.72	2.07	2.46	2.69
61.33	.63½	0.16	r	s	r	r	s
61.33	...64	0.13	0.26	0.48	r	r	3.60
61.33	.64½	r	0.21	s	r	r	s
61.33	...65	r	r	0.33	r	r	4.38

6.250.000 Japanese Yen-100ths of a cent per unit.

Option & Underlying	Strike Price	Apr	May	Jun	Apr	May	Jun
JYen	... 66	r	r	r	r	r	0.16
73.05	...69	r	r	r	0.11	r	r
73.05	...70	r	r	r	0.15	0.48	r
73.05	.70½	r	r	r	0.29	r	s
73.05	.71½	1.54	r.	r	s	0.56	r
73.05	...72	r	r	r	r	1.21	1.35
73.05	.72½	0.95	r	r	1.09	r	s
73.05	...73	0.78	1.29	1.62	1.13	r	s
73.05	.73½	0.56	r	r	r	r	s
73.05	...74	r	r	1.10	r	r	r
73.05	...75	0.24	0.51	r	r	r	r
73.05	...77	0.07	r	0.41	4.63	r	r
73.05	...79	0.02	.	r	r	r	r

62.500 Swiss Francs-cents per unit.

Option & Underlying	Strike Price	Apr	May	Jun	Apr	May	Jun
SFranc	...65	s	s	r	s	s	0.23
71.15	...66	s	s	r	s	s	0.41
71.15	...69	r	2.66	2.64	r	r	1.02
71.15	...70	r	r	r	0.62	1.00	1.38
71.15	...71	0.98	r	r	1.04	r	s'
71.15	.71½	r	r	s	1.31	r	s
71.15	.72½	0.48	r	s	r	r	s
71.15	...74	s	r	0.65	s	r	r
71.15	...75	r	r	0.42	r	r	r
71.15	...76	r	0.18	r	r	r	5.40
71.15	...77	r	r	0.28	r	r	6.27

62.500 Swiss Francs-European Style.

Option & Underlying	Strike Price	Apr	May	Jun	Apr	May	Jun
71.15	...69	r	r	r	r	0.70	r
71.15	...70	r	r	r	0.56	1.06	r
71.15	...71	r	r	r	1.02	1.44	1.88
71.15	...73	r	r	r	2.36	2.76	3.18
71.15	.74½	0.16	r	r	s	r	s
71.15	...74	s	r	r	r	r	3.82
71.15	...76	r	r	r	r	r	5.52
71.15	...78	r	0.07	0.14	r	r	r

Total call vol. 15,913   Call open int. 314,354
Total put vol. 11,087   Put open int. 258,104
r—Not traded. s—No option offered.
Last is premium (purchase price).

Figure 8.1 Representative currency option prices
Source: Wall Street Journal, 21 March 1991. Reproduced with permission

8.2   Use of currency options in hedging

8.2.1   INTRODUCTION

Let us begin by clarifying what is meant by 'hedging'. It is simply the reduction of risk. If a company knows that it will need to convert some dollars into sterling at a future date, there is a risk of an unfavourable move in rates. In Fig. 8.2 this exposure is shown as the $-45°$ line. Should rates remain constant, then the exposure will lead to neither a profit nor a loss. In that case, the current forward rate of 180 ¢/£ will also be the eventual spot rate at which the transaction occurs. Should the ¢/£ rate increase to 190 ¢/£, for example, then the company will suffer a loss of $10/180 = 5.6\%$, because more dollars are required to give the same number of pounds. Should the ¢/£ rate decrease to 170 ¢/£, for example, then the company will make a windfall gain of $10/180 = 5.6\%$.

A hedger is someone who is worried about a potential loss. The hedger is willing to give up the chance of a profit in order to eliminate the chance of a loss. In this example, the company's treasurer may make a forward purchase of sterling at the rate of 180 ¢/£ and so remove the risk. This forward purchase is shown as a 45° line in Fig. 8.1. Adding the forward purchase profit/loss to the exposure profit/loss gives a net zero position at all rates.

Now suppose instead that the treasurer had bought a call option on sterling at an exercise price of 180 ¢/£ and costing 3 ¢/£. Figure 8.3 shows the resulting total exposure. At rates above 180 ¢/£ there is a loss of 3 ¢/£, but at rates below 177 ¢/£ the position becomes profitable.

In what circumstances would the treasurer prefer the asymmetric pay-off on

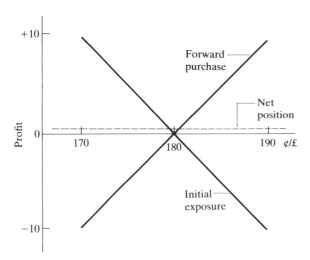

Figure 8.2   Currency hedged with a forward contract

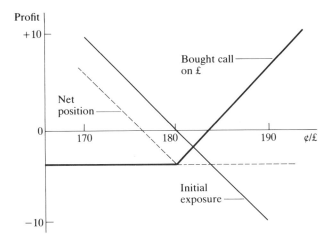

Figure 8.3 Currency hedged with a call option

the option hedge to the zero pay-off on the forward hedge? The answer is: when, after having hedged with a forward contract against a rise in sterling, that currency actually weakens. Is the payment of 3 ¢/£ a reasonable extra cost to incur in order to limit the potential regret? That will depend on risk aversion and the character of the exposure.

One particular kind of exposure to which options are well suited is that arising from a quantity risk. For example, suppose the treasurer hedges an expected amount of currency with a forward contract, but when the time comes there is actually no currency to convert. Buying forward could lead to a huge financial loss. The treasurer's job could be at risk, because the shareholders will want to know why a purely financial loss was made on 'speculative' forward contracts. If call options had been used, the loss would have been limited to the premium.

Nevertheless, a word of warning is in order. If options are written (rather than purchased) the loss is potentially unlimited. The story of the use of currency options by Allied Lyons (a large British company) is given below. It demonstrates how important it is that senior management should understand options before they are used, and the need for an adequate risk-management system.

AN UNENVIABLE RECORD

TRACY CORRIGAN on Allied-Lyons' foreign exchange losses

Allied-Lyons £150m loss in foreign exchange dealings is the biggest incurred by a British industrial company. Sir Derrick Holden-Brown, its chairman, yesterday admitted that the loss stemmed from the use of complex instruments which the company's financial experts failed to understand.

The revelations came in a letter to shareholders following an investigation by KPMG Peat Marwick McLintock, the group's auditors.

Although the loss can be pin-pointed to a short three-week period earlier this year, the root of the problem dates from 1989.

Allied-Lyons treasury team decided to start writing (or selling) call options on foreign currencies, which give the buyer the right to obtain that currency at a fixed price. The buyer stands to lose only the cost of the option; but the seller has potentially unlimited exposure if the market moves the wrong way.

This initiative was set in a dangerous context. The treasury's internal controls were not strictly enforced, its computer systems were outdated, and its staff did not understand the nature of the risks they were taking on.

Sir Derrick, who is to retire early, admitted yesterday that the department had been 'dealing in foreign currency instruments which were inappropriate, and in which it lacked the requisite trading skills'.

The writing of options initially proved a profitable business, and, encouraged by their success, the team adopted increasingly aggressive tactics.

By the second half of last year, the company's internal exposure limit—the maximum it risked losing in the market—of £500m had been breached.

Although the treasury was not officially classified as a 'profit centre', it usually produced moderate annual profits of about £10m. Traditionally perceived by other corporate treasurers and bankers as operating a conservative financial policy, Allied-Lyons had in fact taken trading positions in the financial markets in order to make money rather than just hedge exposure since 1978.

Last year senior management received several warnings that the company's involvement in the foreign exchange markets had increased significantly.

Last summer, the Bank of England brought Allied-Lyons' foreign currency activities to the attention of Sir Derrick during a routine meeting. Subsequently, the company's finance director and treasurer discussed the matter with Bank officials.

But when positions were checked—using what turned out to be inadequate control systems—it was decided that the company's exposure was not excessive and that its positions were broadly balanced.

Another external warning followed, this time from KPMG Peat Marwick McLintock, the company's auditors. That warning, to former finance director Mr Cliff Hatch, was not reported to more senior executives. Exposures were still mostly within the internal limit of £500m.

But in September, a serious breach of that limit at last prompted the company to tackle the problem. The treasury began to reduce its exposure to more prudent levels, but during this process it left itself further exposed.

Between February 21 and March 16 this year, the dollar strengthened strongly against the pound, from $1.95 to $1.79. Most of the losses were incurred because Allied-Lyons left itself with a large and unhedged short position by writing call options on the dollar.

The market moved inexorably against Allied-Lyons, increasing profits for holders of the options, who could exercise their right to buy the dollar at a set rate against the pound, but magnifying Allied-Lyons' losses.

By the time National Westminster Bank was called in to clear up the mess, exposure had reached £1.5bn (calculated on market values at that time).

The systems used by Allied-Lyons to run its positions were not geared for increasingly complex products. Its computer system had been developed to handle straightforward foreign exchange trading. The system was amended in 1989 to cover options, but proved too unsophisticated to track these complex instruments accurately.

This would have been picked up, though, if the nature of call options had been better understood by staff. Until late February, the trading positions were believed to be reasonably balanced.

This was because positions were incorrectly assumed to have been set off against each other, so the real exposure was not known.

Potentially unlimited exposure was believed to be fully hedged by cash positions, or positions in the forward market. But sometimes positions were only partially hedged; in other cases, exposure had been increased. As the treasury traders tried to recover their positions, they left themselves more and more exposed.

As well as its dollar positions, Allied-Lyons had also written options on the yen and the D-mark. But the principal exposure was to the dollar/sterling rate, reflecting—though arbitrarily—the company's largest trading relationship.

KPMG Peat Marwick is now helping the firm reconstitute its treasury team, which, following a reshuffle, will still consist of five staff. Mr Timothy Dalton will stay on as treasurer. A new assistant treasurer is being recruited.

Other UK companies have rushed to reassure shareholders that they do not use options, even though options can safely be used to hedge exposure, rather than to create it.

But when treasuries use options to take trading positions, they are stepping beyond the traditional role of corporate treasuries, which is to protect their companies from loss, rather than secure profit.

Such a strategy takes the corporate treasury into the territory of investment banks, where there are, at least in theory, tight internal controls, daily trading limits, sophisticated infrastructure and expertise in hedging exposure.

Allied-Lyons will not be writing any more options.

Financial Times,
4 May 1991

Below we shall give examples of the use of currency options for hedging, drawing partly from the paper by Giddy (1983).

8.2.2 SALES OR EARNINGS IN OTHER CURRENCIES

Let us suppose that Daimler Benz expects, with a high degree of certainty, that it will sell cars to the value of $100 million in the United States in the next financial year. There might also be another $50 million of additional sales, depending on the state of the US economy. The value in D-Marks of the repatriated earnings will depend on the DM/$ rate. How should the currency risk be hedged, if at all?

Companies have widely differing views about whether currency risks should be hedged (see, for example, Kenyon, 1990). Some ignore them, while others try to hedge them completely. It is likely that the managers of a company are more enthusiastic about hedging than are the shareholders. The former may risk their jobs if rates move, but the latter may hold this company's shares as part of a diversified portfolio. In the Daimler Benz example, the relatively *certain* $100 million of sales could be hedged by buying D-Marks forward against the dollar for appropriate dates throughout the year. The $50 million, which is *not certain* but expected, could be hedged by buying calls on the D-Mark for that amount.

Having decided to use options, it remains to choose an appropriate exercise price. Figure 8.4 demonstrates that the lower the exercise price chosen for the Daimler Benz hedge, the smaller the total cost of hedging but the larger the opportunity loss if ¢/DM fall rather than rise. The outcome after buying calls on the initial exposure is a net position equivalent to a put. Panel (b) in Fig. 8.4

(a) Call options and original exposure

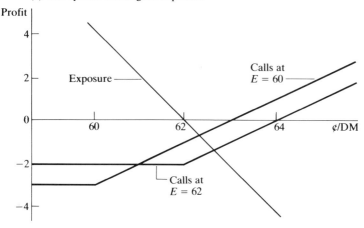

(b) Net exposures with call options

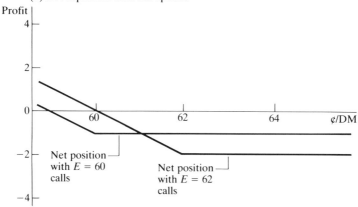

Figure 8.4 Hedging the Daimler Benz exposure with call options

shows that there is potentially more regret from using the 60 cent exercise-price calls then from using the 62 cent exercise-price calls. However, while the 60 cent calls cost more to buy (panel (a)), their net cost in conjunction with the exposure is less (panel (b)). There is no simple rule for choosing the best exercise price: it will depend on how much a fall in the ¢/DM rate would be regretted. If that regret were large for Daimler Benz, then the more costly (net) 62 cent calls would be preferred.

8.2.3 TENDERING FOR A CONTRACT

We have already introduced the concept of a quantity risk. One of the simplest examples of such a risk arises when tendering for a contract in a foreign currency. Suppose that a French company is tendering for a dollar-denominated contract. It faces two kinds of risk. The first is that it does not get the contract, i.e. a quantity risk; the second is that the dollar weakens, so that the French franc value of the contract is reduced, i.e. a price risk. There are then four possible outcomes:

  (i) contract won, dollar strengthens;
  (ii) contract won, dollar weakens;
  (iii) contract lost, dollar strengthens;
  (iv) contract lost, dollar weakens.

Suppose the currency risk is covered by a forward sale of dollars. If the company wins the contract (cases (i) and (ii)), then the franc earnings are predetermined through the forward sale of dollars. If the company loses the contract, then there is a 'naked' exposure on the forward sale of the dollars, leading to a windfall loss if the dollar rises (case (iii)) and a windfall gain if the dollar falls (case (iv)).

If, instead, the currency risk is covered by a call option on the franc, then if the dollar falls the option is exercised, but if the dollar rises the option is abandoned. The exposure is then limited to the call-option premium, which may also be included in the tender as a cost.

As only one company is going to win the contract, it makes sense for competing companies (reporting in one currency) to join together in buying the currency option. Sometimes banks are willing to reduce the option premium on 'tender insurance' if, in the event that the contract is lost (case (iv)), they have the right to any currency gains.[1]

8.2.4 CATASTROPHE INSURANCE

Although exchange rates are not as volatile as most asset prices, the large amount of capital in play makes exchange risk a huge concern for companies. For a company that is largely dependent on foreign markets, it could be a 'catastrophe' if a foreign currency weakened considerably. A recent example would be European car manufacturers, whose sales to the US were hit in 1990 by the fall in the value of the dollar.

This is a variation of sales in other currencies, already discussed in Sec. 8.2.2. The difference is one of strategy. Instead of using options that are near-to-the-money, a company may want to buy some 'insurance' that the rate does not move to an extremely unfavourable level. Thus, Porsche might be willing to accept a strengthening of the D-Mark from 62 to 70 cents per D-Mark, but would like to cap the rate at that level. The company would therefore buy out-of-the-money call options on the D-Mark. A worst rate of 70 cents per D-Mark might be obtained by buying calls at an exercise price of 69 cents, with a 1 cent premium. This is illustrated in Fig. 8.5. The term 'insurance' is particularly appropriate for such an option,

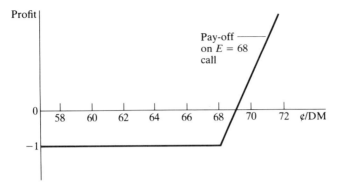

Figure 8.5 Illustration of call option for catastrophe insurance

because it pays out on an event that has a very low chance, but would result in a very large loss.

In 1981 sterling reached a peak of $2.40 per £, then fell to a trough of $1.10 per £ in March 1985. British pension-fund managers already anticipated that the dollar would 'turn' in 1984 and so bought pounds forward to convert their dollar earnings. Instead, the dollar continued to rise in that year and the managers had to report large losses on currency. Had they used options, as some now do, they would have cut their losses.

8.2.5 MULTI-CURRENCY PRICE LIST

Yet another variation on foreign sales arises if a company writes its price list in more than one currency. For example, a Swiss drug company may sell an item at $100, $57, DM291 or Y13 700. The buyer of the drug will then have the option to buy in the cheapest of these currencies. The Swiss company will lose if any of these fall against the Swiss franc and so will need to buy some calls on the Swiss franc against these currencies. In deciding the portfolio of currency options to buy, the Swiss company will need to study the joint behaviour of the four currencies—do they rise and fall together, or not? To the extent that they move together, an option on one currency will cover the risk on another. Clearly, any hedge is going to be approximate, but better than no hedge at all.

8.2.6 CREDIT RISK AND OPTIONS

Forward currency contracts do not cost anything at the time they are initiated; they only require that the currency is bought or sold at maturity at the prearranged price. There is therefore an incentive for the loser to default. Futures contracts overcome this by requiring the payment of a deposit, which is regularly updated. Options overcome the credit risk by requiring immediate payment of the premium. It follows that a company that is a bad credit risk may not be able to obtain forward cover from a bank, but it will always be able to purchase a futures contract or an option.

8.3   Some tailored currency options

Banks are always developing new risk-management products based upon options, in an attempt to gain business from companies. Each bank has a brand name for its own particular product, but they really differ very little (cf. soap powder!). Often the term 'forward' is used in currency products, since that is reassuring to the customer. In this section we shall unravel some of the most commonly marketed arrangements.

Before doing that, one general feature needs to be explained. Because of tax and administration, company treasurers do not like to pay the option premium immediately. They prefer that the premium is paid at maturity and then not made explicit but deducted from the currency rate achieved. Thus, for example, instead of paying 2 cents up front, the premium would be $2(1 + r)^t$ paid at maturity, where r is the relevant interest rate and t is the number of years to maturity. If t were one year and r were 10%, then the deferred premium would be 2.1 cents. If the contract related to the purchase of D-Marks at an exercise price of 62 cents per D-Mark, then upon exercise the treasurer would. pay $62 + 2.1 = 64.1$ cents per D-Mark.

In the following examples we shall, for simplicity, assume that the risk arises on the $/£ rate. The sources for some of these examples are Courtadon (1988), Edwardes and Levy (1987) and Abuaf (1987).

8.3.1   CONDITIONAL FORWARD

Under a conditional forward the customer has a contract to buy sterling at a forward rate of G, but has the right to pull out of the purchase if the rate falls

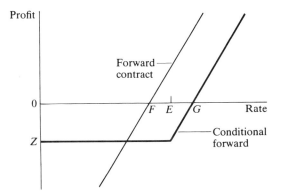

Figure 8.6   A conditional forward on sterling

below G, paying a penalty of a maximum of Z. For example, at a spot rate of $1.55 per £ the offer might be to buy sterling at $1.64 in six months' time. If the pound finishes at $1.64 or above, the deal goes through. If the pound finishes at $1.62, a $0.02 penalty is due. If the pound finishes at less than $1.60, a maximum penalty of $0.04 is due.

In this example, $G = \$1.64$ and $Z = \$0.04$. Figure 8.6 illustrates that this is nothing more than a call option on the pound. The deferred premium, Z, is $0.04 and the exercise price is $G - Z = \$1.60$. The forward rate, F, is shown in the figure for comparative purposes.

8.3.2   BREAK FORWARD

The position is described as follows: 'Having bought pounds at the fixed rate, the treasurer can then sell back the pounds at the break rate'. This is just the same as the conditional forward, i.e. a call option, except that the penalty is now expressed as the ability to sell back at the exercise price. For example, the pounds are bought forward at $1.64 ($G$) and may be sold back to the bank at $1.60 ($E$).

8.3.3   RANGE FORWARD

The deal is that if the $/£ rate rises above G_2, then the customer takes the incremental gain, but if the $/£ rate falls below G_1, then the customer takes the incremental loss. Between G_1 and G_2 the customer makes neither a profit nor a loss.

This is just a combination of a put sold at exercise price G_1 and a call bought for the same premium at exercise price G_2 (see Fig. 8.7). For example, if the spot rate is $1.55 per £, then G_1 might be $1.46 and G_2 might be $1.60. The rate has

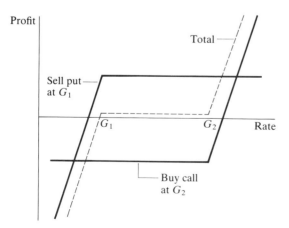

Figure 8.7   A range forward

been given a floor of $1.46 and a cap of $1.60. Sometimes this is called a collar. The trick for the bank is to choose the exercise prices such that the call and the put are of equal value, so the entire deal costs nothing.

From the viewpoint of the treasurer, the range forward would be a hedge if he or she were long of dollars. The cap at $1.60 protects against a large rise in the pound, while the floor at $1.46 is a rate at which the treasurer would be happy to give up any further dollar gains.

8.3.4 PARTICIPATING FORWARD

In this arrangement, there is protection from currency movements in one direction, while gains made from a move in the other direction are shared by the bank and customer. The critical rate is G in Fig. 8.8. If the rate falls below G then the customer gets the rate G. If the rate rises above G, then the gain is shared. It is a 'participating' forward arrangement, because the customer participates in the gain at some prearranged proportion, such as 50%.

Figure 8.8 assumes that the customer is short of dollars and requires protection from a fall in the $/£ rate. A forward sale would give a pay-out at $-45°$ running through the forward rate F. In order to guarantee the rate G, the customer is buying a put on the pound at an exercise price of G. At the same time the customer is selling a call on $q\%$ of the pounds at an exercise price G. In order to make the net cost of the arrangement zero, the cost of the put at G and $q\%$ of a call at G must be the same. Formally,

$$p(G) = qc(G),$$

where p is the put, c is the call, q is the participation rate and G is the exercise price.

As an example: if spot sterling were $1.55 per £, and $G = $1.46, then the $1.46

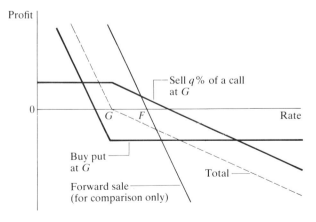

Figure 8.8   A participating forward deal

put for six months might cost $0.036. A $1.46 call would be worth $0.099, so the participation rate would need to be $q = 0.036/0.099 = 36\%$.

The beauty of this arrangement is that it costs nothing, while protecting the downside and giving up part of the gain on the upside. Readers might think that this is familiar. It is very similar to the Mocatta gold deal discussed in Chapter 2.

8.4 The put/call/forward parity relationship

Recall that for a stock (Chapter 3) put/call parity for European options required:

$$p = c - S + PV(E). \tag{8.1}$$

A bought put could be replicated by buying a call, selling a share and lending the present value of the exercise price. In general, a spot price is simply the present value of a forward price, i.e.

$$S = PV(F). \tag{8.2}$$

Substituting for S in Eq. (8.1), we obtain

$$p = c - PV(F) + PV(E)$$
$$p = c - PV(F - E). \tag{8.3}$$

Equation (8.3) indicates that buying a put costs the same as buying a call and borrowing the present value of the difference between the forward rate and the exercise price. It is the put/call/forward parity relationship for any kind of asset.

While (8.3) holds for *costs*, buying a call and borrowing $PV(F - E)$ will not replicate the *pay-off* from a put. What is missing is a forward sale. We can best see this by using an arbitrage proof of the kind already used in Chapter 3.

Let there be two portfolios. The first, A, consists of a bought put. The second, B, consists of a bought call, a borrowing of the present value of $(F - E)$ and a sold forward contract. The pay-offs at maturity of the two portfolios, given an asset price at maturity of S^*, are shown in Table 8.2.

Table 8.2 Portfolio pay-offs at maturity

		Pay-off at maturity	
		$S^* > E$	$S^* \leq E$
(A)	Buy put	0	$E - S^*$
(B)	Buy call	$S^* - E$	0
	Borrow $PV(F - E)$	$-(F - E)$	$-(F - E)$
	Sell forward	$F - S^*$	$F - S^*$
	Total	0	$E - S^*$

The pay-offs to the two portfolios are the same, so they must cost the same. Hence,

$$p = c - \text{PV}(F - E) - \text{Value of forward contract.}$$

But the value of a forward contract at the time it is written is zero, so we have

$$p = c - \text{PV}(F - E)$$

which is the parity relationship in (8.3).

Put/call/forward parity has some useful implications. The first is that European puts and calls written at the forward price will cost the same. This follows from (8.3) because $\text{PV}(F - E) = 0$ when $F = E$. The second implication is that buying a call and selling a put for exercise at the forward rate will cost nothing and be exactly equivalent to a long forward position. Conversely, a short forward position may be established by selling a call and buying a put, both being for exercise at the forward rate.

8.5   Valuation of currency options

8.5.1   GARMAN/KOHLHAGEN FORMULA

A currency is just like a stock that pays a continuous dividend. For example, if I am a dollar investor who buys sterling, then the newly purchased asset will pay the sterling rate of interest. We already saw in Chapter 6 that there was a model (due to Merton) for valuation in the presence of continuous dividends. If we take the foreign currency interest rate to be R and the domestic (dollar) interest rate to be r, then the model may be written

$$c = S\,e^{-Rt}N(d_1) - E\,e^{-rt}N(d_2), \tag{8.4}$$

where $N(d_1)$ and $N(d_2)$ have the Black/Scholes interpretation except that $S\,e^{-Rt}$ replaces S at all times. In full, they are

$$d_1 = \frac{\log(S/E) + (r - R + 0.5\sigma^2)t}{\sigma\sqrt{t}} \tag{8.5}$$

and

$$d_2 = d_1 - \sigma\sqrt{t}. \tag{8.6}$$

Equation (8.4) is often referred to as the Garman/Kohlhagen formula (Garman and Kohlhagen, 1983), but it is really just a repeat of Merton's dividend model (see also Biger and Hull, 1983; Grabbe, 1983).

Equation (8.4) may be equivalently expressed in terms of the forward currency rate, F, rather than the spot currency rate, S. To reach this goal, we first need to invoke the well-known interest-rate parity relationship. This says, effectively, that if I borrow \$1, convert it into a 'foreign' currency, hold it for a period and then convert it back to dollars at a predetermined forward rate, my net gain will be zero. If the gain were more than zero, I would have found a riskless arbitrage. Interest-rate parity may be expressed for discrete intervals as

$$F = \frac{S(1 + r)^t}{(1 + R)^t}. \tag{8.7}$$

In the limit of continuous time, it becomes

$$F = S\,e^{(r - R)t}. \tag{8.8}$$

Rewriting (8.6) in terms of the spot rate we have

$$S = F\,e^{-(r - R)t}. \tag{8.9}$$

If we substitute (8.9) into (8.4) we obtain

$$c = F\,e^{-(r - R)t}\,e^{-Rt}\,N(d_1) - E\,e^{-rt}\,N(d_2),$$

hence

$$c = [FN(d_1) - EN(d_2)]e^{-rt}. \tag{8.10}$$

Equation (8.10), which is the formula for a call option based upon the forward rate, was introduced by Black (1976). It is pleasingly simple. Once again it should be noted that it is necessary to adjust the d_1 and d_2 terms relative to their values in the Black/Scholes formula. $F\,e^{-rt}$ replaces S at all occurrences, so we have

$$d_1 = \frac{\log(F/E) + 0.5\sigma^2 t}{\sigma\sqrt{t}} \tag{8.11}$$

and

$$d_2 = d_1 - \sigma\sqrt{t}. \tag{8.12}$$

As Eqs (8.4) and (8.8) are exactly equivalent, they produce the same answers.

8.5.2   EARLY EXERCISE AND THE GARMAN/KOHLHAGEN FORMULA

A problem with the currency options equations based on either spot or foward rates is that they are for European options. Whether early exercise is valuable or not will depend on the sizes of the two interest rates. For example, consider the limiting case in Eq. (8.4) when volatility is zero. The $N(d_1)$ and $N(d_2)$ terms are both unity, and so we have

$$c \geq \max(S\,e^{-Rt} - E\,e^{-rt}, 0). \tag{8.13}$$

Hence, early exercise would be worth while under zero volatility if $(S - E)$ exceeded $(S\,e^{-Rt} - E\,e^{-rt})$. This is possible, although unlikely. It will be more likely if the foreign interest rate R exceeds the dollar interest rate r, as shown in Fig. 8.9(a). However, Fig. 8.9(b) shows that it may occur for in-the-money options even if the foreign interest rate R is less than the dollar interest rate r.

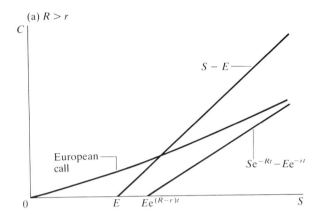

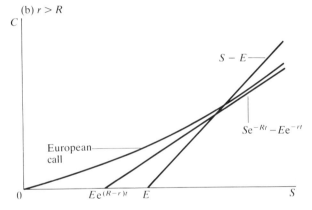

Figure 8.9   Arbitrage bounds for currency calls

The critical portions of Figs 8.9(a) and 8.9(b) are those for which the $(S - E)$ line lies above the $(S e^{-Rt} - E e^{-rt})$ line.

We have already seen that a call on one currency is a put on the other, e.g. the right to buy D-Marks is also the right to sell dollars. It is not surprising, therefore, that if early exercise has value for calls it also has value for puts, particularly when $r > R$. The diagrams to show this would be analogous to those in Fig. 8.9 (see Gemmill, 1986).

The size of the early-exercise problem should not be exaggerated. Studies of the Philadelphia Exchange options have indicated that prices are consistent with the Garman/Kohlhagen formula (8.4)—see, e.g., Shastri and Tandon (1986), Bodurtha and Courtadon (1986). Table 8.3 indicates the potential error for the case where the foreign (sterling) interest rate is 14% and the domestic (US) interest rate is 9%. The largest error arises at- and in-the-money. Very large errors may be avoided by imposing the intrinsic-value bound of $(S - E)$

Table 8.3 Example of call prices on currency

S	c	c*	C	% Error C − c*
95	0.649	0.649	0.694	6.48
100	1.562	1.562	1.696	7.90
105	3.146	3.146	3.490	9.86
110	5.499	5.499	6.278	12.41
115	8.580	10.000	10.144	1.42
120	12.251	15.000	15.000	0.00

Notes:
1. S is the spot rate in $/£
2. c is the European call price from Eq. (8.4)
3. $c*$ is c adjusted for the lower bound of $S - E$
4. C is the correct American call value
5. $E = 105$
6. $t = 200$ days
7. $r = 9\%$ (continuous)
8. $R = 14\%$ (continuous)
9. $\sigma = 0.15$.

(see last column). The 'correct' prices in the table were calculated with the binomial method (see below).

8.5.4 CALCULATING PRICES WHICH ALLOW FOR EARLY EXERCISE

8.5.3.1 *Binomial method*

The simplest way to allow for early exercise is to use the binomial method. Just as in Chapter 4, we have the asset tree and call tree (Fig. 8.10).

As before, assume that a call is sold and the currency bought in the hedge ratio h at a rate S. The pay-off on the portfolio is not quite the same as before, since it now includes interest on the currency position at a rate R per period. If S rises the portfolio pays

$$- C_u + hSU(1 + R).$$

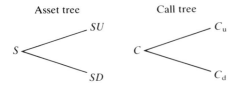

Figure 8.10 Asset tree and call tree

If S falls the portfolio pays

$$- C_d + hSD(1 + R).$$

Equating pay-outs, we find that the hedge ratio is

$$h = \frac{C_u - C_d}{[(1 + R)(U - D)]S} . \qquad (8.14)$$

Solving for C under the requirement that the portfolio pays the risk-free dollar rate, r, leads to

$$C = \frac{m^* C_u + (1 - m^*) C_d}{1 + r} , \qquad (8.15)$$

where

$$m^* = \frac{[(1 + r)/(1 + R)] - D}{U - D} . \qquad (8.16)$$

The method is implemented in the usual way, starting at the final period and working backwards, with a minimum of S–E imposed at each node.

8.5.3.2 *Barone-Adesi/Whaley method*

This method has already been described in Chapter 6 for use in pricing American put options on shares (see Barone-Adesi and Whaley, 1986). It is much faster than the binomial method and is well suited to currency options that have continuous interest-rate terms. It uses the Garman/Kohlhagen equation (8.4) instead of the Black/Scholes equation (5.4), but otherwise the procedure is just the same as that described in Chapter 6.

8.6 Summary

This chapter began with an overview of the markets for currency options. It emphasized that the interbank market is much larger than that to be seen on the organized exchanges.

If options have had an impact on the management of companies, it is probably due to the existence of currency options. Treasurers routinely hedge with currency options, when they are worried that a rate will go in one direction but they wish to limit their regret if the rate goes in the other direction. In particular, hedging with options may be preferred if there is a quantity risk as well as the usual rate risk.

Banks have well-developed marketing sections that tailor currency options for the use of companies. The 'products' on offer have been given reassuring names, such as 'conditional forward' and 'participating forward'. These are just repackaged options, sometimes alone and sometimes in combinations.

Many companies prefer to synthesize their own tailored options rather than to buy them from banks.

Valuation of currency options is relatively easy. A modification of the Black/Scholes model works tolerably well and is very widely used. However, early exercise may have value for both calls and puts, so valuation by the binomial method or the Barone-Adesi/Whaley method is recommended.

Note

1. Hambro's Bank in London has an arrangement named 'EXTRA' of this kind. The reader might like to examine whether Hambro's can hedge its position, or has to take an exposure on whether the company will win the contract.

References

Abuaf, N. (1987), 'Foreign exchange options: the leading hedge', *Midland Bank Corporate Finance Journal*, **5**, 51–8.

Bank of England (1989), 'The market in foreign exchange in London', *Bank of England Quarterly Bulletin*, **29**, 531–5.

Barone-Adesi, G. and Whaley, R. (1986), 'The valuation of American futures options: theory and empirical tests', *Journal of Finance*, **41**, 127–50.

Biger, N. and Hull, J. (1983), 'The valuation of currency options', *Financial Management*, **12** (Spring), 24–8.

Black, F. (1976), 'The pricing of commodity contracts', *Journal of Financial Economics*, **3**, 167–79.

Bodurtha, J. and Courtadon, G. (1986), 'Efficiency tests of the foreign currency options market', *Journal of Finance*, **41**, 151–62.

Courtadon, G. (1988), *Recent Trends in Foreign Currency Option Valuation*, Citicorp Investment Bank, New York.

Edwardes, W. and Levy, E. (1987), 'Break-forwards: a synthetic option hedging instrument', *Midland Bank Corporate Finance Journal*, **5**, 59–67.

Garman, M. and Kohlhagen, S. (1983), 'Foreign currency option values', *Journal of International Money and Finance*, **2**, 231–7.

Gemmill, G. (1986), 'A primer on the pricing of options on currencies and short-term interest rates', *Investment Analyst*, **81** (July), 16–22.

Giddy, I. (1983), 'The foreign exchange option as a hedging tool', *Midland Bank Corporate Finance Journal*, **1** (Fall), 32–42.

Grabbe, O. (1983), 'The pricing of call and put options on foreign exchange', *Journal of International Money and Finance*, **2**, 239–53.

Kenyon, A. (1990), *Currency Risk and Business Management*, Blackwell, Oxford.

Shastri, K. and Tandon, K. (1986), 'Valuation of foreign currency options: some empirical tests', *Journal of Financial and Quantitative Analysis*, **21**, 145–60.

9
Stock-index options

9.1 Introduction

Stock-index options were first introduced by the Chicago Board Options Exchange (CBOE) in 1983 and rapidly became the most heavily traded of the stock-based options. They developed in parallel with stock-index futures contracts, the main one of which in the United States is the S&P 500 future on the Chicago Mercantile Exchange. Unlike the options so far described, they are settled in cash and valued at x per point. For example, the S&P 100 option on the CBOE is valued at $100 per point. At an index level of 360, therefore, one option relates to a $36 000 position in the 100-share portfolio which comprises the index.

Trading in stock-index futures is a way of increasing or decreasing exposure to whole markets. Stock-index options have the added attraction of their asymmetric returns. This chapter describes the instruments and their simple uses, then Chapter 10 discusses portfolio management with index options and, in particular, portfolio insurance.

9.2 Stock-index options markets

Most of the nations that have well-developed stock markets now have their own stock-index options contracts. However, so far there has been little success in introducing 'foreign' index options on domestic markets—for example, Japanese Index options in the United States. The main contracts by turnover in 1991 are listed in Table 9.1.

In addition to the options on indices, many index warrants exist. These are issued in fixed quantities by banks or other intermediaries and have longer times to maturity. They are often listed on exchanges, like shares: for example, many Euromarket warrants are listed on the Luxembourg Exchange.

Figure 9.1 is an extract from the *Wall Street Journal* of 14 March 1991, which

Thursday, March 14, 1991

OPTIONS

Chicago Board

S&P 100 INDEX

Strike Price	Calls—Last Mar	Apr	May	Puts—Last Mar	Apr	May
265	93¼	....	....	....	....	....
280	....	....	....	....	⅛	....
285	....	....	....	....	⅛	....
290	67⅜	....	....	....	3/16	⅜
295	64	....	....	1/16	3/16	9/16
300	60½	58	....	1/16	¼	¾
305	53	54	56¼	1/16	5/16	13/16
310	46	49	51¼	1/16	⅜	1
315	40⅝	44⅜	....	1/16	½	1¼
320	35⅜	37½	41¼	1/16	⅝	1¾
325	30¾	32⅜	....	1/16	13/16	2⅛
330	25¾	27½	32¼	1/16	1 1/16	2⅜
335	20¾	26	28½	1/16	1½	2 15/16
340	15¾	18⅞	....	1/16	2⅛	4½
345	10¾	14½	18½	⅛	3⅛	5⅜
350	5⅞	10⅞	13½	⅜	4⅜	7½
355	2⅛	8	11	1⅜	6⅜	9¼
360	½	5½	8¼	4⅞	9½	11¼
365	1/16	3¾	7	9⅜	11	14¼
370	1/16	2 7/16	4¼	10¼	16	15¼
375	1/16	1 9/16	3¼	....	....	19

Total call volume 236,408 Total call open int. 426,357
Total put volume 175,221 Total put open int. 668,666
The index: High 360.18; Low 352.99; Close 355.31, −0.94

S&P 500 INDEX

Strike Price	Calls—Last Mar	Apr	Jun	Puts—Last Mar	Apr	Jun
305	73	....	....	....	....	....
310	67	....	....	1/16	....	....
315	63½	....	64½	1/16	....	....
320	53⅜	....	....	....	....	....
325	51¾	....	55	1/16	....	1⅜
330	46	....	47¼	1/16	....	1⅞
335	41¾	....	....	1/16	....	....
340	32¾	....	41	1/16	....	3⅛
345	28½	34⅛	37⅜	1/16	⅜	3½
350	23⅜	29¾	29½	....	1	3¾
355	18⅜	24½	....	1/16	1⅞	5¼
360	13½	19	22	1/16	2½	5⅜
365	7¾	16⅜	18¾	3/16	3½	7¾
370	3⅞	10¼	18½	¾	4¾	9¼
375	1⅛	7	15¾	2⅞	7¼	11⅛
380	¼	6½	10	6½	10½	12
385	1/16	3⅜	9	9	13¼	15
390	1/16	2	6⅜	....	17⅛	....
395	....	1⅞	....	....	....	....
400	....	1⅛	4¼	....	....	24¼
425	....	....	¾	....	....	....

Total call volume 70,758 Total call open int. 567,429
Total put volume 35,725 Total put open int. 672,767
The index: High 378.28; Low 371.76; Close 373.50, −1.07

LEAPS-S&P 100 INDEX

Strike Price	Calls—Last Dec92	Dec 93		Puts—Last Dec 92	Dec 93	
27½	....	....	....	13	....	....
30	....	....	....	1¼	....	....
32½	6	....	....	1⅞	....	....
35	4¼	....	....	2⅜	....	....
37½	3⅛	4	....	....	....	....

Total call volume 37 Total call open int. 12,197
Total put volume 616 Total put open int. 43,147
The index: High 36.02; Low 35.30; Close 35.53, −.10

Pacific Exchange

FINANCIAL NEWS COMPOSITE INDEX

Strike Price	Calls—Last Mar	Apr	Jun	Puts—Last Mar	Apr	Jun
220	....	....	40⅛	....	....	....
240	14¾	....	....	....	....	....
245	11¼	13⅜	....	....	....	....
250	6½	....	....	....	....	....
255	2¾	6⅛	....	1 15/16	5	....
260	13/16	4½	....	....	....	....
265	....	2 7/16	....	....	....	....
270	....	....	4	....	....	....

Total call volume 412 Total call open int. 3,007
Total put volume 183 Total put open int. 1,302
The index: High 258.27; Low 253.21; Close 254.55, −0.70

N.Y. Stock Exchange

NYSE INDEX OPTIONS

Strike Price	Calls—Last Mar	Apr	May	Puts—Last Mar	Apr	May
180	....	....	....	....	3/16	....
185	....	....	....	....	7/16	....
190	....	15	....	....	9/16	....
192½	....	....	....	....	1⅛	....
195	9¾	12½	12⅞	....	....	....
197½	....	8½	....	....	....	....
200	4⅜	6½	....	1/16	1⅞	4
205	⅜	4 15/16	6⅜	1	4½	....
210	1/16	....	....	....	6⅜	....

Total call volume 707 Total call open int. 4,050
Total put volume 277 Total put open int. 5,195
The index: High 206.47; Low 203.48; Close 204.28, −0.32

European Options Exchange

Dutch Stock Index

Strike Price	Call-Last Nov	Apr	Jan	Put-Last Nov	Apr	Jan
260	....	14.50	23.00	....	2.20	10.00
265	....	10.70	....	....	3.50	....
270	....	7.70	18.00	....	5.50	14.50
275	....	5.50	....	....	7.80	....
280	....	3.40	12.00	....	11.30	23.00

Total call volume 12,871 Total call open int. 76,276
Total put volume 4,452 Total put open int. 7,375
The index: High 271.89; Low 268.08; Close 271.84, +6.26

London's Stock Exchange

FT-SE 100 SHARE INDEX

Strike Price	Call—Settle Mar	Apr	May	Put—Settle Mar	Apr	May
1900	601	613	619	½	1½	2
1950	551	563	571	½	2	2½
2000	501	515	521	½	2½	3½
2050	451	466	474	½	3	4
2100	401	418	425	½	3	6
2150	350	368	377	½	4	8
2200	301	320	334	1½	5	11
2250	253	275	288	1½	8	15
2300	204	230	244	2½	13	21
2350	155	185	204	4½	18	29
2400	108	142	164	7½	27	39
2450	67	107	129	16	39	54
2500	36	74	97	38	60	75
2550	16	50	71	69	88	102
2600	6	31	52	113	124	134

Volume 7,175; Calls:5,499; Puts:1,676
Open Interest 108,983

FUTURES

FTSE 100 (LIFFE) £25 per index point

	Open	High	Low	Settle	Change	Lifetime High	Lifetime Low	Open Int
Mar 91	2471.0	2503.0	2470.0	2501.0	+ 48.0	2543.0	2077.0	17,896
Jun 91	2513.0	2543.0	2513.0	2541.0	+ 47.5	2549.0	2116.0	13,509
Sep 91	....	....	....	2579.5	+ 47.5	2350.0	2180.0	90

Est vol 8,117; open int 31,495, na.

S&P 500 INDEX (CME) 500 times index

	Open	High	Low	Settle	Chg	High	Low	Open Interest
Mar	376.20	378.80	371.50	373.60	− 2.20	384.00	298.00	46,477
June	379.40	382.20	374.50	376.95	− 2.10	386.00	300.90	127,029
Sept	382.00	384.70	377.50	379.60	− 2.10	386.90	304.00	1,478
Dec	....	....	....	382.45	− 1.75	388.90	316.50	672

Est vol 89,482; vol Wed 77,164; open int 175,656, 1,429.
Indx prelim High 378.28; Low 371.76; Close 373.50 −1.07

NIKKEI 225 Stock Average (CME)—$5 times NSA

June	27350.	27410.	27180.	27220.	− 35.0	27450.	21765.	4,299

Est vol 690; vol Wed 517; open int 4,302, +171.
The index: High 26591.47; Low 26366.45; Close 26542.33 +124.01

NYSE COMPOSITE INDEX (NYFE) 500 times index

Mar	205.40	206.80	203.00	204.65	− .50	207.85	163.85	1,642
June	207.20	208.75	204.70	205.95	− 1.05	209.60	165.85	395
Sept	208.25	209.55	208.10	207.30	− 1.50	210.50	173.10	295

Est vol 7,736; vol Wed 7,422; open int 5,916, −72.
The index: High 206.47; Low 203.48; Close 204.28 −.32

MAJOR MKT INDEX (CBT) $250 times index

Mar	624.00	632.50	621.00	624.25	+ .50	632.50	516.50	5,777
Apr	626.00	634.50	623.75	627.00	+ .75	634.50	547.75	3,109
May	627.10	634.50	623.75	627.10	+ .75	634.50	612.90	190

Est vol 6,500; vol Wed 3,984; open int 9,077, −64.
The Index: High 631.35; Low 619.39; Close 623.56 +2.05

CAC-FORTY STOCK INDEX FUTURE (MATIF)
Frf 200 per index pt

	Open	Settle	Change	High	Low	Yield	Open Int.
Mar	1815.0	1835.0	+ 37.0	1835.0	1812.0	....	8,935
Apr	1833.0	1850.0	+ 34.0	1847.0	1829.0	....	1,892
May	1845.0	1862.0	+ 23.0	1848.0	1845.0	....	5
Jun	1839.0	1856.0	+ 29.0	1848.0	1838.0	....	500

Est vol 7,817; open int 11,332

—OTHER INDEX FUTURES—

Settlement price of selected contract. Volume and open interest of all contract months.

KC Mini Value Line (KC)—100 times index
Jun 300.50 −.50; Est. vol. 100; Open int. 284
KC Value Line Index (KC)—500 times index
Jun 300.30 −.70; Est. vol. 725; Open int. 2,527
The index: High 299.56; Low 297.03; Close 297.29 −.02
CRB Index (NYFE)—250 times index
May 219.35 −1.00; Est. vol. 367; Open int. 1,561
The index: High 220.88; Low 219.79; Close 219.88 −.89

FUTURES OPTIONS

S&P 500 STOCK INDEX (CME) $500 times premium

Strike Price	Calls—Settle Mar-c	Apr-c	Ju-c	Puts—Settle Mar-p	Apr-p	Jun-p
365	8.60	15.20	19.40	0.00	3.35	7.70
370	3.75	11.55	16.05	0.15	4.70	9.25
375	0.60	8.45	13.10	2.00	6.50	11.20
380	0.00	5.95	10.55	6.40	9.00	13.55
385	0.00	4.05	8.30	11.40	12.05	16.20
390	0.00	2.75	6.45	16.40	....	....

Est. vol. 9,489; Wed vol. 1,617 calls; 3,640 puts
Open interest Wed; 42,238 calls; 79,051 puts

NYSE COMPOSITE INDEX (NYFE) $500 times premium

Strike Price	Calls—Settle Mar-c	Apr-c	May-c	Puts—Settle Mar-p	Apr-p	May-p
204	0.85	4.80	6.00	0.20	2.95	4.25

Est. vol. 485, Wed vol. 78 calls, 154 puts
Open interest Wed 681 calls, 1,365 puts

NIKKEI 225 STOCK AVERAGE (CME) $5 times NSA

Strike Price	Calls—Settle Apr-c	May-c	Jun-c	Puts—Settle Apr-p	May-p	Jun-p
27000	925	....	1300	705	....	1080

Est. vol. 5, Wed vol. 9 calls, 16 puts
Open interest Wed 341 calls, 485 puts

CBT—Chicago Board of Trade; CME—Chicago Mercantile Exchange; KC—Kansas City Board of Trade; LIFFE—London International Financial Futures Exchange; NYFE—New York Futures Exchange, unit of New York Stock Exchange.

Figure 9.1 Index trading
Source: Wall Street Journal, 14 March 1991. Reproduced with permission

Table 9.1 Major stock-index options contracts in 1991

Nation	Index	Exchange	Value per point	Index (approx.) 4/91	Volume (million contracts)
USA	S&P 100	CBOE	$100	360	63.9
	S&P 500	CBOE	$100	380	11.9
	S&P 500 fut.	CME	$500	380	1.8
	XMI	AMEX	$100	625	3.9
Japan	Nikkei 225	Osaka	Y1000	27 000	11.8
Netherlands	Dutch	EOE	Df200	270	2.4
France	CAC 40	MONEP	Ff200	1840	2.3
Switzerlnd	SMI	SOFFEX	Sf50	1660	6.2
UK	FTSE 100	LTOM	£10	2500	1.8
Germany	DAX	DTB	DM10	1600	2.0

Key: CBOE   Chicago Board Options Exchange
      CME   Chicago Mercantile Exchange
      AMEX   American Exchange
      Osaka   Osaka Exchange
      EOE   European Options Exchange
      MONEP   Marché des Options Négociables de la Bourse de Paris
      SOFFEX   Swiss Options and Futures Exchange
      LTOM   London Traded Options Market
      DTB   Deutsche Terminbörse.
Sources: Adapted from data in: *Futures and Options World*, February 1992; *International Futures and Options Databook*, published by Futures and Options World/Reuters.

gives prices for several of the stock-index options. Looking at the Chicago S&P 100 options, there was a very large range of exercise prices at that time, from 265 to 375, which reflected the listing of new series as the market had risen early in 1991. The actively traded options were those near to the current index level of 355.31. Taking the at-the-money 355 series as an example, March calls cost $2\frac{1}{8}$ index points, April calls 8 points and May calls 11 points. March puts cost $1\frac{5}{8}$ points, April puts $6\frac{5}{8}$ points and June puts $9\frac{1}{4}$ points. At $100 per point, the April call, for example, would have cost 8 × $100 = $800.

9.3 Uses of stock-index options

9.3.1 SIMPLE SPECULATION

As with other kinds of options, stock-index options may be used to increase or decrease exposure to a particular market, i.e. to speculate or hedge. The very large number of exercise prices enables a wide range of finely tuned strategies to be implemented. We shall consider a simple speculation in S&P 500 index options (traded on the CBOE) for the period 14 March to 15 April 1991. Table 9.2 gives prices for the June 360 and 380 options on the two days. The changes

Table 9.2 S&P 500 June option prices

	14 March (Index = 373.50)		15 April (Index = 381.19)	
Expiry price	Calls	Puts	Calls	Puts
360	22	$5\frac{3}{8}$	$24\frac{3}{4}$	3
380	10	12	11	$7\frac{1}{4}$

Note: Options expired on 21 June, 99 days from 14 March and 67 days from 15 April.

in the level of the index and of the 360 options are also plotted in Fig. 9.2.[1]

The index rose by 7.69 points (from 373.50 to 381.19) over this one-month period. However, before transactions costs the buyer of a 360 call would have gained only $2\frac{3}{4}$ points and of a 380 call only 1 point. What was happening? The answer is not only that the option prices moved less than the index due to the 'delta effect', but their values were eroded by time decay. In March the options had 14 weeks of life remaining, whereas in April they had less than 10 weeks to maturity. The seller of the options would have gained from the erosion. In particular, as the market rose the seller of put options would have doubly gained, both from the market movement and from the decay in time value. For example, the seller of a 380 put would have gained $4\frac{3}{4}$ (40%) before transactions costs.

All the familiar spreads and straddles of Chapter 2 apply equally to index options as to simple share options. For example, a vertical 360/380 bull spread taken out on 14 March would have cost $22 - 10 = 12$ points. Its resale on 15 April would have paid $24\frac{3}{4} - 11 = 13\frac{3}{4}$ points. The profit would have been $1\frac{3}{4}$ points, i.e. \$175, which would not have been sufficient to cover transactions costs.[2]

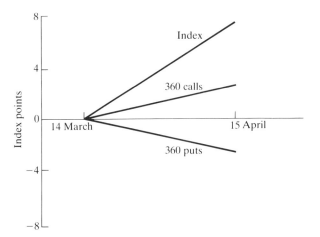

Figure 9.2 Changes in S&P 500 Index options and the index

9.3.2 SPECULATION IN SPECIFIC RISK

Security analysts spend much of their time deciding which shares are under-valued and which are overvalued relative to the market as a whole. Index options (or futures) can be used in conjunction with a share position to obtain an exposure to the relative performance of a share. For example, suppose I am expecting that the software company, Borland, will outperform the American market as a whole over the next month. I can take a position in the *specific* risk and return of this company by purchasing some shares and then buying puts on the S&P 500 Index (or selling index futures). The puts provide protection against a general fall in the market, while the total position will be profitable if Borland outperforms the market.[3]

We can see how this strategy would have performed over the 14 March–15 April period. Borland's share price on 14 March was $46.5. We assume that the investor buys 10 000 shares for $465 000. Now he or she has to decide which index puts to buy and how many. The S&P 500 Index is at 373.50. By purchasing some June 360 puts protection is obtained if there is a market fall by mid June of more than $13.5/373.5 = 3.61\%$. The number to buy depends on their value ($100 per point) and how far the Borland share price moves if the index moves by 1%. Borland is a rather volatile share, so it might be expected to move by 1.4% per 1% move in the index. This relationship is known as the beta of the share.

Hence the number of 360 puts to buy is

$$\frac{\text{Portfolio value}}{\text{Index value}} \times \text{Borland beta} = \frac{\$465\,000}{373.50 \times \$100} \times 1.4$$

$$= 17.43$$
$$\approx 17 \text{ puts (after rounding).}$$

The cost of 17 June 360 puts is $17 \times 5\frac{3}{8} \times \$100 = \$9138$.

On 15 April the Borland share price had risen by more than 29% to $60.25 so the 10 000 shares were worth a total of $602 250, a gain of $137 500. By contrast,

Table 9.3 Speculation in Borland's specific risk

	Shares	Options
14 April	Buy 10 000 at $46.5 = $465 000	Buy 17 June 360 puts at $5\frac{3}{8}$ = $9138
15 May	Sell 10 000 at $60.25 = $602 500	Sell 17 June 360 puts at 3 = $5100
Profit/loss	+ $137 500	− $4038

the S&P 500 Index only rose by 2.06%. The June 360 puts were worth only 3 points each, i.e. $17 \times 3 \times \$100 = \$5100$ in total, a loss of $4038. The total strategy therefore resulted in a gain of $133 462 (before the deduction of transactions costs). The whole strategy is summarized in Table 9.3.

9.3.3 PORTFOLIO HEDGES

Stock-index options can be used to remove almost all of the risk on a whole portfolio. However, it is simpler to achieve this kind of symmetric hedge with futures contracts because the options need to be rebalanced regularly. The hedger in options is also exposed to any change in volatility that might occur, which would raise or lower the options' prices but would leave futures unaffected. Nevertheless, dealers find themselves every day with positions in shares, futures and options and may want to hedge the total book. In that case a delta hedge is needed, and so we shall describe it in some detail.

In hedging a portfolio with options, it is first necesary to calculate the number of options required. In the Borland example above, we noted that the relationship between returns on a share and returns on an index is shown as the share's *beta*. A portfolio is just a mix of shares and the portfolio beta may be calculated as a weighted average of the share betas.

We now have a way to predict the portfolio movement relative to the index, but we still need to account for how far the option moves if the index moves by 1 unit. This is the delta.

Hence, we have:

$$\text{Number of options} = \text{beta} \frac{\text{Portfolio value}}{\text{Index value}} \frac{1}{\text{Option delta}}$$

An example is given in Table 9.4, once again using the S&P 500 option prices for 14 March and 15 April. It is assumed that a $1 million portfolio with a beta of 1.25 is to be hedged against a fall in value. This is accomplished by buying June 360 puts, which have a delta of -0.30. The calculation of the number of puts to buy is shown in the table: it is given as 112, costing $60 200 on 14 March. The position is reversed on 15 April when the portfolio is no longer at risk. The portfolio has risen in value by $25 736, in line with its beta and the increase in the index. There is a loss on the put options of $26 600, so the hedged position loses $864 in total (i.e. 0.1% of the portfolio value).

This hedge is surprisingly good, given that the portfolio value changed by $26 000. Some reasons why it might have been expected to be less effective would be: (i) the option position was not rebalanced; (ii) the options might have been mispriced; (iii) the volatility might have changed; and (iv) the beta is only an estimate of the portfolio/index relationship.

For most investors it makes little sense to (symmetrically) delta-hedge a portfolio with options. Index futures should be used instead. Index options are much more useful if the investor wants to cut losses at a particular price level.

Table 9.4   Hedge of portfolio with S&P 500 options

	Shares	Options
14 March	Worried that market may fall Index = 373.50 Portfolio value = $1m. Portfolio beta = 1.25	Buy puts to hedge May 360 put delta = − 0.30 Buy $1.25 \times \dfrac{1\,000\,000}{373.5 \times \$100} \times \dfrac{1}{0.30}$ = 112 puts at $5\frac{3}{8}$ costing $60\,200
15 April	No longer worried about fall Index = 381.19 Portfolio value = $1\,025\,736	Sell 112 360 puts at 3, giving $33\,600.
	Gain on spot = $25\,736	Gain on options = − $26\,600

For example, he or she might want to protect the $1 million portfolio on 14 March from an index of less than 350 at the end of June. This would require the purchase of an appropriate number of June 350 puts at $3\frac{3}{4}$ each. The number of puts would be the same as above, except that there would be no delta effect:

$$\text{Number of options} = \text{beta} \, \frac{\text{Portfolio value}}{\text{Index value}}$$

$$= 1.25 \, \frac{1\,000\,000}{373.5 \times 100}$$

$$= 33 \text{ (rounded)}.$$

The cost would be $33 \times 3\frac{3}{4} \times \$100 = \$12\,375$. Hence, for a cost of 1.24% (of the $1m. at risk) the portfolio would be insured against an index fall of 6.29% (from 373.50 to 350 or below). Such 'insurance' uses of index options will be discussed in greater detail in Chapter 10.

9.4   Valuation of stock-index options[4]

In valuing stock-index options, the adjustments required to the Black/Scholes model are caused by the same factors that we have already discussed in Chapters 6 and 7—i.e. dividends, transactions costs and the character of the index distribution. These factors will be reviewed in turn.

9.4.1 DIVIDENDS

As an index is merely the sum of its components, so its level will fall on the ex-dividend days of the component shares. Dividend effects are extremely

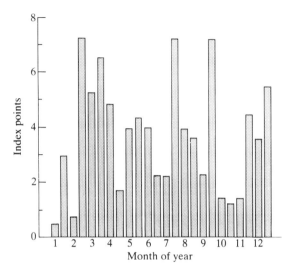

Figure 9.3   The dividend stream on the FTSE 100 Index in 1990
Source: Adapted from data supplied by London Stock Exchange.

important for shares, as was discussed in Chapter 6, particularly in countries such as the UK where payments are semi-annual rather than quarterly (as in the USA). If an index has a relatively small number of component shares, then dividend payments may remain rather lumpy. This is the case for the French CAC 40, for example. On the other hand, the most general indices, such as the S&P 500, spread out the dividends so that payments are rather smooth. Hence, the larger the number of shares in an index and the more frequent the payment of dividends, the smaller the impact of dividends on the index at any one date. Figure 9.3 shows the pattern of dividend payments on London's FTSE 100 Index during 1990. Ex-dividend days coincide with new account periods on this market, so there were 24 of them in 1990. The largest dividend was only 0.35% of the index, but the pattern was quite irregular.[5]

If dividends are a relatively smooth series, they are unlikely to make the early exercise of calls worth while. It follows that Merton's dividend model (of Chapter 6) may be used for valuation, in which the stock (index) price is discounted by the dividend yield over the life of the option.

The Black/Scholes model becomes

$$c = S\,e^{-\delta t}\,N(d_1) - E\,e^{-rt}\,N(d_2), \tag{9.1}$$

where δ is the continuous dividend rate or yield and d_1, d_2 are as before, except that $S\,e^{-\delta t}$ replaces S everywhere.

Nevertheless, there can be large differences between option values based upon continuous dividends and those based upon actual dividends. Brenner *et al.* (1987) demonstrate that, even for the large NYSE Index, the difference is likely to be from 2% at-the-money to 6% out-of-the-money. For the smaller MMI Index the comparable errors are 5.4% and 15.2% respectively. In addition, there remains the problem of undervaluation of the puts, which are American.

A solution is to use the familiar binomial model, which can accommodate any number of discrete dividends. It also has the advantage of correctly valuing the American puts. If speed is important, the calls can be valued with the pseudo-American model of Black (see Chapter 6), while the binomial model is used only for the puts.

9.4.2 TRANSACTIONS COSTS AND THE INFLUENCE OF FUTURES PRICES

Transactions costs have a larger impact on the prices of index options than on the prices of options on individual shares. Pricing models are based on arbitrage between the asset and the options, but it is difficult on most markets to transact simultaneously in all the component shares of an index.[6] Marketmakers in options do not therefore hedge their positions with portfolios of shares but with index futures, for which the transactions costs are very low.[7] The consequence is that index futures and index options are drawn closely into arbitrage equilibrium, but they may both 'wander' within a 'twilight zone' of no arbitrage in relation to the underlying index.[8]

Taking account of discrete dividends, the equilibrium relationship between spot and futures prices is

$$S_t = \frac{F_T}{(1 + r)^{T-t}} + \sum_{k=t+1}^{T} \frac{D_k}{(1 + r)^k},$$ (9.2)

where S is the spot price, F is the futures price, t is the spot time, T is the maturity time, D is a dividend, r is the rate of interest and k denotes the time of a dividend payment.

Quite often in the United States and the United Kingdom the present value of the futures price, as calculated from Eq. (9.2), has been lower than the spot index (see Yadav and Pope, 1990). The opposite has happened in Japan.[9] When there is this disequilibrium, it is difficult to know whether option prices should be based upon the spot index or the present value of the futures price. Marketmakers generally prefer the latter, because they are using the futures market to hedge their option positions.

9.4.3 THE DISTRIBUTION OF RETURNS ON AN INDEX

The Black/Scholes model is based upon a lognormal distribution for the asset price. If share prices follow such a distribution, then an index, which is the sum of lognormal distributions, cannot in theory be lognormally distributed. Equivalently, the returns on an index cannot be normally distributed if the returns on its component shares are normally distributed. Does this matter? Probably not.

Table 9.5   Implied volatilities at various exercise prices for October FTSE 100
options on 28 September 1988

	Implied volatility	
Exercise price	Calls	Puts
1700	0.25	0.21
1750	0.21	0.19
1800	0.17	0.17
1850	0.15	0.18
1900	0.14	0.15

Note: Options priced with a binomial model, using the present value of the implicit futures price
for October. The latter was calculated by interpolation from the spot index and the December
futures price.

The evidence on the shape of index distributions is that their returns are as near,
if not nearer, to a normal distribution than those of shares.[10]

A more important consideration is that observed index-option prices tend to
show an upward bias at low striking prices. An extreme example is illustrated in
Table 9.5 using implied volatilities for calls and puts on London's FTSE 100
Index. Options at the lowest exercise price of 1700 had implied volatilities of
0.25 (calls) and 0.21 (puts). Options at the highest exercise price of 1900 had
implied volatilities of 0.14 (calls) and 0.15 (puts). Rather than 'volatility with a
smile', which was discussed in Chapter 7, this looks more like 'volatility with a
sneer'.

On average over the whole 1985–90 period, options on the FTSE 100 Index
that were 3% below the money were priced with a volatility of 12% more than
options that were 3% above the money. Similar results appear to hold for US
Index options.[11] It is possible that this reflects the hedging behaviour of
marketmakers. They tend to buy out-of-the-money puts in order to protect
their inventory (of shares and options) from a large fall in the market.

9.5   Summary

Index options were only introduced in the United States in 1983. They have
been a huge success and are rapidly penetrating the various European and
Asian markets. They are settled in cash and allow the user to speculate or hedge
on a whole index 'at one shot'. Sophisticated strategies, such as speculation in
the specific risk of a company, are facilitated. Their use in insurance strategies
will be reviewed in detail in the next chapter.

If dividends are a smooth stream, fair values for European options may be
derived with Merton's dividend model. However, most index options are
American and dividends are lumpy, so a model which allows for early exercise
is required. For calls, the Black/Scholes model with pseudo-American adjust-

ment is fast, but the binomial model is more accurate. For puts, the binomial model is recommended.

Index-options prices are likely to 'wander' around fair value rather more than share-options prices, because transactions costs make arbitrage with an index expensive. The result is that marketmakers use futures for hedging their options, so futures prices may have a strong influence on the prices of index options. One systematic peculiarity is that low-exercise-price options are often priced on volatilities above those of high-exercise-price options. This may reflect the behaviour of marketmakers who buy out-of-the-money puts to control their portfolio risks.

Notes

1. It should be noted that these are the last-traded prices from the *Wall Street Journal* and may not relate to exactly the same time, i.e. they may be non-synchronous.
2. Bid/ask spreads could easily cost 3 points on this deal. We are also assuming that it is possible to trade at the quoted prices.
3. This theme is developed by Figlewski and Kon (1984).
4. Papers on valuation include: Evnine and Rudd (1985), Barone-Adesi and Whaley (1986), Brenner *et al.* (1987), Day and Lewis (1988), Merrick (1988) and Bailey and Stulz (1989).
5. These are dividends net of basic-rate tax. It appears that in London the market falls by this amount on ex-dividend dates. In theory it should fall by the gross dividend, because pension funds and other institutions do not pay tax.
6. The New York Stock Exchange has a 'superdot system' for automatic execution of portfolio trades.
7. Figlewski (1989) demonstrates that the spreads on US Index options are actually much narrower than would be expected from arbitrage with the bundle of shares.
8. The index/futures channel is about 1.4% in the United States (Gould, 1988) and 3% in the United Kingdom (Ward, 1988).
9. See *Financial Times*, 21 January 199_
10. Badrinath and Chatterjee (1988) discuss the shape of index distributions in detail.
11. The British results are from Gemmill (1991). The US results are from Bates (1991).

References

Badrinath, S. and Chatterjee, S. (1988), 'On measuring skewness and elongation in common stock distributions: the case of the market index', *Journal of Business*, **61**, 451–72.

Bailey, W. and Stulz, R. (1989), 'The pricing of stock index options in a general equilibrium model', *Journal of Financial and Quantitative Analysis*, **24**, 1–12.

Barone-Adesi, G. and Whaley, R. (1986), 'Valuation of American futures options: theory and empirical tests', *Journal of Finance*, **41**, 127–50.

Bates, D. (1991), 'The Crash of '87: Was it expected? The evidence from options markets', *Journal of Finance*, **46**, 1009–44.

Brenner, M., Courtadon, G. and Subramanyam, M. (1987), 'The valuation of index options', Joint AMEX/SOFFEX Seminar, Zurich.

Day, T. and Lewis, C. (1988), 'The behaviour of the volatility implicit in the pricing of stock index options', *Journal of Financial Economics*, **22**, 103–22.

Evnine, J. and Rudd, A. (1985), 'Index options: the early evidence', *Journal of Finance*, **40**, 743–56.

Figlewski, S. and Kon, S. (1984), 'Portfolio management with stock index futures', *Financial Analysts Journal* (Jan./Feb.), 52–60.

Figlewski, S. (1989), 'Options arbitrage in imperfect markets', *Journal of Finance*, **44**, 1289–1311.

Gemmill, G. (1991), 'Using option prices to reveal traders' expectations', City University Business School, London.

Gould, F. (1988), 'Stock index futures: the arbitrage cycle and portfolio insurance', *Financial Analysts Journal* (Jan./Feb.), 48–62.

Merrick, J. (1988), 'Hedging mispriced options', *Journal of Financial and Quantitative Analysis*, **23**, 451–64.

Ward, V. (1988), 'Market structures obstruct path of FTSE arbitrage', *Futures and Options World* (May), 27–9.

Yadav, P. and Pope, P. (1990), 'Stock index futures pricing: international evidence', *Journal of Futures Markets*, **10**, 573–603.

10
Portfolio insurance

10.1 Introduction

The basic idea of portfolio insurance is that an investor gives up some of the potential gain from a rise in share prices in order to guarantee a minimum rate of return. Although it was criticized by the Brady Commission investigation into the Crash of 1987 (Brady Commission, 1988), portfolio insurance under

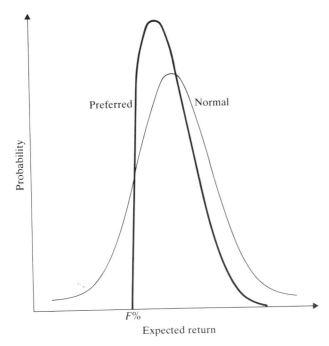

Figure 10.1 Comparison of normal and preferred distributions of returns

other names has existed for many years and will continue to do so. It reflects the desire of investors in a rising market to increase the proportion of equity held in a portfolio and to do the opposite in a falling market. As Rubinstein (1988) says: 'Dynamic asset allocation will not go away, because it reflects investors' preferences which have not changed.' The investors prefer the asymmetric distribution of returns in Fig. 10.1 to the symmetric one. They would like to guarantee a minimum return of $F\%$ and, in exchange, are willing to reduce the chance of extremely high returns.

This chapter begins by demonstrating in Sec. 10.2 how the strategy may be established with either puts or calls. The pay-offs are then compared in Sec. 10.3 with the more traditional approach of 'buy and hold'. Simple rules for implementing the strategy are discussed in Sec. 10.4 and the reasons why futures are often used in implementation are discussed in Sec. 10.5. As usual, the chapter closes with a summary.

10.2   Basic procedures[1]

To implement portfolio insurance, a fund manager must begin by choosing an investment horizon and a floor. Assume that a British fund is holding a diversified portfolio which is representative of the stockmarket as a whole. Let the size of fund at current prices be £10m., the FTSE Index be 2000 and short-term interest rates be 10%. Suppose that the fund manager wants to guarantee that the value of the fund will not fall below £9m. In other words, he or she wants to be protected from a fall in FTSE below 1800. The simplest way to achieve this would be to buy puts on the index at an exercise price of 1800. At £10 per index point and a FTSE level of 2000, a fund of £10m. would need to buy £10 000 000/(£10 × 2000) = 500 put contracts to do this. If the index were then to fall to 1700, for example, the puts would each pay 100 points and so the five hundred together would pay a total of 500 × £10 × 100 = £0.5m. The shares would be worth (1700/2000) × £10m. = £8.5m. and the puts would pay £0.5m., so the total fund would be valued at £9m. It appears that the insurance would work.

However, insurance is not free. The price of an 1800 put with one year to maturity might be 40 points, giving a total insurance cost of 500 × 40 × £10 = £0.2m. This implies that the manager would need £10.2m (rather than £10m.) to implement the strategy. If we rescale by a factor of (10/10.2), then a £10m. fund would need to buy 490 puts costing £0.196m. and invest £9.804m. in shares. The fund would guarantee a terminal value of £8.823m. at index levels of 1800 or below.

The full range of potential pay-offs to this strategy after one year is listed in Table 10.1 and plotted in Fig. 10.2. The figure is drawn in the same way as previous pay-off diagrams, except that portfolio value rather than option pay-out is given on the vertical axis. As an example, at an index level of 2000 at maturity the portfolio value would be £9.804m., comprising shares worth that

Table 10.1   Terminal values for £10m. fund insured with puts

(Values in £m.)

Level of index	All-share portfolio value	Insured portfolio		
		Value of shares	Value of puts at $E = 1800$	Total value of fund
1400	7.0	6.863	1.960	8.823
1500	7.5	7.353	1.470	8.823
1600	8.0	7.843	0.980	8.823
1700	8.5	8.333	0.490	8.823
1800	9.0	8.823	0	8.823
1900	9.5	9.314	0	9.314
2000	10.0	9.804	0	9.804
2100	10.5	10.294	0	10.294
2200	11.0	10.784	0	10.784
2300	11.5	11.275	0	11.275
2400	12.0	11.765	0	11.765

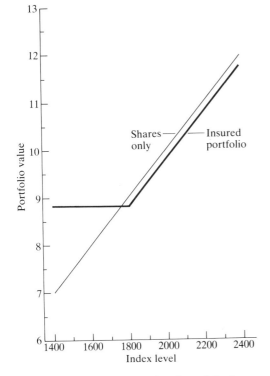

Figure 10.2   Simple example of portfolio insurance

amount and puts worth nothing. At an index level of 1900, the shares would be worth $(1900/2000) \times £9.804 = £9.314$m. and the puts would again be worthless. At an index level of 1700, the shares would be worth £8.333m. and the puts would pay £0.490m., so the portfolio would be worth $(1700/2000) \times £9.804 = £8.823$m., i.e. its guaranteed minimum value.

The pattern in Fig. 10.2 is the same as that for a call option. Here it was achieved by buying the shares and buying puts. It could equally well have been achieved by buying a call and investing the remaining funds at the risk-free rate. Remembering put/call parity (in the absence of early exercise and dividends), we have

$$p = c - S + PV(E)$$

or

$$S + p = c + PV(E).$$

It should therefore be possible to replicate the share plus put strategy $(S + p)$ with a call plus lending strategy $(c + PV(E))$. Such an approach is known as the purchase of 'fiduciary calls'. The minimum guaranteed in the example with puts was £8.823m. To guarantee that amount at 10% interest would require a risk-free investment in Treasury bills of £8.021m. for one year. That leaves £1.979m., which may be used for buying call options. Put/call parity implies that the price of the calls at an exercise price of 1800 would be:

$$c = p + S - PV(E) = 40 + 2000 - \left(\frac{1800}{1.1}\right)$$

$$= 403.6 \text{ points each.}$$

The number of calls that could be bought would then be £1 979 000/(£10 × 403.6) = 490. Not surprisingly, the number of calls to buy is the same as the number of puts that we calculated before.

Let us check the result. If the index falls to 1800 after one year, then the calls pay nothing and the risk-free investment pays £8.823m. If the index stays at

Table 10.2 Terminal values for £10m. portfolio insured with calls (Values in £m.)

Level of index	Value of T-bills	Value of of 490 calls at $E = 1800$	Total value of fund
1600	8.823	0	8.823
1700	8.823	0	8.823
1800	8.823	0	8.823
1900	8.823	0.490	9.313
2000	8.823	0.980	9.803
2100	8.823	1.470	10.293

2000, then the calls pay 200 points each, a total value of $200 \times £10 \times 490$ = £0.98m.: adding this to the risk-free £8.823m. gives a grand total of £9.803m. Hence the fiduciary calls do replicate the results of the share/put approach of Table 10.1. The full set of potential outcomes is summarized in Table 10.2.

Our example assumed that the manager was willing to lose up to 12% of the value of the portfolio (i.e. the guaranteed sum was £8.823m. on an initial value of £10m.). Suppose instead that she was not willing to accept any loss at all over the one-year horizon. This would require that $£10\,000\,000/1.1 = £9.091$m. be invested at the risk-free rate, leaving £0.909m. to be invested in calls. If calls at an exercise price of 2000 cost 250 points for one year, then she could buy $£909\,000/(£10 \times 250) = 363.6$ calls. For each point that the FTSE Index exceeded 2000 in one year's time, the manager would gain $£10 \times 363.6 = £3636$. Had she invested the entire £10m. in shares, each point's rise in FTSE would have paid $(1/2000) \times £10\,000\,000 = £5000$. The result is that the manager is only participating in $3636/5000 = 72.72\%$ of any rise in the market. She gives up 27.28% of any rise in order to be insured against any fall.

The higher the guaranteed value of the fund, the smaller is the participation in any rise. If a 5% gain to £10.5m. were to be guaranteed, then $£10\,500\,000/1.1 = £9.545$m. would have to be invested in the risk-free asset. A 5% gain is equivalent to an index level of 2100. If 2100 calls cost 160 points, then £0.455m. would buy 284.4 calls. For each point rise in the index above 2100, the manager would obtain $£10 \times 284.4 = £2844$, which is only $2844/5000 = 56.88\%$ of the gain from being fully invested in shares. The manager's participation rate is now reduced to 56.88%.

The highest guarantee that is possible is the value of the initial investment compounded at the risk-free rate. For example, if the guarantee is £11m., then all £10m. will have to be invested at the risk-free rate of 10% to achieve it and no calls can be purchased. The participation in any rise is then 0%. At the other extreme, if the manager is prepared to accept any imaginable fall in value of the portfolio, then the entire £10m. will have to be invested in calls with an exercise price of zero, which is the same as placing the entire £10m. directly in shares.

Table 10.3 Summary of calculations on £10m. portfolio

(Values in £m.)

	Fund size	Guarantee	Exercise price	Calls No.	Calls Cost	T-bills cost	Participation rate (%)
e	10.0	0.000	0	–	10.000	–	100.00
d	10.0	8.823	1800	490	0.196	8.021	98.00
c	10.0	10.000	2000	364	0.909	9.091	72.72
b	10.0	10.500	2100	284	0.455	9.545	56.88
a	10.0	11.000	–	–	–	10.000	0.00

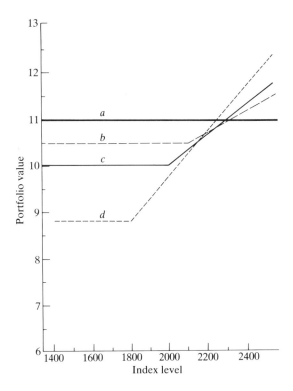

Figure 10.3   The relationship of participation to level of guarantee

Figure 10.3 demonstrates how, for the £10m. fund, the rate of participation declines as the guarantee rises. The calculations are summarized in Table 10.3.

Another way of describing a particular portfolio-insurance strategy is to express the final value as a function of (i) the floor, and (ii) the participation rate in any rise of the index above the floor. This is the same as defining the equation for a particular line in Fig. 10.3:

$$\text{Portfolio value} = \text{Floor} + \max\{0, w[(g \times \text{Index}) - \text{Floor}]\},$$

where w is the participation rate and g is initial portfolio value per index point.

For our £10m. portfolio at an initial index level of 2000, g is $10/2000 = £0.005$m. Assuming a floor of £10.5m., the equation would then read:

$$\text{Portfolio value} = 10.5 + \max\{0, 0.5688[(0.005 \times \text{Index}) - 10.5]\}.$$

At an index level of 2100, this gives

$$\begin{aligned}\text{Portfolio value} &= 10.5 + \max\{0, 0.5688[0]\} \\ &= £10.5\text{m}.\end{aligned}$$

and at an index level of 2200 the result is

$$\text{Portfolio value} = 10.5 + \max\{0, 0.5688[(0.005 \times 2200) - 10.5]\}$$
$$= 10.5 + \max\{0, 0.2844\},$$
$$= £10.7844\text{m}.$$

10.3 Portfolio insurance vs Buy and hold

Guaranteed funds are not new. The insurance industry has marketed investments with guaranteed lump-sum pay-outs for many years. In Britain these are known as endowment policies and they benefit from the absence of capital-gains tax if held for 10 years. Mortgages on houses are often repaid with such funds.

Let us assume that an endowment policy is written for just one year and the future in-payments by the customer have a present value of £10 000. If the guarantee is £10 000, then the money would be partitioned in much the same way as for portfolio insurance. At 10% interest, £9091 would be placed in one-year Treasury bills. The remaining £909 would be placed in shares, to give the non-guaranteed 'bonus' on the policy. This is exactly the same as a 'buy and hold' strategy.

Table 10.4 contrasts the possible terminal values on the endowment, in which shares are purchased to the value of £909, with the terminal values for the portfolio insurance strategy of buying calls worth £909 at an exercise price of 2000. This is also plotted in Fig. 10.4.

The main difference is that the endowment policy has very little uplift. Its rate of participation is merely $0.909/10 = 9.09\%$. By contrast, the rate of participation of the call strategy is $0.364/0.5 = 72.72\%$. Were the index to fall,

Table 10.4 Terminal values for endowment policy vs portfolio insurance, given an investment of £10 000 for one year

(Values in £000)

Level of index	Value of T-bills	Value of 0.3636 calls at $E = 2000$	Total value of fund with calls	Value of shares in endowment	Total value of endowment
1600	10.0	0	10.000	0.727	10.727
1700	10.0	0	10.000	0.773	10.773
1800	10.0	0	10.000	0.818	10.818
1900	10.0	0	10.000	0.864	10.864
2000	10.0	0	10.000	0.909	10.909
2100	10.0	0.364	10.364	0.955	10.955
2200	10.0	0.727	10.727	1.000	11.000
2300	10.0	1.091	11.091	1.045	11.045
2400	10.0	1.454	11.454	1.091	11.091
2500	10.0	1.818	11.818	1.136	11.136

Note: The minimum guaranteed pay-out is £10 000.

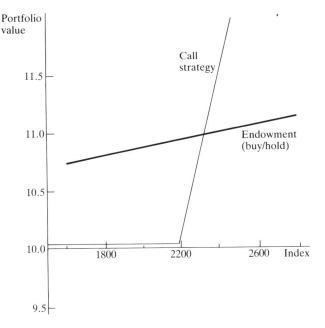

Figure 10.4   Terminal values for insured portfolio: calls vs endowment (buy and hold)

the endowment would pay slightly more (e.g. at an index level of 1600 it pays £10 727 compared with £10 000); but were the index to rise, the endowment would pay less (e.g. at an index level of 2500 it pays £11 136 compared with £11 818).

The endowment (or buy and hold) is a very conservative insurance strategy. It is equivalent to portfolio insurance based on calls that have a zero exercise price, such calls being the same as shares. In terms of the distribution of expected returns, it results in a high probability of returns close to, or slightly above, the floor. This is contrasted in Fig. 10.5 with portfolio insurance, which has the same floor but a higher expected return. Buying shares has an even higher expected return, but no guaranteed floor.

10.4   Simple rules for portfolio insurance

It is not necessary to use options to obtain portfolio insurance. The options may be replicated by equivalent (delta) positions in the shares or in futures on the shares. Even a knowledge of options is not essential. Perold and Sharpe (1988) suggest a 'constant proportions portfolio insurance' (CPPI) strategy. The idea is that the dollar value invested in stocks should be a constant proportion of the value of the fund less the value of the floor. This may be written

$$\text{\$ in stocks} = k(\text{Value of fund} - \text{Floor})$$

where k is the multiplier.

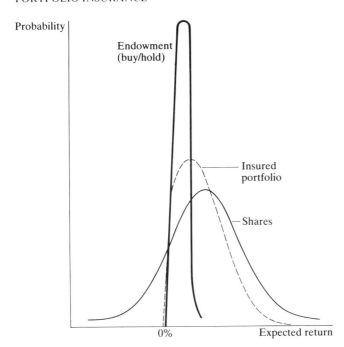

Figure 10.5 Comparison of probability distributions for endowment, portfolio insurance and shares

Consider a fund of $100 with a floor of $75 and a multiplier ($k$) of 2. Let the stockmarket be initially at a level of 100. The required initial investment in stocks, according to the CPPI equation, is $2(100 - 75) = \$50$. Now let the stockmarket fall to 90. The shares in the fund are now worth only $(90/100) \times 50 = \$45$, so the total fund value has fallen to $95. The rule now requires $2(95 - 75) = \$40$ in stocks, so $5 of stocks must be sold and invested in bonds, for which the new total is $55. If the stockmarket continues its fall to 80, then the stocks in the fund fall in value from $40 to $35.56 and the fund is worth $35.56 + 55 = \$90.56$. The rule now requires $2(90.56 - 75) = \$31.11$ in stocks, so $4.45 of stocks are sold and invested in bonds, for which the total is now $59.45.

Table 10.5 shows how the proportions of the fund in stocks and bonds change, assuming 10 point moves in the stockmarket. The first sequence is for a falling market and the second for a rising market. The table shows that the stockmarket would need to fall to 10 before the whole fund was invested in bonds. At the other extreme, if the stockmarket rose to 180 in steps of 10, then instead of lending money by holding bonds the strategy would imply borrowing money to gear-up the position.

The results of Table 10.5 are plotted in Fig. 10.6. The strategy is convex from below, in contrast with the buy and hold (endowment) strategy, which is linear.

Table 10.5 Example of constant proportions portfolio insurance with a floor of $75 and a multiplier of 2: initial fund worth $100 and initial stockmarket at 100

Stockmarket level	$ value of fund	$ in stocks (revised)	$ in bonds (revised)
100	100	50	50
90	95	40	55
80	90.56	31.11	59.45
70	86.67	23.34	63.33
60	83.33	16.67	66.66
50	80.55	11.10	69.45
40	78.33	6.66	71.67
30	76.66	3.33	73.33
20	75.55	1.10	74.45
10	75	0	75
100	100	50	50
110	105	60	45
120	110.45	70.91	39.54
130	116.36	82.72	33.64
140	122.72	95.45	27.27
150	129.54	109.08	20.46
160	136.81	123.62	13.19
170	144.54	139.07	5.47
180	152.72	155.44	− 2.72

Had the multiplier in the CPPI strategy been set at 1, then it would simply have been the same as buy and hold. Had the multiplier been set at 0, then all investment would have been in bonds. Under CPPI with $k > 1$, as the stockmarket rises, so does the proportion of the portfolio invested in stocks. The larger is k, the more rapid is the switch from stocks to bonds (and vice versa).

CPPI has some advantages over options-based portfolio insurance. It is simple and it has no fixed horizon. With an options-based strategy, at maturity either the portfolio is fully invested in stocks or it has zero stocks. If the horizon is rolled forward and the floor ratcheted up or down as the fund value rises and falls, then the strategy is convex at low market levels and concave at high market levels.[2] On the other hand, in a volatile but non-directional market, CPPI will result in much buying and selling of shares. The total of transactions costs depends on the path of share prices, i.e. is 'path-dependent', and can only be estimated at the outset. In contrast, the use of options would result in a known cost at the outset.[3]

10.5 Problems in implementing portfolio insurance

Prior to the Crash of October 1987, and probably still today, most portfolio insurance is arranged through replication strategies rather than directly with

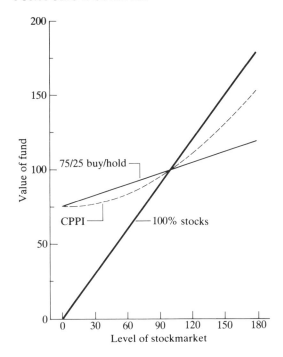

Figure 10.6 Comparison of CPPI with other strategies

options. For example, a fund manager will replicate the purchase of a call on the S&P 500 by buying S&P 500 futures in the hedge (delta) ratio. As the level of the index (and index futures) changes, so the delta will change and the futures position must be adjusted.

There are several potential reasons for using futures-based replication rather than options. The first is that the index-futures market is generally more liquid than the index-options market, so there is a saving in bid/ask spreads. The second is the lack of options that have maturities of more than a few months ahead. The CBOE and some other markets have introduced longer-dated options, but so far there is little volume.[4] An alternative is to use index warrants, which are listed on some exchanges. For example, there is a selection of warrants on British, French, US, German, Japanese and Swiss indices which are traded on the Euromarkets. These have lives of up to three years, but usually about 18 months at issue. They are created by banks, who back them with replication via futures. A third reason for preferring replication with futures is that rolling an option forward at its maturity into the next maturity does not replicate a longer term option at the original exercise price (see Choie and Novometsky, 1989). By contrast, futures can easily be rolled forward and appropriate deltas maintained. A fourth reason for not using options is that European puts are not generally available (although they are available in

London on the FTSE 100). American puts are worth more than European puts, but a portfolio hedger has no desire to exercise early, and so is paying for something that is not required. Use of American puts therefore makes hedging more expensive. The fifth, and final, reason for preferring replication is that options may not be available at the required exercise price for the desired strategy.

Nevertheless, direct buyers of options had a large advantage over 'replicators' at the time of the Crash. Replication requires frequent adjustment of a futures position. If the stockmarket rises or falls rapidly, the change in the delta may require large purchases or sales of futures. These will be difficult to execute if everyone is trying to transact at the same time. On 16 October 1987 the S&P 500 Index fell by 5.5%. Portfolio insurers finished the day with large, unexecuted futures sales that were needed to maintain their strategies. On 19 October as these sales were attempted, the market fell and precipitated the need for further sales. The fall in the stockmarket of 21.1% on 19 October was certainly accelerated by portfolio insurers trying to sell. However, such sales were only about 12% of total volume on that day (Rubinstein, 1988) and to accuse portfolio insurance of being main culprit (as in the Report of the Brady Commission, 1988) would seem to be excessive. One argument against the Brady explanation is that portfolio insurance using futures hardly existed outside the United States at that time, yet almost all stockmarkets fell by more than 15% on 19 October (e.g. UK, Germany and France).[5]

To summarize, strategies based upon replication with futures are more flexible than those based upon options, but they are unable to guarantee as perfectly the minimum value of the portfolio.

10.6 Summary

Portfolio insurance is a particular investment strategy that guarantees a minimum return at a particular horizon, but also allows much larger returns to be achieved. The mechanism is either: (i) to buy shares, the value of which is guaranteed by also buying (or replicating) put options; or (ii) to buy Treasury bills for the guarantee and to buy (or replicate) call options for the uplift. The lower the guarantee, the smaller the cost of insurance and the greater the potential uplift if the market rises.

Portfolio insurance is really a modern variation on a guaranteed endowment (or buy and hold) policy. The difference is in the use of options rather than just shares to give more uplift. It is a strategy which, instead of being risky, is consistent with the preferences of a conservative investor.

Developing rules for portfolio insurance is comparatively simple. The problems arise in implementing the rules. One of the main difficulties of direct implementation with options is that most exchanges trade short-term American options, whereas the strategy requires long-term European options. European index warrants are now becoming more common, in response to this need.

Implementation via options-replicating futures positions is easy if markets move smoothly. However, if there is a sudden move in the underlying market, the 'insurers' may all rush to buy or sell at the same time, thus causing a stampede which contributes to an even more violent move. As the Brady Commission Report stated, there can be an illusion of liquidity that is not there when required.

Prior to the Crash of October 1987, fund managers were happy to hold very large proportions of equity in their portfolios, because they thought that they could rapidly sell futures if the market fell. They were naive. Nevertheless, portfolio insurers probably emerged from the Crash with higher valued portfolios than those who remained fully invested throughout. It is a strategy that is not going to disappear, because 'guaranteed funds' are what many investors want.

Notes

1. This section draws upon Rubinstein (1985). Other papers on methodology are by Leland (1980), Brennan and Solanki (1981), Kritzmann (1986), Black and Jones (1987), Bookstaber and Langsam (1988) and Perold and Sharpe (1988).
2. See Perold and Sharpe (1988) and Benninga and Blume (1985).
3. Using an options-replicating strategy, however, would also incur unknown transactions costs and so be path dependent.
4. The CBOE options are known as LEAPS.
5. For a discussion of portfolio insurance inducing market volatility, see Genotte and Leland (1990).

References

Benninga, S. and Blume, M. (1985), 'On the optimality of portfolio insurance', *Journal of Finance*, **40**, 1341–52.

Black, F. and Jones, R. (1987), 'Simplifying portfolio insurance', *Journal of Portfolio Management*, **14**, 48–51.

Bookstaber, R. and Langsam, J. (1988), 'Portfolio insurance trading rules', *Journal of Futures Markets*, **8**, 15–32.

Brady Commission (1988), *Report of the Presidential Task Force on Market Mechanisms*, submitted to the President, Secretary of the Treasury and Chairman of the Federal Reserve, January, US Government Printer.

Brennan, M. and Solanki, R. (1981), 'Optimal portfolio insurance', *Journal of Financial and Quantitative Analysis*, **16**, 279–300.

Choie, K. and Novometsky, F. (1989), 'Replication of long-term with short-term options', *Journal of Portfolio Management*, **15**, 17–19.

Genotte, G. and Leland, H. (1990), 'Market liquidity, hedging and crashes', *American Economic Review*, **80**, 999–1021.

Kritzmann, M. (1986), 'What's wrong with portfolio insurance?', *Journal of Portfolio Management*, **12**, 13–16.

Leland, H. (1980), 'Who should buy portfolio insurance?', *Journal of Finance*, **35**, 581–94.

Perold, A. and Sharpe, W. (1988), 'Dynamic strategies for asset allocation', *Financial Analysts Journal* (January/February), 16–27.

Rubinstein, M. (1988), 'Portfolio insurance and the market crash', *Financial Analysts Journal* (January/February), 38–47.

Rubinstein, M. (1985), 'Alternative paths to portfolio insurance', *Financial Analysts Journal* (July/August), 42–52.

11
Interest-rate options

This chapter is divided into four sections. In the first we consider some general features of options on short-term and long-term interest rates and list those that are actively traded on exchanges. In the second we give some brief hedging examples. In the third we consider simple methods for valuing options on short-term rates and options on bonds. Finally, in the fourth section, we outline a more sophisticated method of valuation, because the simple methods have theoretical shortcomings.

11.1 Interest rates

Interest rates are generally divided into short-term and long-term categories. The short-term rates are often known as money-market rates and extend up to one year. These include rates on Treasury bills, interbank trading of deposits, and certificates of deposit. The most widespread benchmark for them is the London Interbank Offered Rate on dollars (LIBOR). The long-term rates are implicit in the prices of bonds, which may have lives of up to 30 years if issued by governments. There is also an array of corporate, quasi-governmental and mortgage bonds which generally have lives of about 10 years at issue and pay higher rates than the benchmark government bond of the same maturity.

Figure 11.1 illustrates the behaviour of both three-month and 30-year US interest rates over a five-year period. The two series are certainly correlated, but they are by no means locked together in a fixed relationship.

11.1.1 GENERAL FEATURES OF OPTIONS ON SHORT-TERM RATES

Options on short-term interest rates are very widespread, but, just as for currencies, only a small proportion of the total is actively traded on any exchange. Instead, they are traded over the counter as *caps, floors and collars*. A *cap* is an agreement that the rate payable on a floating-rate loan shall not exceed a fixed percent regardless of rates in the market. For example, if a company has

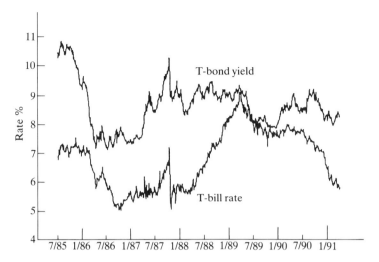

Figure 11.1   US Treasury bill rate and Treasury bond yield

borrowed at **LIBOR** and also purchased a cap at 10%, then the maximum rate payable in any one period will be 10%. This is illustrated in Fig. 11.2. The cap may last for one pricing period, e.g. one quarter, or for all the pricing periods of the loan, e.g. five years of quarterly repricing. The cap for each repricing is a call option on interest rates, so the whole cap arrangement is a portfolio of call options on interest rates.

A *floor*, as its name suggests, is an agreement that the lowest rate payable on a loan shall not be less than some level. It can also last many periods. At each

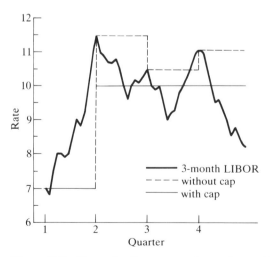

Figure 11.2   Example of a cap on a 1-year loan with quarterly repricing

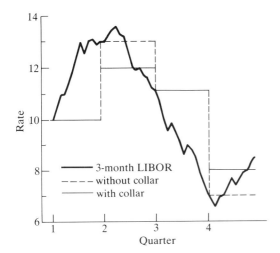

Figure 11.3 Example of a collar on a 1-year loan with quarterly repricing

repricing it has the pay-out of a put option on interest rates for the relevant period (e.g. for the next quarter). A floor is therefore a portfolio of put options on interest rates.

A *collar* is also aptly named. It is just a combination of a cap and a floor, so that interest rates payable on a loan are constrained to lie both above a floor and below a cap. Borrowers may not be willing to pay explicitly for a cap, but they may be willing to finance the cap by agreeing a floor. In effect they have bought set of call options on interest rates, the cap, and sold a set of put options on interest rates, the floor. The bank that is organizing the collar must then make sure that the floor finances the cap. This is very similar to some of the currency deals we saw in Chapter 8, except that the collar is not a 'one-shot' arrangement but a series of such 'shots'. Figure 11.3 demonstrates the impact of a collar.

11.1.2 GENERAL FEATURES OF OPTIONS ON LONG-TERM RATES (BOND OPTIONS)

Traded options on bonds have developed as a complement to bond futures contracts on the same markets. They therefore require exercise into a futures contract rather than into a real-world bond. Bond futures markets are very active. For example, the Treasury bond futures contract on the Chicago Board of Trade is regularly the world's largest futures contract by turnover. There are similarly active bond futures on (among others) Japanese bonds (TSE), French bonds (MATIF), German bonds (LIFFE, DTB), British bonds (LIFFE) and Italian bonds (LIFFE). This success of futures-based options for bonds, rather than ordinary options, is the result of three factors.

1. Futures existed before the options and had already developed a reliable system for delivery of bonds at maturity of a contract. It is easy for the writer of an exercised option to make or take delivery of a futures contract in a liquid market.
2. Futures and options are traded on the same floor, which reduces costs and facilitates the flow of information.
3. In most cases, it is easier to determine an approximately 'fair' price for bond-futures options than it is for simple bond options, as we shall see in Sec. 11.3.

Nevertheless, the bond options traded on exchanges are but a small part of the universe of bond options that exist. Each time a new corporate bond is issued, it has a clause allowing the issuer to buy it back early at some fixed price. For example, the bond might be issued at a price of 100 and repurchase might be allowed after five years at a price of 105. The issuer inserts this clause so that, if interest rates fall, the bond may be repurchased and a new one issued at a lower yield. An early-redemption clause is therefore a call option on the bond. The clause will reduce the price of the bond at the time of issue. A similar kind of option is held by fixed-rate mortgage borrowers who have the right to repay early, which is particularly the case in the United States. Early repayment will occur if long-term interest rates fall, so that the borrower can arrange a new mortgage at a lower rate. Once again it is the borrower who has the option, but in this case he or she has the right to sell it back to the issuer, so it is a put option on the bond.

Table 11.1 Major interest-rate options contracts in 1991

Option	Exchange	Volume (million)
On short-term rates		
3-month Eurodollar	CME	7.874
3-month sterling	LIFFE	1.594
US T-note	CBOT	0.890
3-month PIBOR	MATIF	1.374
On bonds		
US T-bonds	CBOT	21.926
French gov. bond	MATIF	8.412
German Bund	LIFFE	2.452
UK gilt	LIFFE	0.843

Key: CBOT   Chicago Board of Trade
     CME   Chicago Mercantile Exchange
     MATIF   Marché à Terme des Instruments Financières
     LIFFE   London International Financial Futures Exchange.
Source: Adapted from data in *Futures and Options World*, February 1992.

11.1.3 MARKETS FOR INTEREST-RATE OPTIONS (BOTH SHORT AND LONG TERM)

Traded options on interest rates have not had the success of the equivalent futures contracts. The list in Table 11.1 is rather short. By far the most important options are those on dollar rates: bond futures options on the CBOT and Eurodollar futures options on the CME. However, the second-ranking contract is that for French bonds on the MATIF, which is surprising given its relatively recent introduction. Many other options on interest-rate futures exist,

FUTURES OPTIONS

T-BONDS (CBT) $100,000; points and 64ths of 100%

Strike	Calls–Last			Puts–Last		
Price	May-c	Jun-c	Sep-c	Apr-p	Jun-p	Sep-p
92	4-54	4-58	4-48	....	0-06	0-48
94	2-55	3-04	3-19	0-02	0-16	1-16
96	1-00	1-32	2-07	0-10	0-45	1-62
98	0-07	0-34	1-14	1-17	1-44	3-04
100	0-01	0-10	0-43	3-11	3-18	4-30
102	....	0-03	0-23	....	5-11	6-07

Est. vol. 85,000, Fri vol. 57,221 calls, 56,940 puts
Open interest Fri 353,486 calls, 295,895 puts

T-NOTES (CBT) $100,000; points and 64ths of 100%

Strike	Calls–Last			Puts–Last		
Price	May-c	Jun-c	Sep-c	May-p	Jun-p	Sep-p
97	2-34	2-39	....	0-01	0-07	0-52
98	1-34	1-48	1-63	0-02	0-15	1-07
99	0-41	1-01	1-29	0-07	0-32	1-33
100	0-09	0-31	0-62	....	0-60	....
101	0-01	0-12	0-41	....	1-42	....
102	....	0-04	0-15	....	....	....

Est. vol. 4,000, Fri vol. 1,911 calls, 1,688 puts
Open interest Fri 15,989 calls, 13,615 puts

MUNICIPAL BOND INDEX (CBT) $100,000; pts. & 64ths of 100%

Strike	Calls–Settle			Puts–Settle		
Price	Jun-c	Sep-c	Dec-c	Jun-p	Sep-p	Dec-p
90	2-25	2-24	2-28	0-13	0-49	1-12
91	....	1-47	....	0-26	1-05	....
92	0-61	1-17	....	0-48	1-36	....
93	0-34	0-58	1-06	1-19	2-11	2-45
94	0-15	0-39	....	2-01	2-54	....
95	0-09	....	....	2-57	....	....

Est. vol. 720, Fri vol. 100 calls, 0 puts
Open interest Fri 13,287 calls, 13,389 puts

5 YR TREAS NOTES (CBT) $100,000; points and 64ths of 100%

Strike	Calls–Last			Puts–Last		
Price	May-c	Jun-c	Sep-c	May-p	Jun-p	Sep-p
99	....	1-61	....	....	0-03	....
100	0-61	1-05	....	0-01	0-10	....
101	0-10	0-28	....	....	0-31	....
102	....	0-09	....	....	1-11	....
103	....	....	....	....	....	....
104	....	....	....	....	....	....

Est. vol. 370, Fri vol. 133 calls, 165 puts
Open interest Fri 3,089 calls, 1,834 puts

EURODOLLAR (IMM) $ million; pts. of 100%

Strike	Calls–Settle			Puts–Settle		
Price	Jun-c	Sep-c	Dec-c	Jun-p	Sep-p	Dec-p
9325	0.47	0.37	0.23	0.03	0.18	0.48
9350	0.27	0.23	0.15	0.08	0.28	0.64
9375	0.12	0.14	0.09	0.18	0.43	0.82
9400	0.04	0.07	0.06	0.35	0.60	1.03
9425	0.01	0.03	....	0.57	....	....
9450	....	0.02	....	....	....	....

Est. vol. 33,798, Fri vol. 23,706 calls, 20,570 puts
Open interest Fri 176,115 calls, 197,499 puts

TREASURY BILLS (IMM) $1 million; pts. of 100%

Strike	Calls–Last			Puts–Last		
Price	Jun-c	Sep-c	Dec-c	Jun-p	Sep-p	Dec-p
9400	0.42	0.39	....	0.02	0.14	....
9425	0.24	0.25	....	0.08	0.25	....
9450	0.09	0.14	....	0.18	....	....
9475	0.02	0.08	....	0.36	....	....
9500	0.01	0.03	....	0.60	....	....
9525	....	....	....	....	....	....

Est. vol. 179, Fri vol. 11 calls, 6 puts
Open interest Fri 2,343 calls, 1,927 puts

EURODOLLAR (LIFFE) $1 million; pts. of 100%

Strike	Calls–Settle			Puts–Settle		
Price	Jun-c	Sep-c	Dec-c	Jun-p	Sep-p	Dec-p
9325	0.51	0.40	0.25	0.02	0.19	0.49
9350	0.29	0.25	0.16	0.05	0.29	0.65
9375	0.13	0.15	0.09	0.14	0.44	0.83
9400	0.04	0.08	0.05	0.30	0.62	1.04
9425	0.01	0.04	0.02	0.52	0.83	1.26
9500	....	0.02	....	0.76	1.06	....

Est. Vol. Mon, 150 Calls, 0 Puts.
Open Interest Fri 2,685, Calls, 2,706 Puts.

LONG GILT (LIFFE)£ 50,000; 64ths of 100%

Strike	Calls–Settle			Puts–Settle		
Price	Jun-c	Sep-c	....	Jun-p	Sep-p	....
90	2-26	3-30	....	0-22	1-10	....
91	1-44	2-54	....	0-40	1-34	....
92	1-05	2-19	....	1-01	1-63	....
93	0-41	1-52	....	1-37	2-32	....
94	0-24	1-27	....	2-20	3-07	....
95	0-14	1-05	....	3-10	3-49	....

Est. Vol. Mon, 1,320 Calls, 2,133 Puts.
Open Interest Fri 20,405, Calls, 14,827 Puts.

SHORT STERLING OPTIONS (LIFFE) £500,000; pts of100%

Strike	Call–Settle		Put–Settle	
Price	Jun-c	Sep-c	Jun-p	Sep-p
8800	0.72	.	.	.
8825	.	.	0.05	.
8850	0.31	.	0.11	.
8875	0.19	.	0.23	.
8900	0.10	.	0.39	.
8925	.	.	.	0.27
8950	0.02	0.25	.	0.42

Est. vol.5,353; Calls: 2,771; Puts: 2,582
Open Interest; Calls: 26,847; Puts: 32,159

LONG-TERM FRENCH BOND (MATIF) FFr. 500,000; pts of 100%

Strike	Call–Settle			Put–Settle		
Price	Jun	Sep	Dec	Jun	Sep	Dec
102	....	....	....	0.02	....	....
103	....	....	....	0.05	....	0.62
104	....	....	....	0.10	....	....
105	2.21	2.65	....	0.23	0.72	....
106	1.40	....	....	0.45	....	....
107	0.80	....	....	0.85	....	....
108	0.40	0.99	....	1.43	....	....
109	0.19	0.69	1.00	....	....	....
110	0.08	....	....	....	....	....

Volume 22,658; Calls:14,234; Puts:8,424
Open Interest 295,791

Figure 11.4 Exchange-traded interest-rate options
Source: Wall Street Journal, 15 April 1991. Reproduced with permission

but their trading is, as yet, subdued. Prices for some exchange-traded options are given in Fig. 11.4, which is an extract from the *Wall Street Journal*.

11.2 Using interest-rate options

The uses of interest-rate options are similar to those for other kinds of option, so this section will ignore speculation and give only hedging examples.

The typical hedger in options on *short-term interest rates* is a company treasurer who would like to cap the rate payable on a short-term borrowing. The risk to be hedged is of rising rates each time a loan matures and a new one is taken out (known as a rollover). An example of a cap on one rollover of a DM loan is given in Table 11.2.

As in previous examples, we need to ask why this treasurer bought a cap (call option) on rates rather than arranging a forward rate agreement.[1] The explanation is that the treasurer is worried that rates may rise, but does not want to lose too much if rates fall. The treasurer is worried about the potential 'opportunity loss' from hedging.

Turning to *bonds*, Table 11.3 illustrates how the downside risk on some French bonds might be hedged, using the MATIF bond option contract. On 1 May a fund manager holds bonds with a face value of Ff100m. with a yield of 8.80%. The manager hedges by buying 240 puts (on the futures contract) that are out-of-the-money (futures price = 106.88, whereas puts bought at $E = 106$).

The yield on the bonds had risen to 9.20% by 1 June and the hedge was then lifted. The put price had risen from 1.80 to 3.00, but there was still a net loss of $3.01 - 1.48 = $ Ff1.53m., i.e. 1.41% on this hedge. The reason was that it started 1% out-of-the-money and there was decay in the put value. However, the manager was still 1.38% better off than with no hedge.

Readers are advised not to become too absorbed in the intricacies of hedging bonds. In deciding how many puts to buy, the manager had to estimate how far the futures price would move relative to the price of the bond to be hedged. To do this the manager used the bond's duration, which is a measure of its sensitivity to interest rates. This is defined in the appendix to this chapter, where

Table 11.2 Example of a capped rollover

	Real market	Options market
1 May	DM 3-month interbank rate is 8%. Treasurer is worried about a rise for a 1 June rollover	Arranges a cap for 1 June at $E = 8\%$ from the bank, at a cost of 0.12%
1 June	DM rates now 9%	Call pays 1%
	Loss = 1%	Profit = 1% less cost of option (0.12%)

Table 11.3 Hedge of French bonds

	Real market	Options market
1 May	Bonds' face value = 100m.	Futures' face value = 0.5m.
	Duration of bonds = 7.7 Price of bonds = 108.68 Yield = 8.80%	Duration of futures = 6.4 Futures price = 106.88 Yield = 8.93%
	Bonds' market value = 108.68m.	
	Worried that long rates may rise	Buys 245 puts on June futures at $E = 106$, costing 1.80 each
		Total cost = 2.20m.
1 June	Long rates have risen	
	Bond price = 105.67 Yield = 9.20% Bonds' market value = 105.67m.	Futures price = 104.21 Yield = 9.33% Put price = 3.00
		Sell puts for Ff3.68m.
	Loss = Ff3.01m.	Profit = Ff1.48m.

the full hedge calculations are also shown. The important feature is that buying a put option protects against a fall in the price of a bond.

11.3   Simple methods for valuation of interest-rate options

Valuation of interest-rate options is a subject that is still being actively researched. However, there are some quite simple ways in which the familiar Black/Scholes model can be modified in order to give 'reasonable' values. These are the methods used by most practitioners, particularly for the traded options. These simple methods will be reviewed in this section, with separate subsections on: (i) options on short-term rates; (ii) options on futures prices; and (iii) options on long-term rates (bonds). Discussion of more elegant and theoretically correct approaches will be deferred until Sec. 11.4.

11.3.1   SIMPLE MODELS FOR OPTIONS ON SHORT-TERM INTEREST RATES

Why might the Black/Scholes model not apply directly to options on short-term interest rates? There are two reasons. The first is one of inconsistency. The Black/Scholes model assumes that interest rates are constant (are 'non-stochastic' to use the technical phrase). Yet we now want to value options on interest rates, so if they are constant we have a volatility of zero! This could be a severe problem, but it transpires that if the *expected* interest rate for the whole period is used in the Black/Scholes model, the results may not be too mislead-ing. In building a binomial tree for interest rates, the steepness of each branch would depend on interest rates and each pay-off would be discounted at a different, local rate.

The second reason is that short-term interest rates do not follow a lognormal distribution. There is a tendency for them to return to some 'normal' level, the characteristic known as 'reverting to the mean', which we introduced when discussing volatility in Chapter 6. A quick glance at Fig. 11.1 would place the mean in the 6–7% range for US interest rates: rates above 10% or below 5% might be expected to return to more normal levels.[2] This implies that very high or very low rates are unlikely to last long, and this will affect options on rates.

This can be seen with the following example. Suppose we consider a cap at an exercise price of 12%, written when interest rates are 10%. If it protects only one repricing in six months' time, then there may be some chance of rates being above 12%. If it protects a single repricing in four years' time, then the chance of 12% interest rates must be somewhat lower, due to mean reversion, and the cap will be correspondingly less valuable. The solution to this problem is to use the *forward* interest rate in valuing the cap, rather than today's *spot* rate, since the forward rate already reflects mean reversion.

The model that is most widely used for interest-rate options is that of Black (1976) for options on futures. Recall from Chapter 8 that this is

$$c = [FN(d_1) - EN(d_2)]e^{-rt}. \qquad (11.1)$$

The forward rate is used as the underlying asset and the interest rate used for discounting is the spot rate from now until the maturity of the option.

Let us try an example of a September call option. The first question to resolve is: how do we find an appropriate forward interest rate to use for F? The answer is to use either the rate from the futures market or the rate from the forward market. Table 11.4 gives the closing futures prices on 2 May 1991 for 3-month Eurodollars on the Chicago Mercantile Exchange.

The futures contract relates to 100 minus the rate for LIBOR at the second Wednesday of the relevant month. Thus it indicates a 6.08% rate for LIBOR in mid-June, a 6.28% rate for LIBOR in mid-September, etc., as shown in the table. Arbitrage ensures that these futures rates are very similar to the forward rates available. The latter can be calculated from the pattern of spot rates in the cash market.[3]

For a September call option with an exercise price of 7%, we have $F = 6.28$, $E = 7.00$, $t = (132/365)$ years. By interpolation in Table 11.4, the 4-month spot rate (r) is 6%. We set the volatility to 0.16. The value of the call using Black's model is then $c = 0.041\%$. This option is not worth much because it is well out-of-the-money. (The corresponding put option would cost 0.745%.)

We have valued a call option that pays out in the second week of September. If we had been valuing a cap for one repricing in September, it would have cost slightly less because interest on a loan is paid *in arrears*, whereas an option pays

Table 11.4 Eurodollar futures prices (Chicago) and spot interest rates (London) on 2 May 1991

	Maturity	Futures price	Implied rate (100 − Price)
1991	June	93.92	6.08
	Sept.	93.72	6.28
	Dec.	93.22	6.78
1992	Mar.	92.91	7.09
	June	92.46	7.54
	Sept.	92.10	7.90
	Dec.	91.80	8.20
1993	Mar.	91.75	8.25

Period	Spot rate
1 week	$6-5\frac{7}{8}$
1 month	$6-5\frac{7}{8}$
3 months	$6\frac{1}{16}-5\frac{5}{16}$
6 months	$6\frac{1}{8}-6$

Source: Financial Times

up front. The option would pay out three months before the relevant cap. Consequently, we can write:

$$\text{Cap price} = \frac{\text{Call price}}{1 + r_f} \tag{11.2}$$

where r_f is the appropriate 3-month forward rate. Hence the one-shot cap in our example would cost

$$\text{Cap} = \frac{0.041}{1 + (0.0628 \times 0.25)}$$
$$= 0.040\ \%$$

Continuing the example, suppose the cap were to cover the two repricing periods of September and December. The relevant data for December are $F = 6.78\%$, $E = 7\%$, $t = (223/365)$ years, r (7-month spot) $= 6.0625\%$. There is a tendency for more distant volatilities to be below nearby volatilities, so we set the volatility to 0.15. With Black's model we then find that the simple call costs 0.215% (put = 0.427%) and the December one-shot cap would cost $0.215/[1 + (0.0678 \times 0.25)] = 0.211\%$.

The total cost of a cap at 7% covering both September and December repricing of the 3-month loan would therefore cost $0.040 + 0.211 = 0.251\%$.

By using put option prices we could find the cost of a floor at, say, 5.5%, and hence the cost of a 5.5–7.0% collar. By judicious choice of the upper and lower

Table 11.5 Calculation to find the floor of a collar with a 7% cap

		Option costs		
Type	Exercise price	September ($\sigma = 0.16$)	December ($\sigma = 0.15$)	Total
Call	7.00	0.041	0.215	0.256
Put	5.50	0.021	0.010	0.031
	6.00	0.119	0.055	0.174
	6.25	0.221	0.106	0.327
	6.15	0.175	0.083	0.258

rates, the cost of the collar could be set to zero. For example, suppose we want to cap the loan for the two repricing dates at 7%. We have already calculated the cost to be 0.251%, equivalent to two call options costing 0.256% together. By trial and error we are able to find (see Table 11.5) that a floor at 6.15% using put options would cost 0.258%, just about the same as the cap. Hence a 6.15–7.00% collar could be arranged at no net cost (except for the intermediary's fee).

Our example, which has only two repricing dates, is somewhat more simple than most real-world caps but extension to any number of dates is straightforward.

11.3.2 OPTIONS ON INTEREST-RATE FUTURES

11.3.2.1 *Futures on short-term rates*

Traded futures options are priced by practitioners with Black's model, just as above. However, care must be taken with two features of these options. The first is that the options are quoted on futures *prices* and not on interest *rates*. Thus a CALL option on interest RATES at an exercise rate of 6% would be quoted on the market as a PUT option on PRICES at an exercise price of $100 - 6 = 94$. It would be wrong to use the futures price directly as the underlying asset price, because its distribution will not be lognormal. Instead the rate is treated as the asset and calls on rates then become puts on futures prices.

The second feature to keep in mind is that some exchanges such as LIFFE in London have, for options, a futures-style margining system that has an impact on prices. Under this arrangement, the buyer of an option is initially required to pay only a deposit. Should losses be made thereafter in relation to the market price of the option, the buyer has to pay daily, a procedure known as 'marking to market'. As the option matures, so its time value decays and marking to market will gradually lead to the buyer paying the time value of the option to the seller. The in-the-money part of the premium, i.e. the intrinsic value, is paid

Table 11.6 LIFFE Eurodollar futures options on 2 May 1991

Exercise price	Calls		Puts	
	June	September	June	December
93.50	0.42 (0.14)	0.37 (0.16)	0.01 (0.14)	0.14 (0.15)
94.00	0.06 (0.12)	0.12 (0.16)	0.15 (0.12)	0.39 (0.16)
94.50	0	0.03 (0.17)	0.59 (0.12)	0.80 (0.17)

Notes:
1. Decimals in brackets are implied volatilities.
2. June futures price was 93.91, implying a forward rate (F) of $100 - 93.91 = 6.09\%$. June contracts had 41 days to maturity.
3. September futures price was 93.73, implying a forward rate (F) of $100 - 93.73 = 6.27\%$. September contracts had 132 days to maturity.

when the option matures. The deposit remains the property of the buyer, so effectively nothing is paid at the time the option is bought. That is fine for the buyer, but the seller will need to be compensated for not having the premium in hand, and will therefore charge the buyer the compounded value of the usual premium.

Making the approximation that the whole premium is paid at the end (and not just the in-the-money portion), Black's model becomes, for a margined futures option,

$$c = FN(d_1) - EN(d_2). \tag{11.3}$$

The discount term, e^{-rt}, disappears, so that the only interest rate left in the equation is the forward rate, F. This formula does not, therefore, suffer from the inconsistency of assuming that short-term spot rates are non-stochastic, because it includes no such rates.

As an example of traded options on short-term interest rates, some of the September Eurodollar futures options from LIFFE on 2 May 1991 are given in Table 11.6, together with their implied volatilities. We see that calls and puts for the same maturity and exercise price all had the same implied volatilities. For example, the 94.00 (6.00%) call for June had an implied volatility of 0.12, as did the corresponding June put. Surprisingly the June options had slightly lower implied volatilities than the September options, whereas it is more usual for nearby rates to have higher volatilities.

11.3.2.2 *Futures on long-term rates*

Black's model is routinely used for the options on bond futures which are traded on exchanges. Just as for short-term interest-rate options, if there is margining (as on LIFFE) the short-term rate disappears from the formula and the Black result is also the theoretically correct result.

Table 11.7 MATIF French bond futures options on 2 May 1991

Exercise price	Calls		Puts	
	June	September	June	December
106	1.39 (0.055)	2.04 (0.057)	0.18 (0.058)	0.79 (0.055)
107	0.70 (0.055)	1.42 (0.027)	0.47 (0.056)	1.19 (0.055)
108	0.29 (0.057)	0.98 (0.055)	1.05 (0.057)	–

Notes:
1. Decimals in brackets are implied volatilities.
2. June futures price was 107.24. June options contracts had 22 days to maturity.
3. September futures price was 107.24. September options contracts had 120 days to maturity.
4. Short-term interest rate was 8% annual.
Source: Price data from *Financial Times*.

Table 11.7 gives prices and implied volatilities for options on futures for the MATIF's French government bond on 2 May 1991. The implied volatilities, of about 0.055, were surprisingly low. The September 106 call price was probably an error, leading to the even lower implied volatility of 0.027.

11.3.2.3 Summary on simple approaches to valuing options on short-term interest rates and on interest-rate futures

Black's options on futures model may be used to value options on short-term interest rates. It requires that the forward rate and its volatility be known. Caps and floors may be valued as portfolios of call options and put options respectively, with the proviso that the option price is discounted to allow for late payment.

The same model applies to traded options on futures contracts. Where there is margining of the premium, the short rate disappears from the equation. This has the advantage of removing the inconsistency of the model's assumption that short rates are constant.

11.3.3 SIMPLE MODELS FOR OPTIONS ON BONDS

There are three problems in using the Black/Scholes model, adjusted for coupons (dividends), for valuing options on bonds. The first is the assumption that long-term rates are volatile while short-term rates are constant. Figure 11.1 already indicated that the two kinds of rate are not independent. Nevertheless, the assumption that short-term rates are constant may not lead to much bias when valuing short-term options on long-term bonds (e.g. one-year options on 20-year bonds).

The second problem is that the price of the bond will not be lognormally distributed, because it is forced to 100 at the bond's maturity. This is shown schematically in Fig. 11.5.

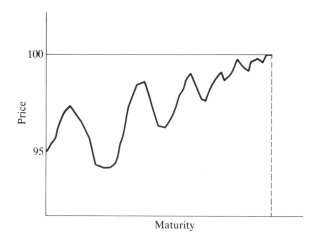

Figure 11.5 Behaviour of a bond price as maturity approaches

The third problem is related to the second. If the bond is 'tied' to a price of 100 at maturity, then the volatility of its price must fall as it matures. This may be seen in the decreasing amplitude of the ripples in Fig. 11.5.

The simple way to price a bond option is, once again, to use Black's model based upon forward prices. All we need to project as inputs are the forward price of the bond and its volatility. These two inputs will be considered in turn.

11.3.3.1 *Projecting the forward bond price*

Figure 11.6 shows the pattern of forward prices for a bond. There is a smooth drift to the final 100, on top of which is superimposed a saw-tooth effect due to

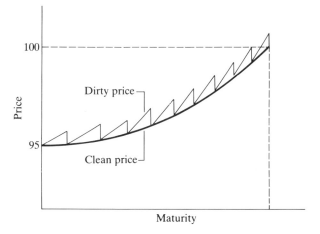

Figure 11.6 Expected bond price pattern including dividend (coupon) payments

the individual coupon payments. Bonds are usually quoted 'clean', i.e. without any accrued interest (coupon), consistent with the smooth line in Fig. 11.6. However, the buyer of a bond will also make an extra payment to the seller, reflecting the accrued interest (consistent with the saw-tooth line in Fig. 11.6). For example, a bond with a once-yearly payment of 8 would mature at a 'dirty' price of 108.

A bond's price is just the present value of its stream of payments. It is customary to discount each payment at a single rate known as the bond's *yield*. (More accurate approaches using *spot* and *forward* rates are discussed in the appendix to this chapter.) The bond price today is then equal to:

$$S = \frac{q}{(1+y_0)^1} + \frac{q}{(1+y_0)^2} + \cdots + \frac{100+q}{(1+y_0)^n} \tag{11.4}$$

where S is today's price, q is the coupon, y_0 is the yield today and there are n periods to maturity.

To project the forward bond price for j periods ahead (F_j) we need to know the yield at that time for bonds with $n-j$ periods remaining. If that yield is y_j, then we have

$$F_j = \frac{q}{(1+y_j)^1} + \frac{q}{(1+y_j)^2} + \cdots + \frac{100+q}{(1+y_j)^{n-j}} .$$

Suppose we have a 10-year bond with a single annual coupon of 8. The market's required yield is 10% for bonds of all maturities and projected to remain 10%. Then (including coupon):

the bond price today is   87.7109
the projected price in one year is   88.4819
the projected price in five years is   92.4184
the projected price in nine years is   98.1818
the price at maturity will be   108.0000

11.3.3.2   *Estimating the volatility of the forward bond price*

We now turn to projecting the volatility. Schaefer and Schwartz (1987) have examined how volatility declines as maturity approaches. This is illustrated in Fig. 11.7(a). Figure 11.7(b) indicates how volatility is a linear function of a bond's *duration*.

Duration is a measure of a bond's sensitivity to interest rates.[4] Assuming the same yield at all maturities, it is calculated as

$$D = \frac{\sum_{i=1}^{n} (iq_i)/(1+y)^i}{S} , \tag{11.5}$$

where D is the duration, i is the number of periods to a payment and q_i is a payment (including the final 100).

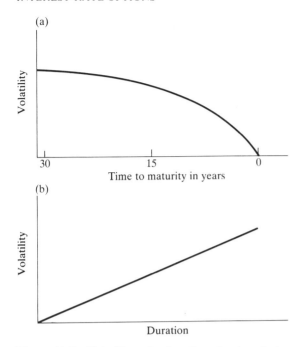

Figure 11.7 Volatility of a bond's price in relation to (a) its maturity and (b) its duration

The relationship between volatility and duration used by Schaefer and Schwartz is

$$\sigma = (KS^{a-1})D, \qquad (11.6a)$$

where K and a are constants. Schaefer and Schwartz suggest that $a = 0.5$. K is estimated from the observed volatility of the bond in question, i.e. Eq. (11.6a) is inverted to give

$$K = \frac{\sigma_h}{(S^{a-1})D_h} \qquad (11.6b)$$

where σ_h is historic volatility and D_h is duration of the bond now. For example, suppose we have a 20-year, 10% bond for which we have estimated the volatility to be 10% ($\sigma_h = 0.10$). If the price (S) is 100, then its duration from Eq. (11.5) is 9.365. Hence K for this bond, from (11.6b), is

$$K = \frac{0.10}{(100^{(0.5-1)})9.365}$$
$$= 0.00107.$$

When this bond has 17 years left to maturity, its duration (D) will have fallen to 8.824 at a price of 100. Its expected volatility will then be

Table 11.8 Comparison of 3-year call values with different bond maturities and different volatility assumptions

Bond (t years)	Duration $t-3$	Base σ	Modified σ	Black price	Modified Black price
5	1.90	0.1	0.020	5.186	1.039
10	5.36	0.1	0.057	5.186	2.969
20	8.82	0.1	0.094	5.186	4.892

$$\sigma = (KS^{\alpha-1})D = (0.00107 \times 100^{(0.5-1)})8.824$$
$$= 0.0944.$$

Hence the projected volatility of the 17-year bond is 9.43%, which is a little less than the current volatility of 10%. A 3-year option on the bond would then use a volatility of 9.44%. As the spot price of the bond is at par (100), so the price will not show any drift and the 3-year forward price will also be 100.

Table 11.8 compares the prices of 3-year calls based upon the assumption of constant volatility versus that of declining volatility. It is assumed that the forward price is 100 at all maturities, all interest rates are 10% and the exercise price is 100.

The calculations illustrate the importance of allowing for the declining volatility when the option is nearly as long as the bond. The modified Black price for a 3-year option on a 5-year bond (1.039) is just 20% of the unmodified Black price (5.186). A huge error would arise if no modification were made. By contrast, the same option on a 20-year bond is worth 4.892 by the modified formula, which is only 6% less than the unmodified value of 5.186. The error on a 10-year bond is somewhere between (see second row of Table 11.7).

11.3.3.3 *Summary on simple approaches to valuing bond options*

As they mature, bond prices are forced towards 100 and show declining volatility. Black's options-on-futures model may be used for valuation, if we can estimate: (i) the forward bond price; and (ii) the relevant volatility of that forward price. The forward bond price may be calculated if we assume a particular yield to exist at the forward date. The volatility at that maturity may be estimated either on an 'ad hoc' basis or by using the relationship between duration and volatility, as demonstrated by Schaefer and Schwartz.

☆ 11.4 More sophisticated models for valuing interest-rate options†

In valuing options on short-term rates we used the *rate* as the asset or 'state variable'. In valuing options on bonds, we used the bond *price* as the state

---

† This section may be omitted without loss of continuity. The text then continues with the chapter summary.

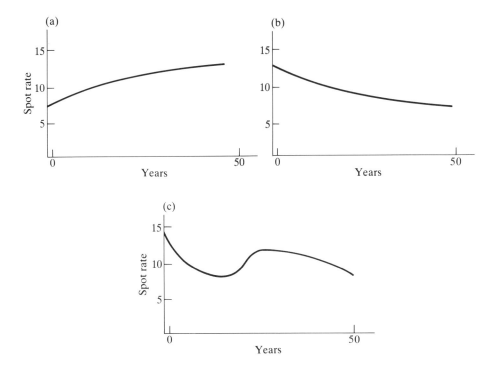

Figure 11.8   Some possible shapes for the term structure of interest rates

variable, but that had some problems. The more sophisticated models are based
upon rates rather than prices and are suitable for options both on short-term
and long-term rates.

If a bond has no risk of default, then its price is uniquely determined by the
1-year, 2-year, . . ., n-year rates that are used to discount its payments. These
rates, $r_{0,i}$, are known as the spot rates of interest:

$$S = \frac{q_1}{(1+r_{0,1})^1} + \frac{q_2}{(1+r_{0,2})^2} + \cdots + \frac{q_n+100}{(1+r_{0,n})^n}, \tag{11.7}$$

where q_i is the ith coupon and 100 is the redemption value.

Once these rates are known, any bond's price can be calculated. Similarly, if
we know how one-period spot rates evolve then we also know how prices must
evolve. Modelling interest rates, therefore, also gives us bond prices.

The pattern of spot rates at any one time is known as the term structure of
interest rates. About two-thirds of the time the rates for more distant periods
are higher than the rates nearby, leading to an upward-sloping term structure,
as depicted in Fig. 11.8(a). For the other one-third of the time, the term
structure is downward-sloping, either smoothly, as depicted in Fig. 11.8(b), or
sometimes with a hump, as depicted in Fig. 11.8(c).

Some researchers, notably Brennan and Schwartz (1982), model simultaneously the evolution of a short-term and a long-term rate. They develop a so-called 'two-factor' model. This is complex and will not be pursued here. The simpler approach is to assume that the whole term structure may be explained by the evolution of the short rate alone. Such models are known as 'one-factor' models.

If follows that in order to value interest-rate options, it is necessary to model the evolution of the term structure. In other words, interest rates, bond prices and option values are all simultaneously determined. There are some well-known models of the evolving term structure by Vasicek (1977) and Cox *et al.* (1985). On the whole, they do not lead to very tractable solutions for options (see Hull and White, 1990a).

Fortunately, a set of models based on the binomial approach has been recently developed, beginning with Ho and Lee (1986), followed by Heath *et al.* (1988, 1989), Black *et al.* (1990) and Hull and White (1990c).[5] Two conditions governing such trees were introduced by Ho and Lee: (i) rates should recombine, so that the number of nodes in the tree does not become huge; and (ii) the tree should evolve in such a way that arbitrage between bonds is rendered infeasible. Our presentation is of the tree developed by Black, Derman and Toy (BDT), which is among the simpler of these models.

What do we know about the term structure and the behaviour of short-term rates that should be incorporated in the model? We know that: short-term rates are mean reverting; negative interest rates should not occur; and a variety of term structures (as in Fig. 11.8) should be possible. The BDT tree achieves all of these, as well as recombining and avoiding arbitrage.[6] The inputs to the model are today's spot rates for each maturity and today's volatilities of these spot rates. Short-term rates are assumed to be lognormally distributed (as in Black/Scholes) at any one time, but through time they revert towards the mean at a rate which depends on their distance from the mean.[7]

For convenience of exposition, BDT refer to the spot rates as *yields*. They are indeed yields on bonds that have no coupons (i.e. zero-coupon bonds). The sample inputs given by BDT for yields and their volatilities are given in Table 11.9.

One-year yields are 10% and have 20% volatility. By contrast, 5-year yields

Table 11.9 Sample term structure of zero-coupon yields and volatilities from BDT

Maturity (years)	Yield (%)	Volatility (%)
1	10	20
2	11	19
3	12	18
4	12.5	17
5	13	16

Bond price

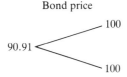

Figure 11.9 One-period tree for prices

are 13% and have only 16% volatility. The term structure of rates is upward-sloping and of volatilities is downward-sloping, which is the usual situation.

For convenience, let the probabilities of up and down steps be equal, i.e. 0.5, and let the upper rate be r_u and the lower rate be r_d. Begin by considering a 1-year bond. Its yield is 10% and its price in one year's time must be 100, regardless of interest rates at that time. This means that its price today must be $100/1.1 = 90.91$. The relevant tree is shown in Fig. 11.9.

Now consider two-step trees for rates and bond prices. Given the yield of 10% for one year, which is also by definition today's short-term rate, what up and down values should be assigned to the 1-year rate for one year's time? From Table 11.9 we know that the 2-year yield is 11%, so the price of a 2-year bond today must be $100/(1.11)^2 = 81.16$. In two years' time the price of this bond must be 100. We can draw two-period trees in outline for prices and rates as in Fig. 11.10, in which the intermediate prices (S_u, S_d) and rates (r_u, r_d) remain to be found.

From risk-neutral valuation, we can discount the future pay-off at today's 1-year rate and equate the result to today's bond price:

$$81.16 = \frac{0.5S_u + 0.5S_d}{1.10}. \tag{11.8}$$

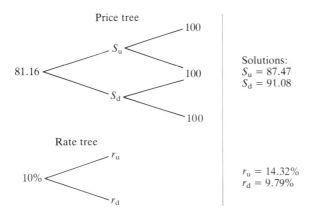

Figure 11.10 Two-period trees for prices and rates

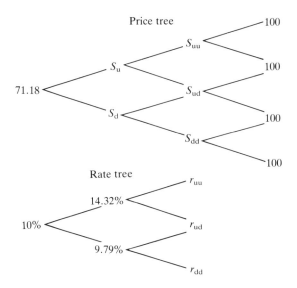

Figure 11.11   Three-period trees for prices and rates

We also know from Table 11.9 that the volatility of 2-year rates is 19%. Because the rates are assumed to be lognormal, this implies that[8]

$$0.5 \log\left(\frac{r_u}{r_d}\right) = 0.19. \tag{11.9}$$

Because of the 100 final pay-off in all states, we know that

$$S_u = \frac{100}{1 + r_u} \tag{11.10}$$

and

$$S_d = \frac{100}{1 + r_d}. \tag{11.11}$$

We can now substitute (11.10) and (11.11) into (11.8) to obtain:

$$81.16 = 0.5\left(\frac{100}{1 + r_u}\right) + 0.5\left(\frac{100}{1 + r_d}\right). \tag{11.12}$$

(11.9) and (11.12) are two equations in two unknowns, r_u and r_d. The simplest way to solve these equations is by trial and error.[9] The result is that $r_u = 14.32\%$ and $r_d = 9.79\%$. From (11.10) and (11.11) we can then calculate the bond prices that correspond to these rates, i.e. $S_u = 87.47$ and $S_d = 91.08$, as listed in Fig. 11.10.

We can now proceed to construct three-period trees for bond prices and 1-year rates. They are drawn in Fig. 11.11, with the rates from the two-period analysis already inserted. The objective is to find the three 1-year rates r_{uu}, r_{ud} and r_{dd}, knowing (from Table 11.9) that their volatility is 0.18 and that the 3-year yield is 12%. The yield immediately gives us the present bond price, which is 71.18 (see Fig. 11.11).

In the previous step, there were two unknowns, r_u and r_d, and two pieces of information, the volatility and the yield. Now there are three unknowns, r_{uu}, r_{ud} and r_{dd}, but still only two pieces of information. There are infinitely many solutions to such a problem! However, by the assumption of lognormal rates, the volatility at any particular step in the tree is the same regardless of the level of rates. Hence we know that $0.5 \log(r_{uu}/r_{ud}) = 0.5 \log(r_{ud}/r_{dd})$, hence $r_{uu}/r_{ud} = r_{ud}/r_{dd}$, or $r_{dd} = r_{ud}^2/r_{uu}$. It follows that if two of the three rates are known, the third is also defined. Hence, we have two unknown rates and not three, so that two pieces of information are sufficient to guarantee a unique solution.

The steps are similar to those for two periods. Beginning at the origin of the tree, we have

$$71.18 = \frac{0.5S_u + 0.5S_d}{1.10}. \tag{11.13}$$

We also know from Table 11.9 that the volatility of 3-year rates is 18%. This implies that

$$0.5 \log\left(\frac{r_{uu}}{r_{ud}}\right) = 0.18. \tag{11.14}$$

We know from above, due to lognormality, that

$$r_{dd} = \frac{(r_{ud})^2}{r_{uu}}. \tag{11.15}$$

Because of the 100 final pay-off in all states, we know that

$$S_{uu} = \frac{100}{1 + r_{uu}} \tag{11.16}$$

$$S_{ud} = \frac{100}{1 + r_{ud}} \tag{11.17}$$

and

$$S_{dd} = \frac{100}{1 + r_{dd}}. \tag{11.18}$$

We also know under risk-neutrality that

$$S_u = \frac{0.5S_{uu} + 0.5S_{ud}}{1.1432} \tag{11.19}$$

and

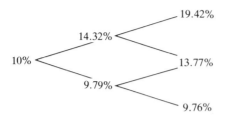

Figure 11.12 Three-period solution for rates

$$S_{\mathrm{d}} = \frac{0.5 S_{\mathrm{ud}} + 0.5 S_{\mathrm{dd}}}{1.0979}. \tag{11.20}$$

Substituting (11.19) and (11.20), then (11.16), (11.17) and (11.18), into (11.13) leaves an equation in terms of r_{uu}, r_{ud} and r_{dd}.

Substituting (11.15) for r_{dd} into this equation leaves two unknowns, r_{uu} and r_{ud}. Equation (11.14) has the same two unknowns and, taking the two equations together, a solution by trial and error may be found. The three-period answer is given in Fig. 11.12. The three rates are 19.42, 13.77 and 9.76%.

Using the same approach, the full five-period solution may be found, as shown in Fig. 11.13.

Now that the tree of 1-year rates has been found, a tree for the price of any bond can be developed. We have used zero-coupon bonds thus far, so a small extension is necessary to bonds that have coupons. Each coupon is treated like a zero-coupon bond, so the bond that has coupons is equivalent to a portfolio of zero-coupon bonds and can be valued as such.

Finally, we can reach the ultimate goal of valuing options on a bond. Figure 11.14 gives the price tree for a zero-coupon bond with a 5-year life, consistent with the rate tree of Fig. 11.13. If we wished to value a 3-year call option on this

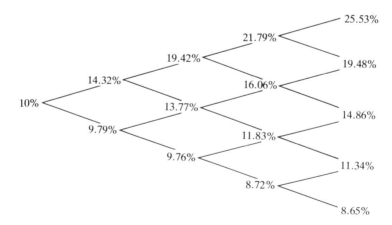

Figure 11.13 Five-period solution for rates

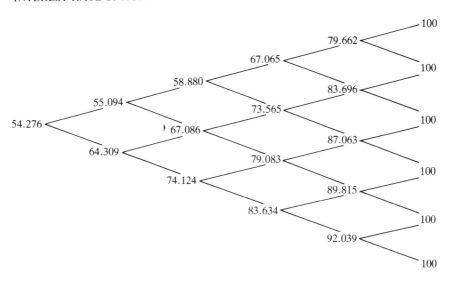

Figure 11.14   Five-year solution for price of a zero-coupon bond

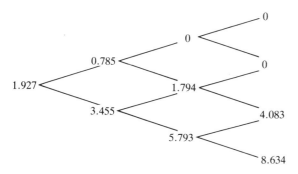

Figure 11.15   Pay-off tree for a 3-year call option on the 5-year zero-coupon bond at $E = 75$

bond at an exercise price of 75, then the pay-offs would be (from the top) respectively 0, 0, 4.083 and 8.634. These can then be discounted back, period by period, at the one-period rates to give the pay-off tree of Fig. 11.15. The value of the call is 1.927. If the call were American, then we would carry back the larger of the exercised or unexercised values from each node.

The grid used here is too coarse to give accurate results. BDT suggest that a coarse grid is used to solve for the tree of one-period rates. These are then used to give a coarse tree of bond values. Interpolation of the latter then gives a finer tree for the relevant period, which is used for option valuation.

11.4.1 COMPARISON WITH SIMPLE METHODS

Does sophistication pay? Suppose we also value the 3-year call on the 5-year zero-coupon bond with our adaptation of Black's model in which the volatility is adjusted and compare it with the BDT result.

The first step is to calculate the forward price of the bond. In three years' time the bond will have two more years to maturity. Three-year yields are 12% (see Table 11.9), so in three years' time the bond price will have risen from today's 54.276 to $54.276(1.12)^3 = 76.254$.[10] The expected pay-off at zero volatility would therefore be $76.254 - 75 = 1.254$, which today is worth 0.893.

From Table 11.9, 5-year *yields* have a volatility of 16%. What does this mean for the volatility of the bond *price*? Comparison of the width of the rate tree in Fig. 11.13 and the price tree in Fig. 11.14 indicates that the price volatility is less. For the 5-year bond the price volatility will be approximately 9.6%.[11] Using the approach based upon duration, described in Sec. 11.3, the volatility for a 2-year zero-coupon bond (with a duration of 2) would be 3.24%. Using Black's model with (i) this volatility, (ii) a forward price of 76.254 and (iii) a short-term interest rate of 12%, we find an estimated call value of 1.70. This may be compared with the BDT estimate (with an extremely coarse grid) of 1.93.

We suspect that the simple modified Black approach and the BDT approach give similar results, but more thorough analyses would be needed to confirm this. The results of Hull and White (1990a) tend to support this view. They show that Black's model with estimated forward volatilities gives results that are reasonably close to the results from the more sophisticated Vasicek and Cox–Ingersoll–Ross models, although there may be some exercise-price bias.

11.4.2 SUMMARY OF SOPHISTICATED METHODS FOR VALUING BOND OPTIONS

A variety of models in the binomial style have recently been developed, one of which is that of Black, Derman and Toy. The inputs to the model are the set of spot rates (also known as zero-coupon yields) and the volatilities of these rates. Assuming risk-neutrality of investors and a lognormal behaviour of the one-period rates, a binomial tree can be developed and solved. From the tree of one-period rates, a tree of one-period prices can be developed for any bond. This is then used to value options on that bond in the conventional way.

The merit of this approach is that it is mathematically simple, if rather protracted. It also ensures that rates do not become negative and it allows for: changing volatility; convergence of bond prices to 100; and mean reversion of the short-term rate. The results appear to be slightly, but not hugely, more accurate than the simple approach based upon Black's forward-price model.[12]

11.5 Summary

Options are traded both on short-term rates and on bonds. Many of these options do not appear on exchanges, but are either traded over the counter as caps, collars, etc., or are implicit in the early redemption features of bonds. Options on short-term rates are rather similar to currency options, being sold to companies as 'rate insurance'. Options on bonds are less homogeneous, since there is a large universe of bonds.

Simple pricing models for interest-rate options assume that short-term and long-term rates are uncorrelated. Options on short-term rates can be valued with Black's options-on-futures model. The same model can be used to value bond options, if care is taken in allowing for the decline in volatility that occurs as a bond matures.

More sophisticated models attempt to explain the development of the whole term structure of interest rates. A few models are based upon the evolution of both short and long rates, but most assume that the panoply of rates evolves on the basis of changes in the short rate only. Such models can be demonstrated and developed as binomial (or sometimes trinomial) trees. As an example, the Black, Derman and Toy model was outlined in this chapter. The model is first tuned to fit the existing term structure of rates and of spot volatilities. After that, the evolution of any bond price is defined and options on the bond can be valued.

Bond-option pricing has been at the frontier of finance over the last few years. There are many complicated models in the literature and new results appear regularly. However, the simpler models probably give results that are satisfactory for most practical situations.

Notes

1. If a futures contract had been used, the treasurer would have needed to sell it, because futures are traded on prices that are (100 − rates).
2. The nominal rate reflects both the real rate and the expected rate of inflation, both of which may be mean reverting.
3. For example, the September futures rate on 2 May can be replicated with a 7-month-and-1-week borrowing and a 4-month-and-1-week lending. That leaves a 3-month borrowing to begin in the second week of September. If we take 3-month and 6-month spot rates as indicative of the 4-month and 7-month rates, from Table 11.4 we see that on 2 May they were: 3 months' lending, $5\frac{15}{16}$; 6 months' borrowing, $6\frac{1}{8}$. Arbitrage requires that the 3-month spot rate compounded by the 3-month forward rate must equal the 6-month rate. Let the implied forward rate be r_f and the 3-month and 6-month rates be r_3 and r_6 respectively. Then we know that:

$$(1 + (r_3 \times 0.25))(1 + (r_f \times 0.25)) = 1 + (r_6 \times 0.5).$$

Solving for r_f we have:

$$r_f = \left[\frac{1 + (r_6 \times 0.5)}{1 + (r_3 \times 0.25)} - 1 \right] \times 4 = 0.0622 \text{ or } 6.22\%.$$

That is reasonably close to the futures-market rate of 6.28% given in Table 11.4, especially as the data come from the *Financial Times* and the futures market close is several hours later than the spot-market observations.
4. See appendix for an explanation of duration.
5. To be precise, Hull and White use a trinomial approach rather than a binomial approach.
6. Hull and White (1990b) argue that the BDT approach does not give the correct volatilities for forward rates. Their trinomial method allows for this. Black and Karasinski (1991) develop a binomial model which also allows for this, using a tree with varying time steps.
7. The continuous-time form of this model and the character of its mean reversion are considered by Hull and White (1990b).

8. In Chapter 5 we saw that in the standard binomial tree with lognormal prices we had $U = e^{\sigma\sqrt{t/n}}$ and $D = e^{-\sigma\sqrt{t/n}}$. For the rate tree $\sqrt{t/n}$ is not relevant, so we have $U = e^{\sigma}$ and $D = e^{-\sigma}$. Hence, $U/D = e^{2\sigma}$ and $\log(U/D) = 2\sigma$. Hence, $\sigma = 0.5\log(U/D)$. Similarly, in the BDT tree for rates we have $\sigma = 0.5\log(r_u/r_d)$.

9. From (11.9) we have $r_u = r_d e^{(0.19)(2)}$. Substitution into (11.12) leads to

$$81.16 = \left[0.5\left(\frac{100}{1 + r_d e^{(0.19)(2)}}\right) + 0.5\left(\frac{100}{1 + r_d}\right)\right]$$

which can be solved easily by trial and error.

10. Implicitly we are assuming that the 2-year spot rate in three years' time will be equal to the forward rate today. The implied forward rate today has to be consistent with 5-year and 3-year rates and is 14.52%. At that rate the bond price is projected to be 54.276.

11. The bond's duration, D, is its elasticity with respect to $(1 + r)$, where r is the relevant rate. Let $R = (1 + r)$. Hence we have the approximation that

$$\sigma_p \approx D\sigma_R,$$

where σ denotes volatility (i.e. standard deviation of percent changes) and subscripts p and R denote price and $(1 + r)$ respectively.

That may allow us to estimate σ_p if we know σ_R, but we want σ_r. We know that σ_R will be much smaller than σ_r, as it is the standard deviation of 1 plus the rate as compared with the standard deviation of the rate itself. We have the further approximation that

$$\sigma_R \approx \sigma_r \cdot r,$$

hence

$$\sigma_p \approx D\sigma_r \cdot r.$$

Hence, in the example,

$$\sigma_p \approx (5)(0.16)(0.12) \approx 0.096.$$

12. For readers who are competent in continuous-time mathematics, the papers by Hull and White (1990a, b) are highly recommended as a complement to the above.

References

Black, F. (1976), 'The pricing of commodity contracts', *Journal of Financial Economics*, **3**, 167–79.

Black, F., Derman, E. and Toy, W. (1990), 'A one-factor model of interest rates and its application to treasury bond options', *Financial Analysts Journal*, **11**, 33–9.

Black, F. and Karasinski, P. (1991), 'Bond and option pricing when short rates are lognormal', *Financial Analysts Journal*, **47**, 52–9.

Brennan, M. and Schwartz, E. (1982), 'An equilibrium model of bond pricing and a test of market efficiency', *Journal of Financial and Quantitative Analysis*, **17**, 301–29.

Cox, J., Ingersoll, J. and Ross, S. (1985), 'A theory of the term structure of interest rates', *Econometrica*, **53**, 385–467.

Heath, D., Jarrow, R. and Morton, A. (1988), 'Bond pricing and the term structure of interest rates: a discrete time approximation', *Journal of Financial and Quantitative Analysis* (forthcoming, 1991).

Heath, D., Jarrow, R. and Morton, A. (1989), 'Bond Pricing and the Term Structure of Interest Rates: A New Methodology for Contingent Claims Evaluation', Cornell University.

Ho, T. and Lee, S. (1986), 'Term structure movements and the pricing of interest rate claims', *Journal of Finance*, **41**, 1011–29.

Hull J. and White, A. (1990a), 'Pricing interest-rate-derivative securities', *Review of Financial Studies*, **3**, 573–92.

Hull, J. and White, A. (1990b), 'One-Factor Interest-Rate Models and the Valuation of Interest-Rate Derivative Securities', Faculty of Management, University of Toronto, November.

Hull, J. and White, A. (1990c), 'Root and branch', *Risk*, **3**, 69–72.

Schaefer, S. and Schwartz, E. (1987), 'Time-dependent variance and the pricing of bond options', *Journal of Finance*, **42**, 1113–28.

Vasicek, O. (1977), 'An equilibrium characterization of the term structure', *Journal of Financial Economics*, **5**, 177–88.

APPENDIX

A11.1 Spot and forward interest rates and the projection of forward bond prices

For a bond with k years to maturity and an annual coupon q, its price today is

$$S = \frac{q}{(1 + r_{0,1})^1} + \frac{q}{(1 + r_{0,2})^2} + \cdots + \frac{100 + q}{(1 + r_{0,k})^k}. \tag{A11.1.1}$$

The rates $r_{0,1}, r_{0,2}, \ldots, r_{0,k}$ are those that apply to payments in $1, 2, \ldots, k$ years' time and are known as the *spot* rates of interest.

Consistent with the spot rates, there is a set of *forward* interest rates. Consider the 2-year spot rate, $r_{0,2}$. This is the market's required annual rate of return for 2-year investments. Equivalently, a sum could be invested for one year at the spot rate $r_{0,1}$ and then re-invested for one more year at the 1-year forward rate for investments beginning in one year's time, $r_{1,2}$. Arbitrage requires that

$$(1 + r_{0,1})(1 + r_{1,2}) = (1 + r_{0,2})^2. \tag{A11.1.2}$$

The 1-year forward rate for one year is then

$$r_{1,2} = \left[\frac{(1 + r_{0,2})^2}{1 + r_{0,1}} \right] - 1. \tag{A11.1.3}$$

Suppose we have a 10-year bond which pays no coupon. Its price in 10 years' time will be 100. If we want to find the 9-year forward price (F_9), then we may discount back the 10-year price by the 1-year forward interest rate which begins in nine years' time, $r_{9,10}$. Then we have

$$F_9 = \frac{F_{10}}{1 + r_{9,10}} = \frac{100}{1 + r_{9,10}}. \tag{A11.1.4}$$

For example, if $r_{9,10}$ is 10%, then F_9 will be $100/1.1 = 90.91$.

If we now assume that the bond pays a coupon of q units once per year, then at its maturity it will pay not only the principal but also a coupon (i.e. $100 + q$). Its forward price at nine years will then be

$$F_9 = \frac{100 + q}{1 + r_{9,10}}.$$

$$(A11.1.5)$$

For example, if $r_{9,10}$ is 10% and q is 8%, then the forward bond price, F_9, will be $108/1.10 = 98.18$.

The other way to find the forward bond price is to compound today's bond price with the relevant spot rates of interest and deduct dividends. For example, if the bond price is now F_0 and the 1-year rate of interest is $r_{0,1}$, then we know that

$$F_0 = \frac{F_1 + q}{(1 + r_{0,1})^1};$$

hence,

$$F_1 = F_0(1 + r_{0,1}) - q.$$

$$(A11.1.6)$$

Similarly for two periods ahead we have

$$F_0 = \frac{q}{(1 + r_{0,1})^1} + \frac{F_2 + q}{(1 + r_{0,2})^2}$$

which leads to

$$F_2 = F_0(1 + r_{0,2})^2 - \frac{q(1 + r_{0,2})^2}{1 + r_{0,1}}.$$

$$(A11.1.7)$$

Further periods ahead may be calculated in the same way.

A11.2   Duration and its use for hedging

A11.2.1   DEFINITION OF DURATION

Duration is the elasticity of a bond's price with respect to $(1 + y)$, where y is the bond's yield. It is the percentage change in the bond's price for a 1% change in $(1 + y)$. Since the yield is the required rate of return on the bond, duration is a measure of the bond's sensitivity to interest rates.

Suppose we have a two-period bond which pays coupons of q_1 and q_2, the latter including the final payment of principal. Let $R = (1 + y)$. Then its price, S, is equal to

$$S = \frac{q_1}{R} + \frac{q_2}{R^2}.$$

$$(A11.2.1)$$

If we take the partial derivative of S with respect to R, we have

$$\frac{\partial S}{\partial R} = -\frac{q_1}{R^2} - \frac{2q_2}{R^3}.$$

$$(A11.2.2)$$

The duration, D, may be defined as

$$D \equiv -\frac{\partial S}{\partial R}\frac{R}{S} . \qquad (A11.2.3)$$

Hence, we find for the bond that

$$D = \frac{q_1/R + 2q_2/R^2}{S} .$$

Generalizing we find that,

$$D = \frac{\sum_{i=1}^{n}(iq_i)/R^i}{S} . \qquad (A11.2.4)$$

In words: 'Duration may be calculated as the weighted sum of the present values of the coupon payments, divided by the bond price, where the weights are simply $1, 2, \ldots, n$ (where n is the total number of coupons).'

A11.2.2 USE OF DURATION FOR THE EXAMPLE HEDGE

The number of futures contracts for a hedge is

$$N = \frac{\text{Face value of bond} \times \text{Price}}{\text{Face value of future} \times \text{Price}} \times \frac{\text{Sensitivity of bond}}{\text{Sensitivity of future}}, \qquad (A11.2.5)$$

where 'sensitivity' means sensitivity of price to changes in interest rates. For small changes in rates, sensitivity of price is

$$\Delta S = DS\left(\frac{\Delta R}{R}\right),$$

where Δ denotes a small change, S is price, D is duration and R is $(1 + \text{interest rate})$.

We can then write N as

$$N = \frac{FV_b}{FV_f} \times \frac{D_b S_b R_f}{D_f S_f R_b} \qquad (A11.2.6)$$

where FV denotes face value, subscript 'b' denotes bond and subscript 'f' denotes future.

For the example of Table 11.2, we then have

$$N = \frac{100}{0.5} \times \frac{7.7 \times 108.68 \times 1.0893}{6.4 \times 106.88 \times 1.0880} = 245.$$

The number of futures to sell for a hedge would be 245, so the number of options on futures required will also be 245.

12
Warrants and convertibles

12.1 Introduction

Warrants and convertibles are considered together because they are both 'option-like' securities issued by companies. Both are listed on exchanges, but their prices are less widely reported than those of the ordinary shares of a company.

This chapter begins by describing these instruments and considering why companies issue them in preference to simple debt or equity. We also give some information on the size of issues in various currencies. This is followed by separate sections on the valuation of warrants and convertibles. The section on valuing convertibles is itself divided into two subsections, the first being an overview and the second being more detailed. This degree of attention reflects the greater complexity of convertibles as compared with warrants. Finally, there is a chapter summary.

12.1.1 WHAT THEY ARE

A warrant is a call option. However, it differs from a traded call option in two main ways. The first is that it has a long life, probably five to ten years at issue. The second is that on its exercise the company will issue new shares, so existing shareholders will experience a dilution of their holding. For example, if 100 shares originally existed and 10 new shares are issued, then each shareholder will now own 1/110 of the revised company. Warrants are usually issued in conjunction with bonds, but are immediately separated and traded on their own. The traditional view of why they exist is that they are 'sweeteners', designed to enhance the attractiveness of particular issues of bonds or equity.

A convertible is somewhat more complicated. It is a bond that guarantees to pay regular coupons and has a fixed redemption date. In addition, the holder has the right to convert the bond into a given number of shares of the company. The convertible is therefore a bond together with a call option on the company's equity. Exercise of the call requires giving-up the bond. As the value of the bond changes, so does the cost of exercise. In the same way as for warrants, exercise results in dilution of the equity, but debt also falls simultaneously. Convertibles have lives of about 10 to 15 years at issue.

12.1.2 WHY COMPANIES ISSUE THEM[1]

As warrants and convertibles *are* issued, they must either provide companies with a cheap source of capital or solve some particular problem that debt or equity alone cannot solve.

The first, and simplest, explanation is that there exists a class of investor who is willing to pay handsomely for these assets, because long-term calls cannot be obtained in any other way. In other words, companies issue a few warrants or convertibles to satisfy a particular clientele. This begs the question of why warrants (and convertibles) are issued by companies which already have traded call options. Perhaps traded calls are too short term and are considered 'speculative', whereas warrants and convertibles are more acceptable to conservative fund managers.

A second possibility is that they are issued by risky companies, whose debt would be very expensive to service. Warrants are a sweetener for taking the debt, while a convertible is an inseparable mix of bond and sweetener. If a company is risky, then its value will be volatile and the call options within these instruments will have substantial value. At the same time, its debt will have a low value. The example in Table 12.1 is taken from Brennan and Schwartz (1986). It depicts two companies that are at different points on the risk spectrum and face different costs of straight debt. The high-risk company would have to pay 2% more on straight debt than the medium-risk company. However, it is able to issue convertible debt at only 0.25% more than the medium-risk company. This argument is supported by evidence that American issuers of convertibles are risky, growth-oriented companies.[2] Outside the United States the issuers are also expanding companies, but they are large and not particularly risky.[3]

A third possibility is that regulation encourages the issue of warrants and convertibles. In many countries there are rules that protect existing shareholders against a company issuing large tranches of new equity. For example, in

Table 12.1 Coupon rates required on new issues of straight and convertible debt

	Company risk (%)	
	Medium	High
Straight debt	14	16
Convertible debt	11	11.25

the UK a company may not issue more than 5% extra equity without giving existing shareholders the first right to buy (so-called pre-emptive rights). By issuing warrants or convertibles a company may be able to circumvent such controls (although that is not the case in the UK). The very large issues of dollar-denominated Japanese warrants in the late 1980s may be attributed to the regulation of rights issues and also to favourable dollar/yen swap rates at that time (see McGuire, 1990).

The fourth possibility is that minimizing tax is important, at least in the case of convertibles. Companies may be able to issue convertibles, deducting the coupons from taxable income, yet counting the convertible as part of equity rather than debt on the balance sheet. For example, in 1990/91 there was a vogue in the UK for 'convertible capital bonds', which were treated as equity on the balance sheet and as debt for tax purposes.[4] Issuers included Sainsbury, the largest supermarket in the UK, and Hanson, the largest conglomerate. There is even the accounting 'trick' that coupon payments are not deducted from declared profit, thus enhancing the company's earnings per share, because the convertible is treated as equity in this context.

What can be concluded? Warrants and convertibles are a relatively cheap source of capital. Tax rules and regulations are the primary reasons for this. Their prices are less sensitive to company risk than is corporate debt, so their use may be favoured by more risky firms. Some investors may also be willing to pay for asymmetry, because transactions costs or unfamiliarity keep them away from traded options, which in any case have only short lives.

12.2   Markets for warrants and convertibles

In 1988 there were $100 bn of convertibles outstanding in Japan, $55 bn outstanding in the United States, $40 bn in the Euromarket and $25 bn in the Swiss market (McGuire, 1990). The ranking in terms of warrants was probably similar. We shall concentrate on Euromarket issues, since they are well reported and, by definition, international.

Table 12.2 gives an analysis of Euromarket issues in 1990.[5] In that year there were 31 issues of convertibles, 112 issues of bonds-plus-warrants and 359 issues of simple warrants. The convertibles raised about $4 bn and the bonds-plus-warrants about $20 bn. The 359 simple warrants included many issued by intermediaries and not by companies, which generally issued bonds-plus-warrants. Intermediaries issue call and put warrants on currencies, oil, stock indices and shares; since, at the same time, they hold the relevant asset, these are known as 'covered warrants'. They are listed just like any other warrant and provide a market in long-dated options.

The main currency of issue was the US dollar for bonds with warrants, but convertibles were about equally divided between dollar, sterling and French franc issues. It should not be assumed that the currency of issue indicates the nationality of the issuer. By far the largest Euromarket issuers of bonds with

Table 12.2 Euromarket issues by currency in 1990

Currency	Bonds + warrants		Warrants-alone	Convertibles	
	Amount ($m.)	Issues	Issues	Amount ($m.)	Issues
US dollar	18 284	88	117	1122	14
D-Mark	1386	21	94	0	0
ECU	0	0	10	0	0
Pound sterling	0	0	47	2041	11
Austrian schilling	137	3	2	0	0
Belgian franc	0	0	1	0	0
Danish krone	0	0	2	0	0
Dutch guilder	0	0	2	0	0
French franc	0	0	52	1115	6
HK dollar	0	0	2	0	0
Italian lira	0	0	9	0	0
Japanese yen	0	0	6	0	0
NZ dollar	0	0	1	0	0
Swedish krona	0	0	13	0	0
Swiss franc	0	0	1	0	0
Totals	19 709	112	359	4278	31

Source: Adapted from data in *Euromoney Bondware.*

warrants have been Japanese companies. For example, from October 1981 to April 1988 Japanese companies made 382 dollar issues worth $37 bn and 239 Swiss franc issues worth $11 bn (see Gemmill, 1989, Table 1). The warrants have yen-denominated exercise prices, which therefore change with the exchange rate between the yen and the currency of issue.

Table 12.3 indicates a halving in bond-plus-warrant issues in 1990, which was due to the opening of the domestic Japanese market for new issues. On the other hand, warrant-alone issues more than doubled in 1990, as intermediaries discovered a profitable role as issuers of covered warrants. Convertible issues

Table 12.3 Numbers of Euromarket issues, 1986–90

Year	Bonds + warrants	Warrants-alone	Convertibles
1986	204	119	77
1987	234	88	131
1988	225	155	49
1989	261	135	39
1990	112	359	31

Source: Adapted from data in *Euromoney Bondware.*

hit a peak in 1987, which was associated with the huge rise in equity markets before the Crash.

12.3   Valuation of warrants

We have already said that warrants are long-term call options. They can be valued with the Black/Scholes model, with certain provisos.

The first proviso is that *dividends* are deducted, or rather the Merton model is used with $S\,e^{-\delta t}$ replacing S, where δ is the dividend yield. Merton's model will be suitable for European warrants, but early exercise of a warrant when there is a large dividend may result in extra value. For example, in one study of German warrants, early exercise resulted in an average of 5% extra value (Schulz and Trautmann, 1990). Using a binomial model with discrete dividends may therefore be advisable.

The second proviso is that a long-term rather than a short-term *volatility* should be used. For example, if the 3-month volatility has been estimated to be 40%, that may not be a good forecast of the volatility over the next five years. As discussed in Chapter 7, there will be reversion to the mean, which might be nearer 25%. A 5-year warrant may then be priced with the average of the volatility expected over the next five years.

The third proviso is the most tricky and concerns the effect of *dilution*. When a warrant is exercised, more shares are issued and the share price falls. Warrant valuation should therefore take account of that fall, as first shown by Galai and Schneller (1978). We shall give a formal analysis followed by an example.

Let there initially be n shares. Let q warrants be issued per existing share. The total number of warrants issued is then nq.

Let X be the exercise price of the warrants. Before the warrants are exercised, the value of the firm's equity, V, is the value of the assets less the value of the debt. When the warrants are exercised, there is an injection of new equity equal to the number of warrants times their exercise price, i.e. nqX, so the net value of the firm will rise to $V + nqX$.

By definition, the share price is equal to the value of the firm divided by the number of shares. Initially it is therefore V/n. After exercise there are $n + nq$ shares, so the value of each share becomes $(V + nqX)/(n + nq)$. The warrant value at maturity (W_T) will therefore depend on this revised share price and we may write it as

$$W_T = \max\left(\left(\frac{V + nqX}{n + nq}\right) - X, 0\right).   \tag{12.1}$$

Dividing through by n leads to

$$W_T = \max\left(\frac{V/n - X}{1 + q}, 0\right).   \tag{12.2}$$

Bringing $[1/(1 + q)]$ outside the expression gives

$$W_T = \frac{1}{1+q} \max\left(\frac{V}{n} - X, 0\right). \tag{12.3}$$

This pay-off is of the familiar kind for a call option, except that there is a dilution factor of $[1/(1+q)]$ and the firm value per share (V/n) replaces the share price, S.

For example, if there are initially $n = 1000$ shares and one warrant is issued per five shares $(q = 0.2)$, then the total number of warrants issued is $nq = 200$. Suppose that the firm has a value of \$5000 when the warrants mature and the warrants have an exercise price of \$4.70. From (12.3) the pay-off to exercising a warrant is

$$W_T = \frac{1}{1+0.2} \max\left(\frac{5000}{1000} - 4.70, 0\right).$$

$$W_T = \frac{1}{1.2}(5 - 4.7)$$

$$= \$0.250.$$

The pay-off on one of these warrants, after dilution, would therefore be 25 cents, as compared with 30 cents if there had been no dilution.

Knowing the final pay-off, we can then write the warrant valuation equation prior to maturity (following Black/Scholes) as

$$W = \frac{1}{1+q}\left[\frac{V}{n} N(d_1) - X e^{-rt} N(d_2)\right], \tag{12.4}$$

where

$$d_1 = \frac{\log(V/nX) + (r + \sigma_v^2/2)t}{\sigma_v \sqrt{t}}$$

$$d_2 = d_1 - \sigma_v \sqrt{t}$$

and σ_v is the volatility of the firm value.

This equation is the same as that of Black and Scholes except: (i) V/n replaces S; (ii) σ_v replaces the equity volatility, σ_s; and (iii) the result is multiplied by the dilution factor $[1/(1+q)]$. In addition (but not shown for simplicity), the firm value should be discounted by the dividend yield for the whole life of the option.[6]

Are we now ready to value warrants? Unfortunately, not quite. We do not know the value of the firm, V, and we do not know the volatility of that value, σ_v. We know that the value of the firm today equals the warrant value today plus the share value today, i.e. $V = W + S$, but we are trying to solve for W and cannot use it as an input. We also know that the firm volatility will be greater than or equal to the share volatility, i.e. $\sigma_v \geq \sigma_s$, because the issue of warrants decreases the gearing.[7] It may be possible to relate σ_v to σ_s (see Schulz and Trautmann, 1990), but that still leaves V unknown.

Do not despair! Schulz and Trautmann (1990) show that a naive valuation of a warrant as a call option, based upon the share price and totally ignoring dilution, is not likely to be far wrong. This result depends on the share price already correctly anticipating the expected dilution. The degree of error is only large if the warrant is both close to maturity (two years or less) and not yet in-the-money.

The reason why this seemingly *ad hoc* approach gives good answers is because of offsetting biases. On the one hand, dilution *reduces* the value of a warrant. On the other hand, firm value is higher than share value and firm volatility is higher than share volatility, so these two factors both *increase* the value of a warrant. The net outcome is that, using the Black/Scholes method, pricing (modified for dividends) is not likely to be far wrong. Hence one may value the warrant as a simple, long-term call option, ignoring dilution. Not surprisingly, that is what practitioners do.[8]

12.3.1 SUMMARY ON WARRANT VALUATION

Warrant valuation is complicated by its dependence on the value and volatility of the firm, both of which are unobservable. However, except for those warrants that are both near to maturity and not in-the-money, simple Black/Scholes pricing based upon the share price and ignoring dilution is quite accurate. Correction for dividends is essential and a long-term volatility should be used. If early exercise is allowed, the binomial method will be more accurate than the Black/Scholes equation.

12.4 Valuation of convertibles

12.4.1 GENERAL OVERVIEW OF CONVERTIBLE VALUATION

As outlined, a convertible bond is just an ordinary bond plus an option to convert into a fixed number of shares. For example, £100 face value of a convertible issued by Sainsbury (the largest British food retailer) in November 1990 could be exchanged for 29.1545 shares over each of the next 15 years. This strange number of shares arose from the fact that the conversion price at issue (exercise price) was set at £3.43 per share. Hence £100 of bond would buy $100/3.43 = 29.1545$ shares. Full details of this particular convertible are given in Table 12.4, together with some market data at the time of issue.

Figure 12.1 shows the pay-off to a convertible at maturity. As convertible debt is usually subordinated to other debt, at very low values of the firm ($< V_1$) it will pay zero. At firm values above V_2 ($= V_1 + B$) it will pay the bond face value (£100). Finally, at firm values above V_3 there is a higher pay-off from conversion than from redemption, because the share price is now above the conversion price. This value is called the conversion or parity value and is simply the value of the shares that can be purchased with the bond.

Table 12.4   Sainsbury 8.5% 2005 Euro-convertible

Date of issue	November 1990
Amount	£150 million
Maturity	7 November 2005
Coupon	8.50%
Conversion ratio	29.1545
Conversion dates	1991–2005
Issuer's recall	from 11/96 onwards at £132
Investor's put	None
Date of evaluation	7 November 1990
Share price	£3.03
Convertible price	£100
Yield on bonds	12.5%
Risk-free interest rate	12.0%

Returning to the Sainsbury example, if at maturity of the convertible the share price were £4.00, the convertible would have a conversion value of 29.1545 × 4.00 = £116.62. By contrast, its redemption would give only £100, so the owner would choose to convert it. At a share price equal to the conversion price of £3.43, the owner would be indifferent between conversion and redemption, both being worth £100.

Figure 12.2 plots the relationship between the value of the convertible and the value of the firm *prior* to maturity, under the assumption that the bond has no risk of default. The convertible is worth more than its conversion value at all possible firm values. This is just the same as the value of a call option being larger alive than dead, as noted in Chapter 3. At low values of the firm, such as K, the convertible is hardly worth more than the underlying bond. When the

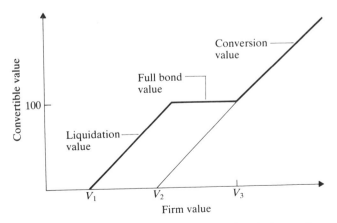

Figure 12.1   Convertible value at maturity in relation to firm value

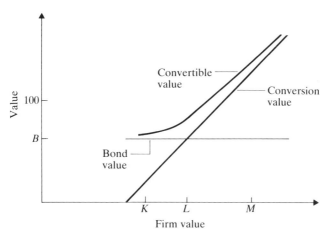

Figure 12.2 Convertible value prior to maturity with no bond-default risk

share price is around the conversion price, so that the firm is valued at L, the convertible has a significant premium above both its bond and conversion values, because there is a good chance of a higher pay-off. Finally, at very high values of the firm, such as M, the convertible approaches its conversion value. The shape of the convertible pay-off is then just like that of a call option on a share, except that the axes are shifted and the value of the firm is the relevant causal variable.

Figure 12.3 complicates the situation further by assuming that the bond is no longer default-free. The curve for the convertible now bends over at low firm values, in order to lie above the risky bond value, but then bends upwards at higher firm values, in order to lie above its conversion value (see also Brennan and Schwartz, 1977).

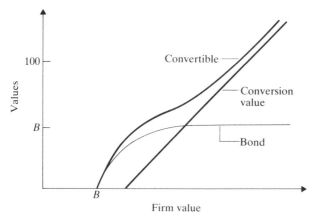

Figure 12.3 Convertible value prior to maturity with risky bond

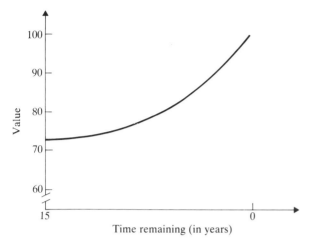

Figure 12.4 Projected bond value for Sainsbury

So far the call option imbedded in the convertible looks much the same as a warrant. It is, but there is one key difference. The *exercise price* of a warrant is fixed, whereas it is the *conversion ratio* of a convertible that is fixed, and its exercise price changes with the bond value. For example, at a yield of 12.5% the Sainsbury issue of Table 12.4 was worth £73.19 as a simple bond. If immediate exercise had been possible, £73.19 of bond could have been sacrificed in order to buy 29.1545 shares, an effective exercise price of 73.19/29.1545 = £2.51 per share. At maturity, with the simple bond worth £100, the effective exercise price would be 100/29.1545 = £3.43 per share. We know that the bond price drifts towards 100 as the bond matures, as illustrated in Figure 12.4, so the exercise price of a convertible also rises through time.

The actual share price for Sainsbury at issue was £3.03, so the option was out-of-the-money. The immediate conversion value was 29.1545 × £3.03 = £88.34. In the market the price of the convertible was £100.00 and its *conversion premium* was quoted as (100.00 − 88.34)/88.34 = 13.2%. This measure is widely used in traditional analyses of convertibles and is listed in newspapers. It indicates how much more expensive it is to buy shares via the convertible than directly.

12.4.2 REDEMPTION AT THE OPTION OF THE ISSUER: THE ISSUER'S RECALL

The issuer usually has the right to redeem the convertible at a given price prior to maturity. Effectively the issuer has a call on the convertible. Often there is a series of calls at different exercise prices in different years. For example, the United Biscuits (UBS) 5.75%, 2003 Euro-convertible, issued in 1988, could be redeemed at the declining sequence of prices listed in Table 12.5. In 1988 it was 105, in 1989 it was 104 (etc.).

Table 12.5   United Biscuits 5.75% 2003 Euro-convertible

Date of issue	September 1987
Amount	£110 million
Maturity	5 April 2003
Coupon	5.75%
Conversion ratio	32.4675
Conversion dates	Anytime to maturity
Issuer's calls	1988, 105; 1989, 104; 1990, 103; 1991, 102; 1992, 101; 1993 +, 100 if share price ≥ £4.158
Investor's puts	1993, 119.45; 1994, 124.45; 1995, 129.90; 1996, 135.85; 1997, 142.32; 1998, 149.38
Date of evaluation	23 May 1988
Share price	258
Convertible price	108
Yield on bonds	10.5%
Risk-free interest rate	9.5%

The firm should (in theory) recall the convertible as soon as it is in-the-money. For example, if the conversion value rose to 105 in 1994 then the firm should enforce its right to recall the convertible at 100. By doing so it minimizes the effective pay-out to the holder of the convertible, since the call option is cut short. The recall would, however, not take effect immediately and the holder of the convertible would prefer to convert into £105 of equity rather than receive only £100 from the firm. The result is that the company's right to recall a convertible forces the holder to convert.[9]

Curiously, the evidence suggests that many firms do not recall their convertibles as soon as possible (see Brealey and Myers, 1991, Ch. 22; Brennan and Schwartz, 1986; Dunn and Eades, 1989). One reason is that it might be unwise to do so immediately, because the share price might drop and so trigger redemption rather than conversion. In our example, UBS might therefore defer its recall until the convertible was worth 110 rather than 105. However, companies in the United States appear to wait until the convertible is 30 or 40% above the recall price (see Ingersoll, 1977). The reason for this is not clear, but it certainly makes convertibles more valuable to investors than would otherwise be the case, and must be a cost for the companies. One explanation is that forcing conversion is a bad signal (see Harris and Raviv, 1985), but need its avoidance be so expensive?

Companies are really somewhat schizophrenic. At the same time as they impose recall provisions, they often limit their impact with minimum-share-price provisions. For example, UBS could not recall its convertible unless the share price exceeded £4.158 (see Table 12.5), which is equivalent to a conversion value of £135. This emasculates the recall provisions except as a means of ensuring conversion rather than redemption. An investor would certainly choose to convert into the equity for a value of £135 than face redemption at £105 or less!

12.4.3   REDEMPTION AT THE OPTION OF THE HOLDER: THE HOLDER'S PUT

Some convertibles also have a put feature. Table 12.5 indicates that the UBS convertible could be sold back to the issuer at a rising profile of prices: £119.45 in 1993, £124.45 in 1994, etc. The *raison d'être* of these so-called 'rolling puts' is to guarantee a particular yield on the convertible. For example, at issue the 1993 put guaranteed a 3% capital gain to 1993, which together with the 5.75% coupon gave a guaranteed convertible yield of 8.75%. Similarly, the 'yield to put' to 1998 was 9.55%. Such puts can be extremely valuable and were very popular prior to the Crash of October 1987. Relatively weak share prices resulted in their exercise in the early 1990s.[10]

12.4.4   DILUTION AND SUMMARY OF OVERVIEW ON CONVERTIBLE VALUATION

We have not considered dilution, which will be similar to that for warrants. We concluded that it could be ignored for warrants, so we shall do the same here.

To summarize, the conversion value and the simple bond value are lower bounds to the convertible value. At maturity the convertible will be valued at the higher of these two. Prior to maturity it will be worth more, because the conversion option is worth more alive than dead. Because early conversion extinguishes the simple bond at a price different from par (100), the effective exercise price changes as the value of the simple bond changes. Dilution of the equity occurs on conversion, but its impact is likely to be anticipated by the share price. The company's right to recall the bond, and the investor's right to resell the bond, may both have a large impact on its price.

12.4.5   CONVERTIBLE VALUATION: SOME EXAMPLES

Example 1   *Sainsbury 8.5% 2005: a relatively simple Euro-convertible*
Traditionally the value of a convertible has been based on conversion value and the relative yields of bonds and equities. Most rules of thumb are based upon a single future share price rather than a distribution of possible share prices, so they can be rather misleading (see Cooper, 1988).

One problem that must be faced is whether to account for a stochastic bond price as well as a stochastic share price. Brennan and Schwartz (1980) show, for a particular example, that the assumption of a stochastic bond price adds only a small amount to the convertible value. We shall therefore allow for bond risk by valuing the simple bond at a yield that includes a risk premium.[11]

The simple option approach is to use Merton's dividend-adjusted model for the investor's call option and add this to the underlying bond value. That approach is used here for the Sainsbury convertible at the time of issue (see Table 12.4).

The Sainsbury convertible had a life of 15 years, but could be recalled by the company in any year after six years if the share price had reached £4.55. Our analysis will therefore be based at first on the assumption that it is recalled after six years, giving it only six years of life. The dividend yield in November 1990 was 3.3%, the 6-year risk-free rate was about 12% and 6-year yields on similarly risky bonds were about 12.5% (i.e. 6.25% semi-annual yield). The share price was £3.03. An average share volatility of 0.2 is assumed.

We first value the simple bond. With a 12.5% yield and a twice-yearly coupon of £4.25, the bond alone was worth

$$B_0 = \frac{4.25}{1.0625^1} + \frac{4.25}{1.0625^2} + \cdots + \frac{104.25}{1.0625^{30}} = £73.19. \tag{12.5}$$

The bond value being given up in six years' time would not be £100 but some smaller amount. If we expect yields to have fallen to 9.5% in six years' time, the underlying bond would then be worth

$$B_0 = \frac{4.25}{1.0475^1} + \frac{4.25}{1.0475^2} + \cdots + \frac{104.25}{1.0475^{18}} = £94.04. \tag{12.6}$$

Exercise after six years would therefore cost £94.04 in bonds and provide 29.1545 shares, so the exercise price for a share would be 94.04/29.1545 = £3.226 (cf. £3.43 at maturity).

Recall that Merton's model is

$$c = S\,e^{-\delta t}N(d_1) - E\,e^{-rt}N(d_2) \tag{12.7}$$

which, for this example, gives

$$c = 3.03\,e^{-0.033(6)}N(d_1) - 3.23\,e^{-0.12(6)}N(d_2).$$

Solving for $N(d_1)$ and $N(d_2)$ gives a call value of

$$c = £0.9638 \text{ per share.}$$

The 6-year call is estimated to be worth £0.9638 per share or 0.9638 × 29.1545 = £28.10 per bond. The total convertible package of bond and option is then estimated to be worth £73.19 + £28.10 = £101.29. In the market it was issued at £100, so we are close to that value. Of course, the choice of volatility, risky yield and dividends is going to be critical here.

This valuation is probably low. The reason is that we have assumed that the call only has a 6-year life, whereas if the share price is below £4.55 at that time the call may last longer. A binomial tree may be constructed which incorporates the investor's call, the issuer's recall and the drifting exercise price. For the Sainsbury convertible this approach results in an estimated price of about £108.

Example 2   *United Biscuits (UBS): a more complex Euro-convertible*[12]
The UBS convertible was issued in 1987, with a coupon of 5.75% and a maturity of 5 April 2003. Valuation is complicated by the series of recall prices

Table 12.6 Sensitivity of UBS convertible to various features

	Bond	Options	Total	Change
Full features	64.84	45.38	110.23	
No recalls	64.64	46.82	111.66	+ 1.3%
No puts	64.84	27.81	92.65	− 15.9%
No puts or recalls	64.84	29.26	94.11	− 14.6%
All interest rates + 1%	59.74	47.14	106.88	− 3.0%
Stock price + 10%	64.84	49.68	114.52	+ 3.9%
Volatility 30%				
and yield + 1%	59.74	56.00	115.74	+ 5.0%
No puts: stock price − 10%;				
all interest rates + 1%	59.74	24.15	83.89	− 23.9%

Note: Initial volatility 20%.

and rolling puts already discussed above. Merton's model cannot be easily adapted to such complexities, but a solution is possible with the binomial model or other numerical methods. In the binomial tree, the issuer's recall provisions place a maximum on the call value at a particular time, which can easily be imposed. The model is first run without any puts. In a second run the puts are evaluated and their value included if it would result in a higher convertible value.

Table 12.6 indicates the relative importance of the different features of the UBS convertible. The base value of the convertible is estimated to be £110.23, of which the net option value is £45.38, or 41%. Without the issuer's recalls (second row), the value of the convertible would rise by a meagre 1.3% (see final column), indicating that the minimum-share-price provisions undo the impact of these rights, as was noted earlier. By contrast, removal of the puts alone (third row) would cause a 15.9% fall in value. Removal of both recall and put provisions (fourth row) would reduce the price by 14.6%. Raising interest rates by 1% (long and short) would lead to a modest fall in value of 3.0%. A simple stock price rise of 10% would raise the price of this convertible by 3.9%, indicating a delta of 0.39 over this range. If the company became more risky, so that its required bond return rose from 10.5 to 11.5% and its share-price volatility rose from 20 to 30%, the convertible would *rise* in value by 5.0%. The reason is that the fall in bond value is more than offset by the rise in option value. This demonstrates the argument of Brennan and Schwartz, made in the first part of this chapter, that convertibles may not be very sensitive to company risk.

Finally, while it is true that convertibles are not as risky as equity, there are occasions when their prices are surprisingly volatile. For example, if all interest rates rose by 1% and the share price fell by 10%, the bond price would fall at the same time as the option value fell. The final row of Table 12.6 is designed to illustrate this for the bond without puts. The meaningful comparison is between the 'no puts' value of £92.65 in row three of the table and the £83.89 value in the final row of the table. The result is a fall in value of 9.5%.[13]

12.4.6   SUMMARY ON DETAILED VALUATION OF CONVERTIBLES

A convertible can be valued as a bond plus an option, using an appropriate risky rate for the bond valuation and Merton's model for the option. If early exercise is possible, then the drift of the bond price to 100 leads to an equivalent drift in the exercise price of the option. This may be accommodated by a binomial model or other numerical procedures. These methods may also allow for the recall rights of the issuer and the puts of the investor, both of which may have rolling exercise prices.

12.5   Summary

A warrant is a long-term call option, usually issued by a company in conjunction with a bond, but also sometimes issued by an investment bank. A convertible is an inseparable mix of a call option and a bond. Companies issue convertibles because they cost less (for tax, regulatory or option reasons) than straight issues of equity or debt. They tend to be issued in rising markets by companies that expect to make acquisitions or have a high growth rate. They allow investors to share in that growth, while limiting the downside risk to the value of the underlying bond.

When warrants and convertibles are exercised, the existing shares are diluted. The standard theoretical approach is therefore to value the calls as options on the value of the firm. However, if the share price already anticipates dilution, then models based simply on current share prices appear to be reasonably accurate. It follows that the Merton dividend model may be used to value warrants. It can also be used for convertibles, as long as allowance is made for the changing exercise price. Convertibles may also have complications such as recall provisions for the issuer and puts for the investor. Binomial (or other numerical) models can accommodate these features.

Notes

1. This section draws on Brennan and Schwartz (1986).
2. For references, see Brennan and Schwartz (1986).
3. An exception to the rule that outside the United States only large companies issue warrants is the large number of warrants on (small) investment trusts in the UK.
4. For a discussion, see the *Financial Times*, 7 March 1991, p. 29.
5. I am grateful to staff of Goldman Sachs and Credit Suisse for help in compiling the Euromarket tables.
6. Note that the dividend yield is one based upon firm value per share and not share price.
7. Crouhy and Galai (1988, p. 19) explain this as follows: 'The equity of a firm issuing warrants is less risky . . . than that of a pure equity firm with identical business risk. . . . A warrant can be replicated in a dynamic framework by issuing additional shares and investing the proceeds in government bonds. This tends to reduce the risk of the assets of the firm and hence of its equity.'

8. For a study of warrants in the United States in which dilution is incorporated and the Black/Scholes model is used, see Lauterbach and Schulz (1990).
9. The holder may also lose a dividend payment when electing to convert and the result may be that the convertible trades at less than its apparent conversion value. I am grateful to Jennie Tanner of Smith New Court for pointing this out.
10. See, for example, an article by Maggie Urry in the *Financial Times* of 14 May 1991.
11. An alternative is to use the 'option to exchange' model of Margrabe, which is explained in Chapter 14. This allows for two risky assets (e.g. bond and share). Whether bond volatility has much impact on the result then depends on the correlation of bond and share prices.
12. A similar example is provided in more detail by Jennergren and Sörensson (1991).
13. Similar circumstances resulted in a large London securities house making a loss in 1990 and ceasing to be a marketmaker in convertibles.

References

Brealey, R. and Myers, S. (1991), *Corporate Finance* (4th edn), McGraw-Hill, New York.

Brennan, M. and Schwartz, E. (1977), 'Convertible bonds: valuation and optimal strategies for call and conversion', *Journal of Finance*, **32**, 1699–1715.

Brennan, M. and Schwartz, E. (1980), 'Analysing convertible bonds', *Journal of Financial and Quantitative Analysis*, **15**, 907–29.

Brennan, M. and Schwartz, E. (1986), 'The case for convertibles', *Chase Financial Quarterly*, **1**, 27–46.

Cooper, I. (1988), 'The relationship between two methods of valuing convertible bonds', London Business School.

Crouhy, M. and Galai, D. (1988), 'Warrant valuation and equity volatility', HEC, Paris.

Dunn, K. and Eades, K. (1989), 'Voluntary conversion of convertible securities and the options call strategy', *Journal of Financial Economics*, **23**, 273–301.

Galai, D. and Schneller, M. (1978), 'Pricing warrants and the value of the firm', *Journal of Finance*, **33**, 1339–42.

Gemmill, G. (1989), 'The pricing of Euromarket warrants on Japanese stocks: a preliminary study', in Guimaraes, R., Kingsman, B. and Taylor, S. (eds), *A Re-appraisal of Market Efficiency*, Springer-Verlag, Berlin.

Harris, M. and Raviv, A. (1985), 'A sequential signalling model of convertible debt call policy', *Journal of Finance*, **40**, 1263–81.

Ingersoll, J. (1977), 'An examination of corporate call policies on convertible securities', *Journal of Finance*, **32**, 463–78.

Jennergren, P. and Sörensson, T. (1991), 'On the choice of model in convertible valuation—a case study', *Omega*, **19**, 185–96.

Lauterbach, B. and Schultz, P. (1990), 'Pricing warrants: an empirical study of the Black-Scholes model and its alternatives', *Journal of Finance*, **45** (4), 1181–1209.

McGuire, S. (1990), *Convertibles*, Woodhead-Faulkner, Cambridge.

Schulz, G. and Trautmann, S. (1990), 'Valuation of Warrants: Theory and empirical tests for warrants written on German stocks', University of Stuttgart.

13

Commodity options

13.1 Introduction

Commodity options are less well known than options on financial assets, but they have existed for much longer. Rees (1972, p. 35) reports that in Amsterdam by the early seventeenth century there were 'optional' contracts on herrings, grains, spices, whale oil and salt. The buyer could either take up the agreed quantity (of herrings), or else pay a predetermined penalty.

Commodity options were, for many years, the 'poor relatives' of commodity futures contracts. The latter were developed in Chicago in the mid-nineteenth century and had the merit of being standardized. This ensured that they were liquid, so a buyer could easily resell a contract. By contrast, commodity options were traditionally struck at the going forward price, so the lack of standardized exercise prices made them difficult to retrade. Standardized exercise prices were not introduced until the 1980s.

Another impediment to the use of commodity options was their ban, in the United States, from the late 1970s to the early 1980s. This stemmed from a variety of frauds in which 'London' (metal) options were sold to unsophisticated investors. The investor either paid a hugely inflated premium or the option was, in fact, not a real one.

Figure 13.1 gives the commodity futures and options prices listed by the *Wall Street Journal* (Europe) on 14 May 1991. There is a very large set of futures contracts and a somewhat smaller set of options contracts. The options are listed as *futures options* because the underlying asset is a futures contract and not the spot commodity. This means that if a call option is exercised the holder receives a futures contract. He or she will not be required by the broker to pay the full exercise price, such as $20 per barrel of oil, but merely to deposit an initial margin, such as $2 per barrel. The latter ensures performance on the contract. Because of margining, exercising commodity futures options does not require much capital. It also has the advantage that a futures contract can be easily resold, unlike a spot contract which might require immediate delivery of 1000 barrels of oil or 50 tonnes of sugar.

FUTURES OPTIONS

—AGRICULTURAL—

CORN (CBT) 5,000 bu.; cents per bu.

Strike	Calls—Settle			Puts—Settle		
Price	Jly-c	Sep-c	Dec-c	Jly-p	Sep-p	Dec-p
230	18¼	21	22½	1	4½	6¾
240	10½	14⅛	17¼	3½	8	10½
250	5½	9½	12¾	8⅛	12¾	16
260	2½	6¼	9¾	15¼	19¾	22½
270	1⅛	4½	6¾	23½	27	29
280	½	3	5	33¼	35½	....

Est. vol. 9,000, Mon vol. 7,830 calls, 4,557 puts
Open interest Mon 87,891 calls, 62,841 puts

SOYBEANS (CBT) 5,000 bu.; cents per bu.

Strike	Calls—Settle			Puts—Settle		
Price	Jly-c	Aug-c	Sep-c	Jly-p	Aug-p	Sep-p
525	46	....	....	¾	1⅞	3½
550	24¾	32¼	....	4¼	7¼	10¾
575	10½	19	23	15¼	18¼	22½
600	4¾	10½	14½	34	35	39¼
625	1⅞	6¼	9¾	55¾	55¼	59
650	1	3¾	6½	79½	77½	....

Est. vol. 12,000, Mon vol. 9,371 calls, 2,080 puts
Open interest Mon 72,962 calls, 38,628 puts

WHEAT (CBT) 5,000 bu.; cents per bu.

Strike	Calls—Settle			Puts—Settle		
Price	Jly-c	Sep-c	Dec-c	Jly-p	Sep-p	Dec-p
270	23¾	32¼	....	⅞	2½	....
280	15½	24½	36½	2½	4	4
290	8¾	18¼	29½	5¾	6¾	5¾
300	4¾	12½	23½	11½	10⅞	9¼
310	2¼	8¼	18	19	16¾	13¾
320	¾	5¼	13	27½	23½	19

Est. vol. 2,000, Mon vol. 1,117 calls, 1,125 puts
Open interest Mon 26,142 calls, 17,953 puts

ORANGE JUICE (CTN) 15,000 lbs.; cents per lb.

Strike	Calls—Settle			Puts—Settle		
Price	Jly-c	Sep-c	Nv-c	Jly-p	Sep-p	Nov-p
110	8.60	10.30	....	0.35	2.15	2.20
115	4.50	7.15	7.50	1.40	3.20	....
120	1.60	4.60	5.20	3.75	5.40	....
125	0.60	2.75	3.10	7.80	....	....
130	0.15	1.50	1.80	12.35	....	....
135	0.10	0.75	....	....	....	....

Est. vol. 70; Mon vol. 12 calls; 12 puts
Open interest Mon ; 2,594 calls; 901 puts

COFFEE (CSCE) 37,500 lbs.; cents per lb.

Strike	Calls—Settle			Puts—Settle		
Price	Jly-c	Sep-c	Dc-c	Jly-p	Sep-p	Dec-p
80	9.28	11.60	15.00	0.08	0.40	0.65
85	4.62	6.35	11.00	0.42	1.15	1.65
90	1.30	4.40	7.93	2.05	3.13	3.58
95	0.35	2.60	5.50	6.15	6.40	6.15
100	0.10	1.65	3.75	10.90	10.45	9.40
105	0.06	1.00	2.85	15.86	14.80	13.50

Est. vol. 973; Mon vol. 531 calls; 107 puts
Open interest Mon; 15,164 calls; 9,957 puts

SUGAR—WORLD (CSCE) 112,000 lbs.; cents per lb.

Strike	Calls—Settle			Puts—Settle		
Price	Jly-c	Oct-c	Dc-c	Jly-p	Oct-p	Dec-p
7.00	0.83	0.84	0.90	0.07	0.25	0.28
7.50	0.44	0.54	....	0.17	0.45	....
8.00	0.20	0.34	0.40	0.46	0.75	0.71
8.50	0.08	0.22	....	0.83	1.14	....
9.00	0.05	0.15	0.20	1.28	1.54	1.53
9.50	0.02	0.11	....	1.77	2.06	....

Est. vol. 5,244; Mon vol. 3,633 calls; 1,387 puts
Open interest Mon; 87,151 calls; 48,189 puts

COCOA (CSCE) 10 metric tons; $ per ton

Strike	Calls—Settle			Puts—Settle		
Price	Jly-c	Sep-c	Dc-c	Jly-p	Sep-p	Dec-p
800	202	235	281	2	6	11
900	100	138	195	3	9	25
1000	28	65	110	26	40	50
1100	5	27	58	110	100	110
1200	1	10	34	201	190	164
1300	1	9	19	301	280	249

Est. vol. 542; Mon vol. 89 calls; 91 puts
Open interest Mon; 4,300 calls; 11,264 puts

—OIL—

CRUDE OIL (NYM) 1,000 bbls.; $ per bbl.

Strike	Calls—Settle			Puts—Settle		
Price	Jly-c	Aug-c	Sp-c	Jly-p	Aug-p	Sep-p
19	1.96	2.09	2.18	.09	.20	.29
20	1.12	1.34	1.44	.25	.44	.56
21	.51	.79	.92	.64	.89	1.01
22	.20	.44	.54	1.33	1.53	1.64
23	.08	.24	.34	2.21	2.32	....
24	.05	.13	.20	3.18	....	....

Est. vol. 15,289; Mon vol. 5,216 calls; 6,014 puts
Open interest Mon; 79,870 calls; 74,215 puts

HEATING OIL No.2 (NYM) 42,000 gal.; $ per gal.

Strike	Calls—Settle			Puts—Settle		
Price	Jly-c	Aug-c	Sp-c	Jly-p	Aug-p	Sep-p
52	.0367	.0462	....	.0022	.0040	.0045
54	.0210	.0307	.0464	.0065	.0085	.0085
56	.0100	.0180	.0324	.0155	.0158	.0145
58	.0040	.0105	.0225	.0245	....	.0246
60	.0017	.0055	.0145	.0472	....	....
62	.0008	....	.0095	.0647	....	....

Est. vol. 2,159; Mon vol. 429 calls; 319 puts
Open interest Mon; 19,731 calls; 11,007 puts

GASOLINE—Unleaded (NYM) 42,000 gal.; $ per gal.

Strike	Calls—Settle			Puts—Settle		
Price	Jly-c	Aug-c	Sp-c	Jly-p	Aug-p	Sep-p
64	.0457	.0272	.0295	.0055	.0190	.0345
66	.0307	.0285	.0220	.0105	.0303	....
68	.0202	.0205	.0165	.0200	.0423	....
70	.0131	.0152	.0125	.0329	....	....
72	.0080	.0111	.0093	....	....	....
74	.0050	.0080	....	....	....	....

Est. vol. 2,172; Mon vol. 835 calls; 256 puts
Open interest Mon; 14,364 calls; 7,920 puts

—METALS—

COPPER (CMX) 25,000 lbs.; cents per lb.

Strike	Calls—Last			Puts—Last		
Price	Jly-c	Sep-c	Dec-c	Jly-p	Sep-p	Dec-p
94	4.55	5.75	7.20	1.15	2.80	4.80
96	3.35	4.70	6.00	1.85	3.70	5.60
98	2.20	3.45	4.90	2.70	4.50	6.60
100	1.40	2.75	4.30	3.85	5.60	8.00
102	0.50	1.45	2.70	7.90	9.35	11.40
104	0.20	0.85	1.70	12.60	13.60	15.10

Est. vol. 725, Mon vol. 249 calls, 282 puts
Open interest Mon 4,064 calls, 2,330 puts

GOLD (CMX) 100 troy ounces; dollars per troy ounce

Strike	Calls—Last			Puts—Last		
Price	Jly-c	Aug-c	Oct-c	Jly-p	Aug-p	Oct-p
340	23.90	24.90	28.90	0.30	1.10	2.60
350	14.90	16.50	21.40	1.10	2.60	4.70
360	7.20	9.70	14.80	3.30	5.80	8.00
370	2.70	5.00	10.10	8.80	11.10	13.20
380	1.00	2.50	6.60	16.60	18.30	19.30
390	0.50	1.30	4.30	26.20	27.00	25.40

Est. vol. 6,500, Mon vol. 4,008 calls, 1,478 puts
Open interest Mon 39,509 calls, 17,019 puts

SILVER (CMX) 5,000 troy ounces; cents per troy ounce

Strike	Calls—Last			Puts—Last		
Price	Jly-c	Aug-c	Sep-c	Jly-p	Aug-p	Sep-p
350	58.4	62.9	64.9	0.6	0.7	2.2
375	34.6	40.3	43.1	1.8	3.0	5.4
400	15.5	22.5	26.2	7.7	10.0	13.5
425	6.2	11.2	15.0	23.4	23.6	27.3
450	2.3	5.5	9.0	44.5	42.7	46.3
475	1.2	3.0	5.8	68.4	65.1	68.1

Est. vol. 5,500, Mon vol. 3,664 calls, 354 puts
Open interest Mon 45,615 calls, 13,815 puts

GOLD (EOE)—10 troy ounces, dollars per troy ounce)

Strike	Calls—Last			Puts—Last		
Price	May	Aug	Nov	May	Aug	Nov
340	20.00	26.50	34.00	0.30	3.00	5.50
350	9.00	18.50	26.50	0.20	4.20	7.00
360	1.70	13.00	21.00	2.50	9.50	12.00
370	0.10	6.00	16.00	13.00	14.50	18.00
380	0.50	3.80	10.00	23.00	24.00	24.00

Call Volume: 47 contracts — Call Open Interest: 15,323
Put Volume: 42 contracts — Put Open Interest: 3,571

Figure 13.1 Extract of prices
Source: Wall Street Journal, 14 May 1991. Reproduced with permission

FUTURES PRICES

Tuesday, May 14, 1991

Open Interest Reflects Previous Trading Day.

—GRAINS AND OILSEEDS—

	Open	High	Low	Settle	Change	Lifetime High	Lifetime Low	Open Interest
CORN (CBT) 5,000 bu.; cents per bu.								
May	238	240	236½	240	+ 2¾	306½	235	1,695
July	245¾	247½	244	247¼	+ 2	308¼	241½	91,839
Sept	245	247	243¾	247	+ 2½	287½	240¼	21,586
Dec	244¾	247	244¼	247	+ 2¼	275	241½	75,061
Mr92	252½	254½	251½	254½	+ 2¼	275¼	249	9,991
May	256½	258½	256	258½	+ 2½	279½	254	2,172
July	260¾	263½	260¾	263½	+ 2¾	282	257¾	1,341
Est vol 40,000; vol Mon 37,980; open int 203,685, −937.								
OATS (CBT) 5,000 bu.; cents per bu.								
May	125½	128¼	125½	128¼	+ 3	183¾	111¼	51
July	127½	129½	126¾	129¼	+ 2	164¾	117	10,569
Sept	133¼	134¾	133	134¾	+ 1½	153	122½	2,375
Dec	141¾	143½	141	143½	+ 2½	151½	131	1,075
Est vol 1,250; vol Mon 778; open int 14,104, +13.								
SOYBEANS (CBT) 5,000 bu.; cents per bu.								
May	564	564	559	563	− 2¼	711	559	1,173
July	572	573	567½	570¾	− 2	718	567½	57,011
Aug	578	578	572	575½	− 2½	695	572	7,519
Sept	578½	578½	573	575½	− 3¾	670	573	5,671
Nov	586½	586½	579	583½	− 3¼	674	579	23,728
Ja92	596½	597	591	595¾	− 3¼	649½	591	4,931
Mar	608	608	603	606¾	− 2½	660	603	732
May	617	617	613½	616	− 3½	662½	613½	471
July	623	623	619	621½	− 3	666	619	196
Est vol 38,000; vol Mon 29,251; open int 101,432, +1,917.								
SOYBEAN MEAL (CBT) 100 tons; $ per ton.								
May	169.50	169.70	168.50	169.50	....	208.00	164.00	1,785
July	171.50	171.70	170.30	171.40	+ .10	209.00	167.90	23,970
Aug	172.80	173.00	171.50	172.60	+ .20	199.00	169.90	7,653
Sept	173.80	174.20	172.80	173.70	....	193.50	171.70	5,297
Oct	174.80	174.80	173.50	174.40	− .30	190.00	172.50	3,147
Dec	177.50	177.50	176.10	176.70	− .80	191.50	174.00	6,471
Ja92	177.50	178.00	177.00	177.10	− .90	190.50	177.00	1,014
Est vol 13,000; vol Mon 8,995; open int 49,418, +870.								
SOYBEAN OIL (CBT) 60,000 lbs.; cents per lb.								
May	19.92	19.92	19.65	19.72	− .28	25.65	19.65	1,361
July	20.12	20.16	19.85	19.91	− .26	25.70	19.85	36,209
Aug	20.30	20.32	20.05	20.10	− .24	25.50	20.05	11,114
Sept	20.48	20.48	20.25	20.28	− .21	25.10	20.25	6,851
Oct	20.63	20.66	20.40	20.44	− .21	24.90	20.40	4,448
Dec	21.00	21.00	20.70	20.80	− .21	24.75	20.70	8,699
Ja92	21.15	21.15	20.85	20.96	− .19	24.15	20.80	1,469
Mar	21.25	21.25	21.25	21.26	− .22	23.55	20.80	663
May	....	....	....	21.53	− .22	23.80	21.70	162
Est vol 15,000; vol Mon 8,752; open int 70,980, −596.								
WHEAT (CBT) 5,000 bu.; cents per bu.								
May	288	288	285½	286	− 2	373	254¼	519
July	296	296	292	293¼	− 2	355	262	30,092
Sept	304	304	300¾	301¼	− 3	326	269½	8,563
Dec	316¼	316¼	313½	314¼	− 2½	325	281½	11,495
Mr92	322½	323¼	321	321¾	− 4½	332½	289¼	2,871
Est vol 13,000; vol Mon 12,312; open int 53,615, +497.								
WHEAT (KC) 5,000 bu.; cents per bu.								
May	293½	293½	293½	293½	− ¾	362¾	256½	10
July	297	297½	294½	295	− 1	320½	262	13,429
Sept	301½	302¼	299½	300¼	− ¾	307¼	268½	3,792
Dec	311½	311½	309½	310½	− ½	318¼	279	4,162
Mr92	316	316	315½	315½	....	318	283	809
Est vol 3,109; vol Mon 5,676; open int 22,287, +856.								

—LIVESTOCK & MEAT—

	Open	High	Low	Settle	Change	Lifetime High	Lifetime Low	Open Interest
CATTLE—LIVE (CME) 40,000 lbs.; cents per lb.								
June	75.30	75.50	75.05	75.10	− .15	78.37	72.15	33,293
Aug	73.35	73.52	73.15	73.20	− .07	75.80	70.35	22,460
Oct	75.05	75.12	74.77	74.90	− .07	76.90	70.70	16,108
Dec	75.45	75.47	75.22	75.25	− .10	77.00	71.75	6,481
Fb92	75.10	75.10	74.92	74.97	− .02	76.70	72.40	1,013
Apr	75.80	75.80	75.65	75.65	+ .02	77.00	74.60	383
Est vol 8,747; vol Mon 6,708; open int 79,808, +577.								
HOGS (CME) 40,000 lbs.; cents per lb.								
June	58.02	58.20	57.60	57.90	− .10	59.30	47.70	11,625
July	56.80	56.85	55.90	56.22	− .47	58.37	48.30	7,509
Aug	53.35	53.50	52.75	53.17	− .05	55.50	46.90	5,080
Oct	48.35	48.37	47.85	48.05	− .12	49.55	42.90	1,028
Dec	48.20	48.20	47.70	47.70	− .15	48.92	44.40	624
Fb92	47.50	47.95	47.50	47.60	− .30	48.35	44.50	135
Apr	46.05	46.05	45.70	45.80	− .35	46.62	45.00	110
Est vol 6,242; vol Mon 5,782; open int 26,122, +43.								
PORK BELLIES (CME) 40,000 lbs.; cents per lb.								
May	61.30	61.55	60.00	60.75	− .52	73.12	49.50	419
July	58.30	58.82	56.65	57.75	− .62	72.80	50.15	7,130
Aug	55.20	55.80	53.60	54.65	− .47	70.05	51.60	2,699
Feb	56.90	56.95	56.10	56.80	− .35	63.15	56.00	211
Est vol 7,056; vol Mon 5,037; open int 10,464, −442.								

—FOOD & FIBER—

COCOA (LDN FOX) Sterling per metric ton; lots of 10 tons

	Close	High	Low	Previous	Vol
May	583- 588	589	582	680- 683	167
Jul	612- 613	613	604	606- 607	2648
Sep	640- 641	642	632	633- 634	1536
Dec......	674- 675	676	667	664- 665	392
Mar	706- 708	708	700	698- 699	399
May	728- 729	730	723	720- 721	43
Jul	749- 750	753	745	742- 743	180

COFFEE (LDN FOX) Sterling per metric ton; lots of 5 tons

	Close	High	Low	Previous	Vol
May	531- 532	533	530	530- 532	439
Jul	558- 559	562	557	559- 560	780
Sep	580- 582	585	580	582- 583	535
Nov	603- 604	606	602	604- 605	376
Jan......	621- 623	626	623	620- 623	87
Mar	640- 641	644	639	639- 641	117
May	....-....	....	....	....-....	....

SUGAR (LDN FOX) U.S. dollars per metric ton; lots of 50 tons

	Close	High	Low	Previous	Vol
Aug91 .	166.0-168.6	170.0	167.0	169.8-170.0	68
Oct	166.0-167.8	169.6	166.0	169.2-169.8	101
Dec....	170.0-180.0	170.4	168.0	170.4-171.8	2
Mar92 .	166.2-169.2	171.4	169.0	171.4-171.6	34
May ...	170.0-180.0	170.8	170.6	174.4-175.4	79
Aug ...	175.0-185.0	179.0	179.0	177.4-180.0	1
Oct	175.0-185.0	....	....	177.4-183.0	....

WHITE SUGAR (Paris) in U.S. dollars per metric ton

	Close	High	Low	Previous
Aug	268.5-270.0	270.5	268.5	270.0-270.3
Oct	240.0-242.0	242.0	240.1	242.6-242.8
Dec...........	239.0-241.0	....	....	241.0-243.0
Mar	241.0-242.5	242.5	....	242.5-244.0
May	243.0-245.0	....	....	245.0-247.0
Aug	248.0-250.0	....	....	250.0-253.0

Est. vol. 724; Vol. Mon.801.

Source : Bourse de Commerce, Paris

	Open	High	Low	Settle	Change	Lifetime High	Lifetime Low	Open Interest
COCOA (CSCE)—10 metric tons; $ per ton.								
May	965	975	965	969	+ 8	1,572	940	34
July	991	1,004	988	1000	+ 8	1,590	978	15,851
Sept	1,018	1,031	1,017	1,029	+ 10	1,515	1,009	8,281
Dec	1,062	1,072	1,060	1,070	+ 8	1,535	1,051	8,622
Mr92	1,105	1,107	1,105	1,111	+ 9	1,538	1,092	6,855
May	1,137	1,137	1,137	1,139	+ 9	1,385	1,120	2,664
luly	....	....	....	1,162	+ 4	1,385	1,145	2,715
ept	....	....	....	1,187	+ 7	1,218	1,169	2,176
Est vol 2,405; vol Mon 3,044; open int 47,198, −322.								
COFFEE (CSCE)—37,500 lbs.; cents per lb.								
ay	86.80	87.40	86.75	88.15	+ 1.05	113.00	84.30	582
uly	88.40	89.30	87.90	89.20	+ .65	111.50	86.90	23,039
ept	90.80	91.50	90.25	91.20	+ .35	113.50	89.50	13,045
ec	93.75	94.70	93.50	94.35	+ .45	116.00	92.50	4,055
r92	97.35	97.35	97.35	97.45	+ .55	107.50	95.50	958
ay	....	....	....	99.15	+ .60	106.00	98.50	168
pt	....	....	....	103.15	+ .15	108.00	101.50	193
Est vol 4,507; vol Mon 3,299; open int 42,096, −270.								
SUGAR—WORLD (CSCE)—112,000 lbs.; cents per lb.								
ly	7.73	7.79	7.69	7.75	− .12	14.90	7.59	55,202
t	7.54	7.61	7.48	7.55	− .09	14.40	7.46	28,464
92	7.67	7.71	7.57	7.67	− .10	10.14	7.56	21,916
y	7.77	7.78	7.69	7.77	− .08	9.77	7.67	2,335
st vol 6,840; vol Mon 14,101; open int 108,008, +793.								
UGAR—DOMESTIC (CSCE)—112,000 lbs.; cents per lb.								
	21.24	21.24	21.22	21.23	− .01	23.41	21.09	3,182
	21.27	21.29	21.26	21.28	....	23.35	21.20	4,390
	21.75	21.78	21.73	21.78	− .01	23.14	21.68	2,870
	22.10	22.10	22.07	22.08	....	23.01	21.95	1,196
	22.08	22.08	22.07	22.10	....	22.80	21.98	1,648
	22.15	22.15	22.12	22.15	+ .01	22.30	22.05	558
	21.24	22.20	22.20	22.20	+ .02	22.39	22.10	371
	....	....	....	22.23	+ .03	22.25	22.22	111
vol 1,160; vol Mon 295; open int 14,326, +72.								
TTON (CTN)—50,000 lbs.; cents per lb.								
	89.00	90.40	89.00	90.33	+ 1.70	90.40	65.67	14,472
	79.70	81.17	79.70	81.17	+ 2.00	81.17	66.75	9,491
	73.40	74.30	73.40	74.19	+ 1.35	74.30	63.85	18,793
	74.20	75.00	74.20	74.98	+ 1.35	75.00	64.70	4,236
	74.45	75.18	74.45	75.18	+ 1.15	75.18	65.10	1,661
	74.60	75.38	74.60	75.39	+ 1.09	75.38	65.50	708
vol 12,000; vol Mon 5,679; open int 49,401, −119.								

Figure 13.1 (*continued*)

	Open	High	Low	Settle	Change	Lifetime High	Lifetime Low	Open Interest
ORANGE JUICE (CTN)—15,000 lbs.; cents per lb.								
May	118.50	118.75	117.90	118.75	+ .55	190.00	101.50	220
July	117.60	118.30	117.10	118.30	+ .90	180.00	102.50	3,688
Sept	118.50	119.20	118.00	119.15	+ .95	127.00	106.00	942
Nov	118.05	119.00	118.00	118.80	+ .55	119.50	111.00	123
Ja92	118.50	119.00	118.50	119.25	+ .45	119.75	113.40	360
Mar	119.20	119.55	119.20	119.55	+ .35	119.70	113.60	193

Est vol 700; vol Mon 268; open int 5,526, −27.

—METALS & PETROLEUM—

	Open	High	Low	Settle	Change	Lifetime High	Lifetime Low	Open Interest
COPPER-HIGH (CMX)—25,000 lbs.; cents per lb.								
May	100.90	101.70	99.10	99.25	− 1.45	117.80	97.00	3,025
June	100.00	100.80	98.50	98.55	− 1.55	115.00	100.10	1,353
July	99.50	100.00	97.40	97.50	− 1.75	113.50	96.50	25,821
Aug	98.00	98.00	98.00	97.40	− 1.65	109.00	97.40	519
Sept	99.00	99.35	97.00	97.00	− 1.85	110.50	95.50	5,028
Oct	99.00	99.00	97.90	96.80	− 1.90	106.90	100.00	433
Nov	98.15	98.15	98.15	96.60	− 1.90	105.00	96.60	245
Dec	98.60	98.60	96.50	96.40	− 1.95	108.50	94.50	4,394
Ja92	98.00	98.00	98.00	96.10	− 1.85	104.50	96.10	213
Feb	97.70	97.70	97.70	95.85	− 1.70	105.10	95.85	112
Mar	97.60	97.60	96.00	95.60	− 1.55	106.80	95.60	1,579
May	96.65	96.80	95.70	95.20	− 1.45	106.20	95.20	1,088
July	96.15	96.15	95.00	94.90	− 1.25	103.80	95.00	572
Sept	96.00	96.00	94.80	94.40	− 1.35	103.45	94.40	237
Dec	95.25	95.25	93.50	93.75	− 1.50	100.50	93.50	196

Est vol 9,000; vol Mon 9,655; open int 44,970, +2,090.

	Open	High	Low	Settle	Change	Lifetime High	Lifetime Low	Open Interest
GOLD (CMX)—100 troy oz.; $ per troy oz.								
May	....	....	....	360.10	+ 1.50	369.00	350.30	4
June	359.70	361.80	358.00	361.20	+ 1.40	466.20	352.60	54,642
Aug	362.50	364.30	361.00	363.90	+ 1.40	468.00	355.80	13,706
Oct	365.80	367.30	364.20	366.90	+ 1.40	476.00	359.30	3,545
Dec	368.70	370.20	367.40	370.00	+ 1.40	483.00	362.00	11,263
Fb92	372.00	372.00	371.30	373.20	+ 1.40	456.00	366.00	4,797
Apr	374.50	374.50	374.10	376.20	+ 1.40	446.00	373.50	4,617
June	....	....	....	379.60	+ 1.40	467.00	381.00	5,116
Aug	....	....	....	383.20	+ 1.40	426.50	377.50	2,435
Oct	....	....	....	386.70	+ 1.30	410.80	389.50	259
Dec	....	....	....	390.50	+ 1.30	431.00	383.50	1,545
Fb93	....	....	....	394.60	+ 1.30	....	....	496
June	....	....	....	402.60	+ 1.30	....	....	555

Est vol 32,000; vol Mon 21,319; open int 102,982, −1,491.

	Open	High	Low	Settle	Change	Lifetime High	Lifetime Low	Open Interest
PLATINUM (NYM)—50 troy oz.; $ per troy oz.								
July	393.50	395.00	392.50	393.50	+ .30	528.50	378.00	9,645
Oct	399.00	399.50	397.00	397.60	+ .30	513.00	383.50	3,571
Ja92	402.00	402.20	401.00	401.60	+ .40	451.50	387.00	1,569
Apr	405.00	405.00	405.00	405.20	....	438.50	396.00	387

Est vol 1,385; vol Mon 1,321; open int 15,184, +9.

	Open	High	Low	Settle	Change	Lifetime High	Lifetime Low	Open Interest
PALLADIUM (NYM) 100 troy oz.; $ per troy oz.								
June	94.60	94.75	94.15	94.55	....	125.25	80.00	1,872
Sept	96.00	96.00	95.25	95.65	....	119.40	80.75	1,701
Dec	97.00	97.40	97.00	96.80	....	114.50	82.50	805

Est vol 48; vol Mon 325; open int 4,412, −16.

	Open	High	Low	Settle	Change	Lifetime High	Lifetime Low	Open Interest
SILVER (CMX)—5,000 troy oz.; cents per troy oz.								
May	397.0	405.5	396.5	404.5	+ 5.6	647.0	355.0	533
June	399.0	399.0	399.0	405.2	+ 5.5	415.5	389.5	173
July	402.0	408.0	399.5	407.8	+ 5.5	667.5	360.0	55,595
Sept	407.0	413.0	405.0	412.7	+ 5.7	654.0	367.5	9,386
Dec	415.0	420.0	413.5	419.6	+ 5.8	623.5	374.0	10,838
Mr92	418.5	427.5	418.5	427.2	+ 5.9	613.0	382.0	4,804
May	426.0	426.0	425.0	432.5	+ 6.0	589.0	385.0	4,824
July	432.0	432.0	432.0	437.8	+ 6.1	557.0	395.0	1,955
Sept	....	....	....	443.6	+ 6.2	482.5	412.0	[illegible]
Dec	....	....	....	452.5	+ 6.3	477.5	408.0	[illegible]

Est vol 17,000; vol Mon 11,831; open int 92,986, −753.

	Open	High	Low	Settle	Change	Lifetime High	Lifetime Low	Open Interest
SILVER (CBT)—1,000 troy oz.; cents per troy oz.								
May	....	....	....	401.0	+ 5.0	422.0	361.0	6
June	397.0	404.0	397.0	403.0	+ 6.0	579.0	356.0	3,379
Aug	403.0	409.0	402.0	408.5	+ 6.0	523.0	363.0	513
Dec	414.0	419.5	412.0	418.5	+ 6.0	575.0	374.0	1,962

Est vol 1,400; vol Mon 199; open int 5,987, +1.

	Open	High	Low	Settle	Change	Lifetime High	Lifetime Low	Open Interest
CRUDE OIL, Light Sweet (NYM) 1,000 bbls.; $ per bbl.								
June	21.00	21.05	20.63	20.74	− .17	31.50	17.10	59,019
July	21.05	21.16	20.77	20.87	− .09	30.40	16.80	55,256
Aug	21.04	21.17	20.82	20.90	− .08	29.50	16.90	32,220
Sept	21.03	21.15	20.08	20.91	− .06	28.72	16.90	24,108
Oct	21.00	21.14	20.90	20.92	− .04	28.40	17.04	17,625
Nov	20.93	21.10	20.90	20.92	− .03	28.10	17.20	12,328
Dec	20.99	21.10	20.90	20.92	− .02	27.70	17.10	22,191
Ja92	20.88	21.07	20.88	20.87	− .01	27.60	17.25	10,958
Feb	20.82	20.98	20.82	20.83	+ .01	27.00	17.50	6,499
Mar	20.77	20.85	20.70	20.79	+ .02	26.75	17.25	7,415
Apr	20.73	20.87	20.73	20.76	+ .03	26.50	17.50	12,890
May	20.72	20.72	20.71	20.74	+ .03	24.60	17.30	1,765
June	20.70	20.71	20.70	20.74	+ .04	24.50	17.70	6,097
July	20.70	20.71	20.70	20.74	+ .04	23.59	17.90	3,689
Aug	20.70	20.71	20.70	20.75	+ .05	20.89	17.75	741
Sept	20.70	20.71	20.70	20.76	+ .06	24.00	17.78	1,441
Oct	20.71	20.72	20.71	20.77	+ .06	20.80	18.85	407
Nov	20.73	20.73	20.72	20.78	+ .06	21.45	19.70	283
Dec	20.74	20.74	20.73	20.79	+ .06	24.00	18.25	2,509
Mr93	....	....	....	20.82	+ .06	20.20	18.64	1,214
June	....	....	....	20.89	+ .04	23.00	18.60	7,530
Dec	....	....	....	21.01	+ .07	23.00	18.70	2,164

Est vol 108,025; vol Mon 89,238; open int 288,266, −6,488.

	Open	High	Low	Settle	Change	Lifetime High	Lifetime Low	Open Interest
HEATING OIL NO. 2 (NYM) 42,000 gal.; $ per gal.								
June	.5455	.5530	.5435	.5475	+.0022	.8575	.4800	18,067
July	.5540	.5605	.5510	.5545	+.0005	.8500	.4800	18,631
Aug	.5635	.5685	.5600	.5622	−.0012	.8507	.4900	13,432
Sept	.5760	.5830	.5755	.5779	−.0010	.8428	.5025	6,869
Oct	.5890	.5905	.5865	.5889	−.0015	.8500	.5130	2,739
Nov	.5985	.6000	.5970	.5989	−.0017	.7800	.5230	2,944
Dec	.6070	.6100	.6050	.6079	−.0021	.8262	.5330	15,610
Ja92	.6100	.6100	.6070	.6092	−.0018	.8200	.5340	4,995
Feb	.5970	.6015	.5970	.5984	−.0016	.6060	.5225	3,261
Mar	.5760	.5760	.5730	.5763	−.0017	.5880	.5415	1,347
Apr	.5580	.5580	.5560	.5567	−.0018	.5660	.5000	395
May	....	....	....	.5417	−.0018	.5505	.4875	601
June	....	....	....	.5347	−.0018	.5400	.4800	172

Est vol 18,358; vol Mon 21,558; open int 89,083, +372.

	Open	High	Low	Settle	Change	Lifetime High	Lifetime Low	Open Interest
GASOLINE, Unleaded (NYM) 42,000 gal.; $ per gal.								
June	.7130	.7140	.6975	.7010	−.0134	.9550	.5490	22,677
July	.6900	.6920	.6775	.6802	−.0102	.8270	.5525	17,386
Aug	.6650	.6650	.6570	.6582	−.0063	.9050	.5350	9,908
Sept	.6385	.6415	.6340	.6350	−.0040	.9025	.5160	5,224
Oct	.6100	.6100	.6060	.6060	−.0030	.8625	.4975	6,417
Nov	.5890	.5950	.5890	.5890	−.0020	.6675	.4860	1,958
Dec	.5730	.5760	.5730	.5730	−.0010	.7525	.4775	1,166
Ja92	.5700	.5700	.5630	.5635	−.0005	.6415	.4700	3,049
Feb	.5700	.5735	.5700	.5685	−.0005	.5755	.5070	4,581
Mar	.5875	.5875	.5875	.5835	−.0015	.5875	.5050	435
Apr	.6295	.6300	.6295	.6195	−.0010	.6300	.5500	535
May	....	....	....	.6130	−.0005	.6155	.5525	444
June	....	....	....	.6000	....	.6020	.5500	895
Aug	....	....	....	.6510	....	.5800	.5070	137

Est vol 27,159; vol Mon 23,060; open int 74,848, −785.

	Open	High	Low	Settle	Change	Lifetime High	Lifetime Low	Open Interest
NATURAL GAS, (NYM) 10,000 MMBtu.; $ per MMBtu's								
June	1.350	1.354	1.349	1.349	....	1.800	1.340	1,312
July	1.360	1.365	1.359	1.359	− .001	1.810	1.347	1,578
Aug	1.380	1.390	1.373	1.378	....	1.840	1.370	1,850
Sept	1.380	1.389	1.371	1.371	− .004	1.860	1.355	2,086
Oct	1.465	1.475	1.460	1.460	− .003	1.840	1.445	1,716
Nov	1.720	1.729	1.720	1.720	+ .003	2.040	1.680	1,723
Dec	2.010	2.015	2.005	2.005	+ .003	2.360	1.964	2,605
Ja92	2.144	2.149	2.136	2.136	− .009	2.360	2.105	2,232
Feb	....	....	....	1.935	....	2.040	1.910	1,418
Mar	1.580	1.580	1.757	1.575	− .005	1.675	1.530	219

Est vol 678; vol Mon721; open int 16,856, −1.

	Open	High	Low	Settle	Change	Lifetime High	Lifetime Low	Open Interest
BRENT CRUDE (IPE) 1,000 net bbls.; $ per bbl.								
June	19.15	19.30	19.02	19.06	− .23	25.70	15.40	27,379
July	19.25	19.50	19.23	19.29	− .10	35.02	15.52	28,540
Aug	19.40	19.66	19.30	19.32	− .22	24.80	15.79	4,979
Sept	19.48	19.65	19.48	19.65	− .05	20.00	15.92	4,755
Oct	19.63	19.70	19.63	19.68	− .07	20.08	17.00	2,119
Nov	....	....	....	19.60	− .05	20.08	18.62	566

Est vol 28,000; vol Mon 24,405; open int 68,338, −4,005.

	Open	High	Low	Settle	Change	Lifetime High	Lifetime Low	Open Interest
GAS OIL (IPE) 100 metric tons; $ per ton								
June	173.00	175.50	171.50	175.25	....	268.50	148.50	17,046
July	171.00	172.50	171.00	172.50	− 1.00	240.00	148.00	10,553
Aug	173.25	174.25	173.00	174.25	− 1.00	227.00	151.00	4,729
Sept	175.50	177.00	174.00	177.00	− .50	183.50	154.00	2,365
Oct	177.50	179.25	177.50	178.75	− 1.25	185.75	156.00	3,873
Nov	179.25	181.00	179.50	180.25	− 1.75	186.00	162.00	2,985
Dec	179.50	181.75	179.25	181.75	− .75	186.50	167.00	5,494
Ja92	177.50	179.50	177.50	179.50	− .75	186.00	176.00	660

Est Vol 8,000; vol Mon 6,478; open int 47,705, −2,559.

LONDON METAL EXCHANGE

Quotations in pounds sterling per metric ton at the close of second ring trading in the afternoon.

	Bid	Chg.	Asked	Chg.
Aluminum—Hi—Spot (z)	1306.00	+ 24.00	1308.00	+ 24.00
3 months	1335.00	+ 22.00	1336.00	+ 22.00
Tin—Spot (z)	5730.00	....	5740.00	+ 5.00
3 months	5810.00	+ 5.00	5820.00	+ 10.00
Copper—Cath—Hi—Spot	1343.00	− 99.00	1345.00	− 99.00
3 months	1308.00	− 37.00	1309.00	− 38.00
Lead—Spot	315.00	+ 4.00	316.00	+ 4.00
3 months	328.75	+ 4.75	329.00	+ 4.50
Nickel—Spot (z)	8435.00	−120.00	8445.00	+220.00
3 months	8467.00	−103.00	8570.00	−105.00
Zinc—Sp Hi—Spot (z)	1079.00	+ 3.00	1080.00	+ 3.00
3 months	1092.00	+ 2.00	1093.00	+ 2.00

z - Prices quoted in U.S. dollars.

Tuesday, official LME volumes: Aluminum-high grade, 33,732*; Copper—Grade A 11,063; Lead, 5,435; Nickel, 3,263; Zinc—high grade, 10,246*. *Quoted in US dollars

:BT—Chicago Board of Trade; CME—Chicago cantile Exchange; CMX—Commodity Exchange, York; CSCE—Coffee, Sugar & Cocoa Exchange, New ; CTN—New York Cotton Exchange; EOE—Euro- Options Exchange; IMM—International Monetary ket at CME, Chicago; IPE—International Petroleum ange; KC—Kansas City Board of Trade; LDN —London Futures & Options Exchange; MCE—Mi- erica Commodity Exchange; NOCE—New Orleans nodity Exchange; NYFE—New York Futures ange, unit of New York Stock Exchange. NYM—New Mercantile Exchange.

Figure 13.1 *(continued)*

Table 13.1 Turnover of major commodity options contracts in 1991

Commodity	Exchange	Volume
Softs		
Corn	CBOT	2 048 422
Live cattle	CME	776 624
Sugar	CSCE	1 512 976
Cotton	NYCE	392 132
Metals		
Gold	COMEX	1 398 451
Silver	COMEX	1 019 093
Aluminium	LME	396 500
Copper	LME	590 586
Energy		
Crude oil	NYMEX	4 968 742
Crude oil	IPE	234 280

Source: Adapted from data in: *Futures and Options World*, February 1992.
Key: CBOT   Chicago Board of Trade
       CME   Chicago Mercantile Exchange
       CSCE   Coffee Sugar and Cocoa Exchange, New York
       IPE   International Petroleum Exchange, London
       LME   London Metal Exchange
       NYMEX New York Mercantile Exchange

Table 13.1 indicates that in 1991 the most important futures options were on oil, sugar, corn and gold. 4.97 million crude-oil futures options were traded on NYMEX, but this was less than one-quarter the volume of trading in crude-oil futures (21.01 million contracts).

Just as for currencies and interest rates, many commodity options are traded over-the-counter (OTC) and are designed to meet the needs of particular hedgers. Most of these options are relatively short term and are often based on the average rate for the relevant period, leading to so-called 'Asian' options (to be discussed in Chapter 14). Longer term deals are usually based on swaps rather than options, in which a floating price is exchanged for a fixed price over several years. It is then possible to buy caps, floors and collars for oil up to five years ahead, which are based on the underlying swap market. Similar arrangements are offered on jet fuel and other fractions of the barrel, despite the fact that futures markets do not exist in all cases. (For discussions of oil-related options, see Chassard (1987) and Trabia (1992).)

A very recent example of caps and floors on a commodity is offered by electricity contracts in England. Just before privatization of the industry in 1990, a complex set of 'one-way' and 'two-way' contracts was negotiated between the power-generation companies and their main customers, the regional distributors. A one-way contract is just a cap or floor on the electricity price over a certain period. A two-way contract is a fixed-price contract or swap. It is equivalent to buying a cap and a floor at the same exercise price, locking-in a single price—hence the use of the term 'two-way'.

Intermediaries, such as Salomon Brothers or Bankers Trust, sometimes issue call and put warrants on oil and other commodities, but secondary trading in the warrants is rather small, as can be judged from the following extract. The warrants are simply long-dated options. The intermediaries have become so important in the oil market that they are known as the 'Wall Street refiners'. They never handle any oil, but only arrange financial transactions related to oil prices.

Salomon announces oil price warrant

By MARTIN DICKSON

A warrant which allows investors to hedge against the price of oil up to seven years ahead was announced yesterday by Salomon Brothers.

Although other securities houses have produced similar products in the oil sector, this is believed to be the first instrument of this kind with such a long life.

Bankers Trust unveiled a similar warrant last October but that issue was for only two and a half years.

Salomon is issuing 5m warrants, developed in conjunction with its commodities trading subsidiary Phibro Energy, at a price of $3.50 a warrant, with a strike price of $20 a barrel.

This means that if the price of oil exceeds $20 a barrel on the various dates over the next seven years when the warrant can be exercised, the holder will be entitled to a cash payment of the difference.

No physical oil is involved.

The reference point to be used in determining the oil price will be the closing price of the sixth month contract on the New York Mercantile Exchange for light sweet crude on the Friday immediately succeeding the exercise date. That price is currently $20.01.

The warrants are exerciseable quarterly during the seven years from March 9 this year to March 14 1997, with the first exercise date being June 7.

The strike price gives a gearing of about 5.72 and represents a total premium of 17.72 per cent.

Mr Neil Bresolin of Phibro Energy said the warrant was designed to allow investors to take advantage of the relative cheapness of long-term oil.

Analysts said that the Bankers Trust warrant, although of a much shorter duration, was slightly more flexible in that investors could exercise it at any time during a six-month period.

That warrant was apparently bought largely in the Asian market.

(*Financial Times*, 24 January 1990)

Another class of commodity option exists within commodity bonds (see Schwartz, 1982). These are bonds that are convertible on maturity into a fixed amount of commodity. For example, a bond might be issued in 1991 with redemption in 2001, at which time it would pay $100 or the value of 5 barrels of oil. In some cases the coupon also has an option feature, such as $10 per annum or the value of 0.5 barrels of oil. *The Economist* estimated in 1989 that there were about 40 international issues of commodity bonds in existence. One infamous issue was the 'Giscard' gold-backed bond, so-named because it was arranged by Giscard d'Estaing when he was French finance minister in 1973. Soon after issue the gold price was set free from the dollar and it zoomed from $35 per ounce to $300 per ounce. Buyers of the bond profited, but the French Treasury probably lost (unless, as it claims, it was hedged by holding gold).

Finally, there are implicit commodity options inherent to natural resources. For example, in valuing a gold mine that has yet to be developed, the traditional approach would be to project gold prices and calculate a net present value for the project. As Brennan and Schwartz (1985) point out, this approach fails to take account of the volatility of the future gold price. It is equivalent to valuing a stock option by taking a single value for the stock price at maturity. The high volatility of commodity prices may make a new mine or other development valuable, even though exploitation at today's prices would not be worth while.

13.2   Using commodity options

This section will be brief, because strategies with commodity options are virtually the same as those with other kinds of option. They are used for speculation and hedging. What may differ is the kind of hedger involved. A few will now be considered.

Suppose that a company plans to develop a new copper mine that will take five years to come into production. Most of the capital will be borrowed. It could ensure its ability to repay the loan by pre-selling its first five years of copper output. Alternatively, it could borrow by issuing a commodity bond, so that the cost of repayment would be automatically linked to the price of copper. As with all convertible bonds, this approach is likely to be cheaper, because the option on copper is valuable. Users of this approach include Mexico, which has issued oil-backed bonds on several occasions. A danger is that the development of the mine or oil-field is delayed, so that there is no production to cover the repayment.

One sector, for which governments provide free put options in almost all of the industrial nations, is agriculture. Farmers are guaranteed minimum prices for their output. Hence the cost of agricultural policy can be considered as the cost of providing put options (see Marcus and Modest, 1986). Consideration of how farmers might use exchange-traded puts is made by Gardner (1985).

There are pilot programmes in the United States in which farmers are encouraged to buy exchange-traded puts rather than depend on government guarantees. Similar ways in which developing countries might use floors and collars for their commodity exports are reviewed by Gilbert and Powell (1988).

Although the discussion has been about producers of commodities, industrial consumers may also wish to cap their purchase prices. Buyers of calls would include: travel companies hedging against a rise in the price of jet-fuel; a school-district hedging against a rise in its winter fuel bill; the cocoa buyer of a company manufacturing chocolate; and a fabricator of copper products.

13.3   Valuation of commodity options

Exchange-traded commodity options are *options on futures*. Since futures prices are virtually identical to forward prices,[1] put/call/forward parity (as proved in Chapter 8) applies:

$$p = c - PV(F - E), \qquad (13.1)$$

where F now denotes a futures price. It follows that if a put and a call are struck at the same futures price (i.e. if $F = E$), the two options will have the same premium.

In deciding on pricing models, there are three particular features of commodities that might need to be taken into account, and we shall consider each in some detail: (i) the term structure of prices; (ii) the term structure of volatility; and (iii) the relationship of volatility to price level.

13.3.1   TERM STRUCTURE OF PRICES

If a commodity is storable, then in order to persuade someone to hold it the forward (or futures) price must cover both interest (r) and the cost of warehousing/insurance/deterioration (w). We therefore have the relationship between forward (F) and spot (S) prices, in the absence of a risk premium, of

$$F = S\, e^{(r + w)t}, \qquad (13.2)$$

where t is the period in years to the maturity of the forward contract, and the variables r and w are expressed in continuous form.

The cheapest place to keep an exhaustible commodity, such as oil or copper, is in the ground, where the warehousing cost is zero. Relationship (13.2) led Hotelling (1931) to formulate the rule that prices for exhaustible resources, which are in the ground, should rise at the risk-free rate of interest. However, what we actually observe for all kinds of commodities, both exhaustible and renewable, is that prices over the long term do not rise at a rate sufficient to fully reward storage (see, e.g., Heal and Barrow, 1980).

We can use quoted futures prices to see directly that storage is not always fully rewarded. A strategy of buying the spot commodity, storing and selling futures is, in principle, riskless and so should pay the risk-free rate. Table 13.2 lists the spot and futures prices for gold on COMEX on 14 May 1991. The profile is of rising prices, but not at a rate sufficient to cover interest and storage. For example, buying June 1991 futures, selling June 1992 futures and taking delivery of the gold for one year from June 1991 to June 1992 would give a reward of 5.09%. The approximate interest cost of doing that was 6.625% at the time, to which must be added a small warehousing and insurance cost. Storing gold was therefore unprofitable.

Why is there a net loss from storage? One possibility is that the futures price may incorporate a risk premium that is necessary to elicit buyers: it is biased

Table 13.2 Spot and futures prices for gold on 14 May 1991

	1991				1992				1993
Spot	June	Aug.	Oct.	Dec.	Feb.	Apr.	June	. . .	June
357.95	361.20	363.90	366.90	370.00	373.20	376.20	379.60	. . .	402.60

Source: Wall Street Journal.
Spot is London price; futures prices from COMEX.

downwards relative to the eventual spot price. The evidence is against such a bias (see, e.g., references in Kamara, 1982). A simpler explanation is that the futures price is an unbiased forecast of the eventual spot price, but there has been a persistent downward drift in real commodity prices (see, e.g., Deaton and Laroque, 1992). The reason is that the supply function has shifted out-wards under the influence of technology at a higher rate than has the demand function, as illustrated in Fig. 13.2. Malthusian forecasts, such as that of the 'Club of Rome' in 1972, assumed fixed supply and exponentially growing

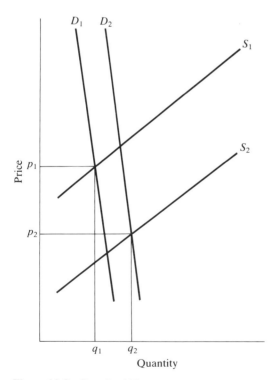

Figure 13.2 Supply shifts exceed demand shifts leading to lower prices

demand, both of which were false. Another example is provided by US agricultural policy, which was at one time mistakenly based upon maintaining the prices of agricultural commodities in a fixed relationship with the prices of other goods: needless to say, the policy was too costly to maintain.

Despite the apparent loss, users of commodities must hold stocks in order to maintain their manufacturing processes. They are said to earn a *convenience yield* (γ) from holding stocks, which is just sufficient to compensate for the loss. The relationship between spot and futures prices may be modified to take this into account:

$$F = S \, e^{(r + w - \gamma)t}. \tag{13.3}$$

Rearranging (13.3), the convenience yield may be expressed as

$$\gamma = r + w - \left(\frac{1}{t}\right) \log\left(\frac{F}{S}\right). \tag{13.4}$$

The convenience yield is like an implicit dividend payment and can be simply incorporated into the Black/Scholes equation. The current spot price is discounted for the convenience yield (γ) and compounded for the direct storage cost (w), to give the options-pricing equation:

$$c = S \, e^{(w - \gamma)t} N(d_1) - E \, e^{-rt} N(d_2), \tag{13.5}$$

where $S \, e^{(w - \gamma)t}$ replaces S in the d_1 and d_2 terms also.

Equation (13.5) is just another form of Merton's dividend model, introduced in Chapter 6. Alternatively, the spot price discounted by the convenience yield and compounded by the storage cost rate may be re-expressed from (13.3) as:

$$S \, e^{(w - \gamma)t} = F \, e^{-rt}. \tag{13.6}$$

Substituting in the options-pricing equation (Eq. (13.5)) we then have Black's (1976) options-on-futures equation once again, which is

$$c = [FN(d_1) - EN(d_2)]e^{-rt}. \tag{13.7}$$

Practitioners do not think in terms of convenience yields and costs of storage. They simply observe, or project, forward prices and use them in this equation (remembering that $F \, e^{-rt}$ replaces S in the original Black/Scholes formulation in the d_1 and d_2 terms).

As another example of the drift (convenience yield), consider the crude-oil futures prices on NYMEX for 4 May 1991, shown in Table 13.3. The price profile is almost flat (see Fig. 13.3). The gross reward to storage from June 1991 to June 1992 would have been precisely zero ($F = S$), yet the one-year rate of interest at the time was 6.625%. Ignoring any other storage costs (i.e. assuming that $w = 0$), the convenience yield for that period was then precisely equal to the interest rate, i.e. 6.625% per annum. Two-year oil options would have been based upon the futures price of $20.89 per barrel for June 1993 and not the compounded spot price, which from a base of June 1991 would

Table 13.3 Spot and futures prices for crude oil on 14 May 1991

	Delivery date	Price ($)	Full carry cost ($)	Loss on storage ($)	Conv. yield (%)
1991	June	20.74	–	–	–
	August	20.80	20.96	0.16	4.72
	October	20.92	21.19	0.27	3.96
	December	20.92	21.42	0.50	4.88
1992	June	20.74	22.12	1.38	6.65
	⋮	⋮	⋮	⋮	⋮
1993	June	20.89	23.58	2.69	6.29

Source: Wall Street Journal. Futures prices from NYMEX.
Notes:
1. The June 91 contract was effectively spot, because oil cannot be traded for more immediate delivery than one month ahead. This is confirmed by the spot quote for WTI oil at Cushing, Oklahoma, which was $20.75 per barrel on that day.
2. Direct storage costs (in the ground) assumed to be zero ($w = 0$).

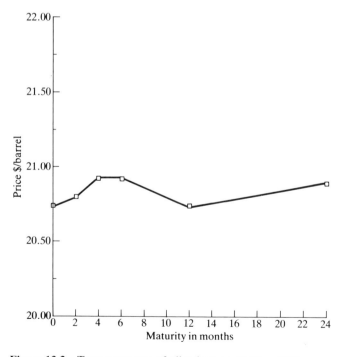

Figure 13.3 Term structure of oil prices on 14 May 1991

have been $20.74(1 + 0.06625)^2 = \$23.58$ per barrel (see column 3 of Table 13.3).

The loss on storage from June 1991 to June 1993 would therefore have been $2.69 per barrel (final row of column 4), or 6.29% per annum (column 5). The latter was the convenience yield: someone was implicitly paying this for not selling the oil in June 1991, but preferring to hold it to June 1993. As the table indicates, the convenience yield was not the same for all horizons, the range being from about 4% to 7%. In the options-pricing equation (Eq. (13.5)), a different γ would be required for each maturity. Equivalently (and more simply), the options-on-futures model (Eq. (13.7)) would have a different futures price at each maturity.

Let us summarize. There is a term structure of forward or futures prices for commodities. Although forward prices tend to be above spot prices, they are usually not sufficiently high to cover the cost of holding stocks. In order to value options on commodities, it is possible to estimate the rate of loss (convenience yield) on storage, which may then be incorporated in the same way as a dividend in Merton's variation of the Black/Scholes model (13.5). More simply, the forward price may be projected and used in Black's options-on-futures model (13.7).

As an example, we shall now value June 1992 options on oil using three different methods. The first two are based on Merton's Eq. (13.5), but they differ in that the first of them allows for early exercise by using the binomial approach. The third method ignores convenience yield and so is a simple Black/Scholes valuation. The data are from Table 13.3, assuming that the options were exactly one year away from maturity, had a volatility of 0.25 and an exercise price of $20 per barrel. The results are given in Table 13.4.

The binomial model with $\gamma = 6.625\%$ is taken as being 'correct', since it allows for early exercise. It gives values of $2.307 per barrel for the call and $1.596 per barrel for the put. The Merton model gives values that are slightly lower, indicating the value of early exercise to be worth an extra 1.73% for the call and 1.44% for the put. The unadjusted Black/Scholes model gives results that are grossly in error: 35% too large for the call and 29% too small for the put. It is therefore *very* important to correct for γ, but correcting for early exercise does not appear (in this example) to matter greatly.

Table 13.4 Example valuation of oil options (prices in $ per barrel)

Method	Call price ($)	Call error (%)	Put price ($)	Put error (%)
Binomial with γ	2.307	0	1.596	0
Merton with γ	2.267	− 1.73	1.573	− 1.44
Black/Scholes	3.112	+ 34.89	1.128	− 29.32

Note: $S = \$20.74$, $t = 1$, $\sigma = 0.25$, $X = \$20$, $\gamma = 0.06625$, $r = 0.06625$.

13.3.2 TERM STRUCTURE OF VOLATILITY

Not only do the forward (or futures) prices show some particular pattern, but their volatilities may be lower for most distant maturities. We might hypothesize a pattern such as that shown in Fig. 13.4. The argument for this pattern of declining volatility, first made by Samuelson (1965), runs as follows. Let us suppose that the price of oil in 20 years' time is expected to be $25, while the price today is $21. A war is now declared in the Persian Gulf, which propels spot prices up to $50 per barrel and 1-year prices to $30 per barrel. However, the 20-year price remains unaffected at $25 per barrel. The prices of distant futures contracts depend on long-term expectations, while nearby futures contracts are affected by both short-term information (such as the war) and long-term information. Nearby futures contracts are therefore affected by a wider set of information than are distant futures contracts, so nearby prices fluctuate much more. At some very distant horizon, expectations, and hence futures prices, are virtually constant.

The empirical evidence from futures contracts on commodities (see, e.g., Duffie, 1989, and a recent study on oil prices by Gabillon, 1991) generally supports this argument. However, it should be noted that we can only observe the volatility of actual futures prices up to 18 months away: more distant futures did not exist until very recently.[2]

The implication for option pricing is that more distant options should be given lower volatilities. As an extreme example, a 20-year option might have a volatility that was a weighted average of those depicted in Fig. 13.4, i.e. about

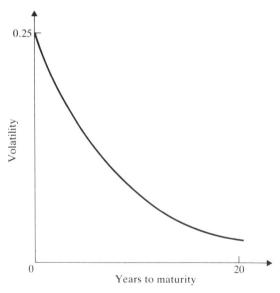

Figure 13.4 Hypothesized term structure of volatilities for a commodity

Table 13.5 Example of five-year cap on oil prices

Horizon	Price ($)	Volatility		Call price ($)	Cap price ($)
		Forward	Spot		
6/91	20.74	0.300	0.300	–	–
6/92	20.74	0.200	0.250	1.828	1.714
6/93	20.89	0.150	0.217	2.199	2.062
6/94	21.00	0.125	0.194	2.312	2.168
6/95	21.00	0.113	0.178	2.289	2.147
6/96	21.00	0.100	0.167	2.257	2.117
					Total = $10.218

0.10. In practice, options on oil are traded over-the-counter only up to about five years ahead, and on exchanges actively only for the next few months.

Table 13.5 illustrates the possible cost of a cap on oil prices for the next five years, priced once per year, as on 14 May 1991. The table assumes the particular term structure of prices given in column 2: the first three prices are those from the futures market and the next three are subjective projections. The assumed volatilities of the forward prices are given in column 3, ranging from 0.30 for spot to 0.10 at the five-year horizon. Column 4 gives the spot volatilities, which are the period volatilities from now until the relevant horizon. These have been calculated as averages from the forward values. For example, the spot volatility to 6/93 is approximated as the average of the forward volatilities for 6/91, 6/92 and 6/93, equalling 0.217. The call prices for 1- to 5-year options are given in column 5. The cost of a cap, shown in column 6, is lower than the cost of a call (column 5) by one year's interest. This is because (as discussed in Chapter 11) the cap pays out one period later than the corresponding call. The total cost of the cap over five years would be an estimated $10.218. This looks high, but it should be remembered that it relates to five barrels of oil and not just one.

A floor could be similarly calculated and combined with the cap to provide a costless collar, as already illustrated for interest rates in Chapter 11.

13.3.3 RELATIONSHIP OF VOLATILITY TO PRICE LEVEL

Many commodities show short periods of high and volatile spot prices followed by long periods of lower and more stable prices. A good example is given by sugar, for which real prices over a 40-year period are plotted in Fig. 13.5. There were high and volatile prices in 1957, 1973 and 1980. Between these years, prices were much lower and rather stable. Another example, already mentioned, was the price of oil immediately before the Gulf War in the spring of 1991. The spot price was driven temporarily to more than $42 per barrel, but thereafter fell back to less than $20 per barrel and was rather stable.

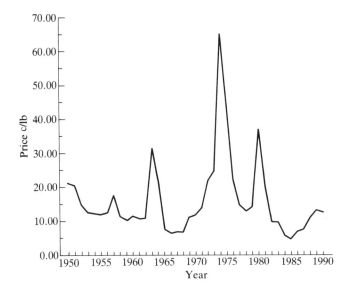

Figure 13.5   Real price of sugar 1950–90
Note: Annual average price deflated by US wholesale price index. Data from International Financial Statistics

Many commodities also display seasonal price patterns. For example, the price of heating oil rises in the winter while that of petrol rises in the summer. Grains have prices that are lowest immediately after the northern-hemisphere harvest in September and rise during the storage period to the following June or July. As stocks are drawn down and prices rise, so prices tend to become (seasonably) more volatile.

There are options-pricing models which allow for volatility to change with price level. One such is known as the *constant elasticity of variance* (CEV) model and was introduced by Cox and Ross (1976). It assumes simply that a 1% rise in asset price leads to a $(\psi - 1)$% rise in volatility. If $\psi = 1$ then there is no change in volatility with price and the model is the same as that of Black/Scholes. If $\psi > 1$ then volatility rises with price, which may be appropriate for commodities (see Choi and Longstaff, 1985, and Milonas, 1986). For example, Milonas (p. 673) found ψ to be about 2.85 for soyabean futures. If $\psi < 1$ then volatility falls with price level, which may be appropriate in some cases for shares. For example, Beckers (1980) found ψ to be on average 0.62 for a sample of US equities.

The effect of rising volatility as price rises is to skew the return distribution to the right, as shown in Fig. 13.6. A binomial implementation of the CEV model, which is based on such a distribution, is explained in the appendix. Table 13.6 gives some illustrative call prices from this model, for options having respectively 4 months ($t = 0.333$) and 1 year ($t = 1.0$) to run,

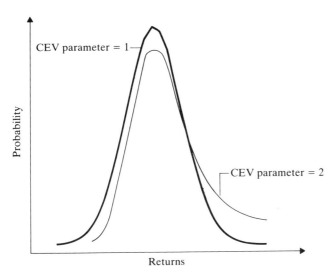

Figure 13.6 Return distribution in a CEV model

Table 13.6 Some representative CEV model call values

t	σ	E	$\psi = 2.0$	$\psi = 1.0$	$\psi = 0.5$	$\psi = 0.0$
0.333	0.2	35	5.72	5.76	5.79	5.81
		40	2.17	2.17	2.17	2.17
		45	0.59	0.51	0.47	0.43
	0.3	35	6.14	6.26	6.32	6.38
		40	3.07	3.07	3.07	3.07
		45	1.40	1.26	1.19	1.12
	0.4	35	6.72	6.90	7.00	7.10
		40	3.97	3.97	3.97	3.98
		45	2.33	2.11	2.01	1.92
1.00	0.2	35	7.27	7.39	7.45	7.52
		40	4.16	4.15	4.16	4.16
		45	2.27	2.07	1.98	1.89
	0.3	35	8.26	8.48	8.60	8.74
		40	5.67	5.67	5.66	5.68
		45	3.96	3.64	3.50	3.37
	0.4	35	9.42	9.74	9.92	10.14
		40	7.20	7.17	7.18	7.21
		45	5.67	5.25	5.07	4.92

Note: S = 40; r = 0.05.
$\psi = 1$ gives B/S values.

with ψ parameters from 0.0 to 2.0 and with no convenience yield.[3] The spot price is set to 40 and the interest rate is 5Y (continuous). The prices with $\psi = 1$ are the same as Black/Scholes values.

The impact on options prices of different ψ-values is relatively small. Nevertheless, at an exercise price of 35, which is in-the-money, the $\psi = 2$ options are worth about 2–10% less than the Black/Scholes ($\psi = 1$) options. Conversely, at an exercise price of 45 which is out-of-the-money, the $\psi = 2$ options are worth about 8–16% more than the Black/Scholes values. These differences could be important for commodities for which there is a small, but significant, probability of stocks being exhausted, leading to a spike in prices.

Yet another approach to rising volatility when stocks are low is to make the convenience yield, γ, a function of S, and to make it stochastic. Gibson and Schwartz (1990) demonstrate the latter approach for oil options. They argue that options prices are significantly changed by their method, but the cost in extra complexity is also large.

13.4 Summary

Commodity options can be valued with models of the Black/Scholes type as long as certain factors are taken into account. The first is that prices tend to fall through time relative to a random walk. This can be treated as a convenience yield, which can be incorporated like a dividend into the model. The second is that long-maturity options should usually be priced with lower volatilities than short-term options. A third, but less important, factor is that volatility may rise with the price level. This reflects the occasional 'spikes' that occur in commodity prices and are associated with very high volatility. The CEV model can be used to adjust for the changing volatility.

On the whole, the modelling problems for commodity options are not insurmountable. The greatest difficulty is in forecasting future price levels and their volatilities for periods of more than two years ahead, because there are almost no distant futures prices.

Notes

1. Apart from the difference in price due to credit risks on forward contracts, futures and forward prices would be the same if there were no chance that interest rates would change over the life of the contract. The reason is that a forward price reflects a fixed rate of interest, whereas margining causes a futures price to reflect an expected, but fluctuating, rate of interest (see Cox *et al.*, 1981).
2. In November 1990 NYMEX introduced contracts on crude oil up to three years ahead.
3. These are the same as prices for stock options and the example is an extension of one in Cox and Rubinstein (1985), p. 364.

References

Beckers, S. (1980), 'The CEV model and its implications for options pricing', *Journal of Finance*, **25**, 661–73.

Black, F. (1976), 'The pricing of commodity contracts', *Journal of Financial Economics*, **3**, 167–79.

Brennan, M. and Schwartz, E. (1985), 'Evaluating natural resource investments', *Journal of Business*, **58**, 135–58.

Chassard, C. (1987), 'Option trading and oil futures markets', Oxford Institute for Energy Studies, Working Paper No. 11.

Choi, J. and Longstaff, F. (1985), 'Pricing options on agricultural futures: an application of the constant elasticity of variance option pricing model', *Journal of Futures Markets*, **5**, 247–58.

Cox, J. and Rubinstein, M. (1985), *Options Markets*, Prentice-Hall, Englewood Cliffs, New Jersey.

Cox, J. and Ross, S. (1976), 'The valuation of options for alternative stochastic processes', *Journal of Financial Economics*, **3**, 145–66.

Cox, J., Ingersoll, J. and Ross, S. (1981), 'The relationship between forward prices and futures prices', *Journal of Financial Economics*, **9**, 321–46.

Deaton, A. and Laroque, G. (1992), 'On the behaviour of commodity prices', *Review of Economic Studies*, **59**, 1–24.

Duffie, D. (1989), *Futures Markets*, Prentice-Hall, Englewood Cliffs, New Jersey.

Emanuel, D. and Macbeth, J. (1982), 'Further results on the constant elasticity of variance call option pricing model', *Journal of Financial and Quantitative Analysis*, **17**, 533–54.

Gabillon, J. (1991), 'The term structure of oil futures prices', Oxford Institute for Energy Studies, Working Paper, No. 17.

Gardner, B. (1985), 'Commodity options for agriculture', *American Journal of Agricultural Economics*, **69**, 986–92.

Gilbert, C. and Powell, A. (1988), 'The use of commodity contracts for the management of developing country commodity risks', in Currie, D. and Vines, D. (eds), *North-South Economic Interactions*, Macmillan, London.

Gibson, R. and Schwartz, E. (1990), 'Stochastic convenience yield and the pricing of oil contingent claims', *Journal of Finance*, **45**, 959–76.

Heal, G. and Barrow, M. (1980), 'The relationship between interest rates and metal price movements', *Review of Economic Studies*, **47**, 161–81.

Hotelling, H. (1931), 'The economics of exhaustible resources', *Journal of Political Economy*, **39**, 139–75.

Kamara, A. (1982), 'Issues in futures markets: a survey', *Journal of Futures Markets*, **2**, 261–94.

Marcus, A. and Modest, D. (1986), 'The valuation of a random number of put options: an application to agricultural price supports', *Journal of Financial and Quantitative Analysis*, **21**, 73–86.

Milonas, N. (1986), 'A note on agricultural options and the variance of futures prices', *Journal of Futures Markets*, **6**, 671–6.

Rees, G. (1972), *Britain's Commodity Markets*, Paul Elek, London.

Samuelson, P. (1965), 'Proof that speculative prices fluctuate randomly', *Industrial Management Review*, **6**, 41–9.

Schwartz, E. (1982), 'The pricing of commodity-linked bonds', *Journal of Finance*, **37**, 525–41.

Trabia, X. (1992), 'New developments in oil options markets', Oxford Institute for Energy Studies, forthcoming working paper.

APPENDIX

A13.1 Binomial implementation of the constant elasticity of variance model

There is an analytical solution to the constant elasticity of variance (CEV) model, which is given by Cox and Rubinstein (1985, p. 363). Simplified formulae derived by Cox for the cases of $\psi = 0$ and $\psi = 0.5$ are given by Beckers (1980). Implementation when $\psi > 1$ is discussed by Emanuel and Macbeth (1982). Here we shall develop a binomial approximation. This has the advantage of being adaptable to a variety of price/volatility relationships and it may also incorporate the value of early exercise.

The instantaneous volatility of returns at the jth step (σ_{Rj}) in the tree is assumed to be related to its long-term value $(\hat{\sigma})$ as,

$$\sigma_{Rj} = \hat{\sigma} \left(\frac{S_j}{S_0} \right)^{\psi - 1}, \qquad (A13.1)$$

where S_0 is the initial asset price, S_j is the asset price after j steps, and ψ is a constant. In logarithms this may be written as

$$\log(\sigma_{Rj}) = \log(\hat{\sigma}) + (\psi - 1)\log\left(\frac{S_j}{S_0} \right). \qquad (A13.2)$$

Relationship (A13.2) may then be estimated from a time-series of the behaviour of the asset price (see, e.g., Beckers, 1980; Milonas, 1986).

The main problem in binomial modelling with a changing volatility is that, because the U and D factors in the tree are not constant at any one time, the tree will not recombine. To overcome this we shall assume that at each step only the two outermost prices take on new values, while the inner prices repeat earlier values. Three steps in such a 'repeating' tree are outlined in Fig. A13.1.

Now the volatility of an asset price (σ_{Sj}) is approximately equal to the volatility of its returns (σ_{Rj}) multiplied by the expected asset price, $\epsilon(S_{j+1})$; that is,

$$\sigma_{Sj} \approx \sigma_{Rj}\epsilon(S_{j+1}). \qquad (A13.3)$$

If we assume a risk-neutral world, then the expected asset price at step $(j + 1)$ in the tree, $\epsilon(S_{j+1})$, is simply the compounded value of the asset price from the previous node, S_j; that is,

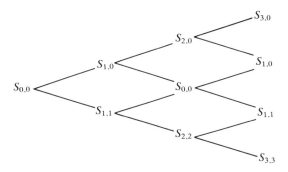

Figure A13.1 Three steps in the repeating tree

$$\epsilon(S_{j+1}) = (1 + r) S_j. \tag{A13.4}$$

Hence, we may write the asset-price volatility at the jth step as approximately

$$\sigma_{Sj} \approx \sigma_{Rj}(1 + r) S_j. \tag{A13.5}$$

Suppose we start with an asset price of $S_{0,0} = 1.0$, a long-term volatility of $\hat{\sigma} = 0.2$, an interest rate of $r = 0.1$ per period, a time step of $(t/n) = 1$ and the parameter $\psi = 2$. Because at the origin $S_j = S_0$, the return volatility (from (A13.1)) starts at its long-term value of 0.2. We set $U = e^{\sigma\sqrt{t/n}} = 1.2214$ and $D = 1/U = 0.8187$ and the tree starts exactly like a conventional one (see Fig. A13.2).

From Eq. (A13.1), the revised volatility of returns at the upper node is

$$\sigma_{Rj} = 0.2\left(\frac{1.2214}{1.00}\right)^1 = 0.2443.$$

The corresponding volatility of the asset price from Eq. (A13.5) is

$$\begin{aligned}
\sigma_{Sj} &\approx \sigma_{Rj}(1 + r) S_j \\
&\approx 0.2443(1.1)1.2214 \\
&\approx 0.3289.
\end{aligned}$$

We know that the downward branch from here must fall to an asset price of 1.00, in order to ensure recombination. We need to find the asset value for the upward branch, $S_{2,0}$, as outlined in Fig. A13.3.

We know that the binomial multiplier m is defined as

$$m_{1,0} = \frac{1 + r - D_{1,1}}{U_{1,0} - D_{1,1}}.$$

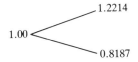

Figure A13.2 First step in CEV tree

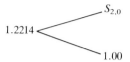

Figure A13.3 Upper branch in example CEV tree

Hence, we know that

$$U_{1,0} = \left(\frac{1 + r - D_{1,1}}{m_{1,0}}\right) + D_{1,1}. \tag{A13.6}$$

We also know, from the definition of a variance, that

$$\sigma_S^2 = m_{1,0}(S_{2,0})^2 + (1 - m_{1,0})(S_{2,1})^2 - [\epsilon(S)]^2$$

$$= m_{1,0}(S_{1,0}U_{1,0})^2 + (1 - m_{1,0})(S_{1,0}D_{1,1})^2 - [S_{1,0}(1 + r)]^2. \tag{A13.7}$$

Equations (A13.6) and (A.13.7) have two unknowns, $m_{1,0}$ and $U_{1,0}$, so they may be solved simultaneously by trial and error. In this case the solution is

$$U_{1,0} = 1.357,$$

so

$$S_{2,0} = 1.3570(1.2214) = 1.6574.$$

At the bottom of the tree the up-multiplier is known, so the two unknowns are the down-multiplier $D_{1,2}$ and the probability $m_{1,1}$. Solution of the two equations at the bottom gives

$$D = 0.8330 \quad \text{and} \quad S_{2,2} = 0.6820.$$

The whole tree over four steps is shown in Fig. A13.4.

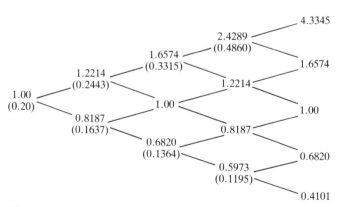

Figure A13.4 Binomial tree for CEV example (with volatilities in brackets)

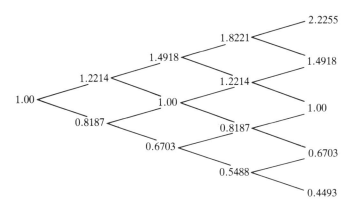

Figure A13.5 Standard binomial tree example

Figure A13.5 is an equivalent Black/Scholes tree, i.e. with $\psi = 1$. After four steps the upward skewness of the first tree relative to the second tree is quite apparent. For example, the uppermost value in the first tree is 4.3350 after four steps, whereas the equivalent in the second tree is 2.2255. Of course, the up and down probabilities in the CEV tree are not constant, unlike those in the Black/Scholes tree.

The CEV model may then be solved in the same way as any other binomial model, care being taken to use the correct multipliers from the tree for each node.

Finally, two problems may arise which need to be circumvented. The first is that asset prices may become negative, so that a minimum may need to be imposed in the tree. The second is that, for a large value of ψ, the tree may become 'explosive', so that a maximum asset price may also need to be imposed.

14
Exotic options

In this chapter we shall consider some kinds of option and methods of valuation that would not have fitted well in the previous chapters. The first topic is the pricing of average-rate or 'Asian' options, which have appeared over the last few years. These have the twin advantages of being relatively cheap and suiting the low-risk preferences of many companies. The second topic is a discussion of how to value options by the Monte Carlo method. This system can be applied to almost any option, and Asian options are used as an example. The third topic is the valuation of 'look-back' options, which allow the holder to exercise at the highest or lowest price achieved over a particular time interval. Not surprisingly, being given the benefit of hindsight leads to some expensive options. The fourth topic is the valuation of an option to exchange one asset for another. The most common of these are options on the spread of prices between two assets or of prices for two futures contracts on the same asset.

14.1 Average-rate (Asian) options

14.1.1 WHAT THEY ARE

Average-rate ('Asian') options are widely available on currencies, oil and metals. As their name suggests, they are options to buy (calls) or to sell (puts) at an average of prices over a given period. Thus, I might buy an Asian call on the dollar at an exercise price of DM1.50, which has a life of three months and costs DM0.10. The call would have a positive final payment if the *average* rate exceeded DM1.50/$ over the period. As another example, I might buy an Asian call on crude oil at an exercise price of $20 per barrel for one year. If the average turned out to exceed $20, then the call would have a final pay-off.

Clearly an average price is less volatile than the series of prices from which it is computed, so Asian options are less valuable than traditional options. Similarly, the more frequent the averaging, the lower the volatility: for example, daily averaging will result in a lower volatility than weekly averaging and hence a lower option value.

There have been several papers on how to price these Asian options. Bergman (1985) wrote about them, but his results were neither widely distributed nor immediately applicable. Ritchken *et al.* (1990) provided a simple introduction. Solutions based upon geometric averages and Monte Carlo methods were obtained by Kemna and Vorst (1990) and extended by Vorst (1990). Carverhill and Clewlow (1990) developed a numerical method of valuation based upon the convolution of density functions via the fast Fourier transform. Levy (1900) and Turnbull and Wakeman (1991) developed approximations based upon the assumption that an arithmetic average is nearly lognormal in its distribution.

We shall show: (i) that there exists a naive and expensive replication strategy for these options; (ii) that a binomial tree for these options is not easy to solve, because it does not recombine; and (iii) that the approximation developed by Vorst (1990), based upon the geometric average, is easy to implement.

14.1.2 NAIVE REPLICATION

If an option can be replicated by a position in the underlying asset, then by choosing the right proportions of the asset and option a hedged position can be established. Solving for the risk-free return on the hedge will allow the option's price to be imputed. The first question is, therefore: How do we replicate an average-rate option? The underlying average asset does not exist, but it can be created as follows. A long position in an average asset is established by buying $(1/n)$ units of the asset per period, where the averaging is to take place over n periods. For example, if 1000 barrels of oil comprise the average asset and averaging is to occur at the end of each of four quarter years, then 250 barrels of oil would be purchased on 31 March, 30 June, 30 September and 31 December. Such a programme would result in the purchase of the 1000 barrels at the period-average price.

Given that we have now created the average asset, it remains to determine its present price (on 1 January). The example average asset is equivalent to a portfolio of four forward contracts, each written at its own forward price. For example, we might have March oil at $20, June oil at $20.50, September oil at $21 and December oil at $21.50. The forward price for the asset would then be the average, i.e. $20.75.

Given that the average asset consists of four quarterly contracts, why not replicate a call option on the asset by purchasing four separate calls—one maturing each quarter? The answer is that this naive approach, consisting of a portfolio of calls, will always cost more than a single call on the portfolio of forward contracts. Here is an example of why this occurs, based upon the oil data. Let us assume that the price of oil is $32 in March and $20 in each succeeding quarter. The average for the year would then be

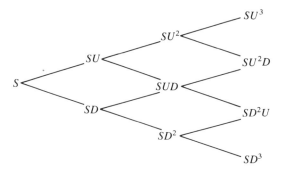

Figure 14.1 Tree for simple asset

$(32 + 20 + 20 + 20)/4 = \$23$ per barrel. If an Asian call option had been written at an exercise price of \$25, then on expiry it would have been worthless. However, if it had been replicated by the purchase of four quarterly call options, each at an exercise price of \$25, then the first call would have paid $32 - 25 = \$7$ per barrel and the other calls, nothing. For the four calls averaged, the total pay-off would have been $(1/4) \times 7 = \$1.75$ per barrel. It is therefore possible for the four calls to make a positive pay-off when the average option does not. Consequently, the four calls must cost more than the average-rate option.

14.1.3 BINOMIAL APPROACH

As it is possible to create the average asset, then it is also possible to establish a binomial tree and solve for the option price. Suppose the simple asset starts at a

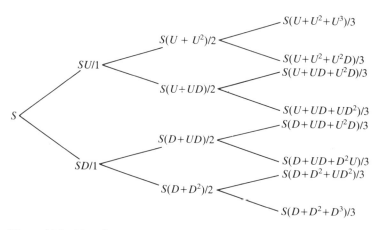

Figure 14.2 Tree for arithmetically averaged asset

price of S and has the familiar up and down multipliers, U and D respectively. The resulting tree for the simple asset is shown in Fig. 14.1, and the corresponding tree for the average asset is shown in Fig. 14.2.

The tree for the *simple* asset (Fig. 14.1) has one extra branch per time step, because the middle branches recombine; for example, $SDU = SUD$. The tree for the *average* asset (Fig. 14.2) does not recombine in this way and there is a doubling of branches at each time step. After only 20 time steps there would be $2^{20} = 1.049$ million possible outcomes to evaluate and at least 50 time steps would be required for accurate results.

14.1.4 GEOMETRIC AVERAGE APPROACH

What should we do? One solution, adopted by Kemna and Vorst (1990), is to use geometric rather than arithmetic averaging. A geometric average is less than or equal to an arithmetic average. The more volatile the series, the greater the difference. Kemna and Vorst derive the call value as the present value of the expected geometric average pay-off. Vorst (1990) then shows how the exercise price may be adjusted to allow for the difference between discrete-arithmetic and continuous-geometric averages.

For currency options, the price of a continuous geometrically averaged call (CG) is:

$$CG = e^{-rT}[e^{M + 0.5V} N(d_1) - XN(d_2)], \tag{14.1}$$

where

$$M = \log(S) + (r - R - 0.5\sigma^2)[t_1 + 0.5(T - t_1)] \tag{14.2}$$

$$V = \sigma^2 \left\{ t_1 + \left[\frac{(T - t_2)(2n - 1)}{6n} \right] \right\} \tag{14.3}$$

$$d_1 = \frac{M - \log(X) + V}{\sqrt{V}} \tag{14.4}$$

$$d_2 = \frac{M - \log(X)}{\sqrt{V}} \tag{14.5}$$

N denotes a cumulative normal variable, T is the time to maturity, t_1 is the time to the first averaging date, n is the number of averaging dates, S is the asset price, X is the exercise price, r is the dollar interest rate, R is the non-dollar interest rate and σ is the volatility of the asset price.

This geometric average option looks complicated, but is just a slight variation on the Black/Scholes equation. It now remains to correct for the difference between geometric averaging in continuous time and arithmetic averaging at some discrete interval such as a week.

If the average is taken with an interval of h years, then the expected arithmetic average, EA, is

Table 14.1   Prices for Asian currency options with weekly averaging

X	r	BS	VOR	MC
190	0.06	15.1913	11.8648	11.8454 (0.00876)
200	0.06	10.2499	6.3623	6.3632 (0.00872)
210	0.06	6.5948	2.9488	2.9737 (0.00847
190	0.08	16.3604	12.5298	12.5118 (0.00913)
200	0.08	11.1954	6.8502	6.8545 (0.00919)
210	0.08	7.3086	3.2437	3.2724 (0.00906)
190	0.10	17.5719	13.2081	13.1944 (0.00959)
200	0.10	12.1866	7.3565	7.3643 (0.00969)
210	0.10	8.0729	3.5589	3.5910 (0.00958)

Notes:
1. BS   The Black/Scholes value adapted for currency (Chapter 8)
2. VOR   The corrected value using Vorst's method
3. MC   The Monte Carlo value
4. Bracketed values are standard deviations for the Monte Carlo results.

X = exercise price; r = domestic currency.

$S = 200$; $\sigma = 0.2$; $R = 0.08$; $T = 28$ weeks; $t_1 = 2$ weeks.

Source: Own calculations except for the MC column which has been adapted from Vorst (1990) with a small adjustment because he uses a peculiar maturity of 197.2 days and here it is 196 days. The adjustment is equal to the difference in VOR results from 196 versus 197.2 days.

$$EA = \left(\frac{S}{n}\right)e^{(r-R)t^1}\left[\frac{1 - e^{(r-R)nh}}{1 - e^{(r-R)h}}\right].\tag{14.6}$$

The expected geometric average in continuous time, GA, is

$$GA = e^{(M + 0.5V)}.\tag{14.7}$$

The revised exercise price, X', to use in Eq. (14.1) is then

$$X' = X - (EA - GA).\tag{14.8}$$

Some results from the use of this method for currency options are given in Table 14.1. The example is of a 28-week option for which averaging begins after two weeks and occurs weekly. Hence there are $n = 27$ averaging dates and $h = \frac{1}{52}$ years per average. The VOR column gives the results with the exercise price corrected as per Eq. (14.8). The MC column gives Monte Carlo valuations, which will be explained in Sec. 14.2 and are taken to be the 'correct' prices. The VOR results are only slightly different from the Monte Carlo results, so the approximation works well. We see that the Asian options are worth about half to two-thirds as much as the ordinary Black/Scholes calls.

If we denote Vorst's call price as C_{vor}, an equivalent put, P_{vor} is worth

$$P_{vor} = C_{vor} - e^{-rT}\,EA + e^{-rT}X.$$

14.1.5 SUMMARY ON ASIAN OPTIONS

Asian options are cheap and match the risk exposure of many companies. Their use continues to grow. They can be valued quite accurately and quickly with Vorst's method or similar approximations.[1] Hedge ratios may be found empirically by recalculating the option price after a one-unit change in the asset price.

14.2 Monte Carlo method of valuation

To demonstrate the Monte Carlo method, we shall continue the previous example of valuing Asian options. In this approach, the basic complexity of the binomial tree of Fig. 14.2 is accepted, but the possible outcomes are sampled rather than fully evaluated. Random paths through the tree are chosen and the option value is computed as the average of the pay-offs. Boyle (1977) first suggested this Monte Carlo approach to option pricing, and it has been widely used to value options with stochastic volatilities (see Hull and White, 1987; Johnson and Shanno, 1987; Scott, 1987). The great advantage of the Monte Carlo approach is that it can be used to value any option. Its great disadvantage is that it is slow.

Consider the Asian tree in Fig. 14.2. The asset price begins at S. Initially it can rise to SU or fall to SD. If it rises, then it may rise further to $S(U + U^2)/2$ or fall to $S(U + UD)/2$. The probability of a rise is the same as that in the simple tree of Fig. 14.1. Assuming a currency (or other interest-paying) option, the probability of a rise is (as shown in Chapter 8):

$$m = \frac{[(1 + r)(1 + R)] - D}{U - D}, \qquad (14.9)$$

where r is the dollar rate of interest and R is the foreign rate of interest.

At each step in the tree, the up-path is chosen with probability m and the down-path with probability $(1 - m)$. A whole series of steps is followed to maturity, at which point there is a particular asset price S^*. The pay-off to this particular path for a call option with exercise price E would then be $(S^* - E)$. This value is stored and a new journey is made through the tree, yielding a new pay-off. After a substantial number of such journeys, e.g. 10 000, the mean of the pay-offs is calculated. The estimated value of the option is then the present value of this expected pay-off.

One question is: How many journeys (replications) are needed? The answer can be obtained by repeating the procedure several times. Each time there is an estimated option value and together they form a sample for which a mean and standard deviation can be calculated. The size of the standard deviation (which is really a standard error since it is the standard deviation of the mean) indicates the accuracy of the result. If it is large relative to the option value, then more replications are required.

In Table 14.1 the standard errors in the MC column are quite small relative to the prices, so one may have confidence in the Monte Carlo results.[2]

14.2.1 SUMMARY ON THE MONTE CARLO METHOD

The method is simple, but slow. It requires the calculation of pay-offs from following a large number of journeys through an options tree. At each step in the tree the choice of up or down movement is chosen at random, but with the correct probability. The present value of the average pay-off is the value of the option.

14.3 Look-back options

A look-back call option gives the holder the right to purchase a fixed amount of an asset at the *minimum* price attained over the option's life. Similarly, a look-back put option gives the right to sell at the *maximum* price attained over the option's life. As Garman (1989) expresses it, this would appear to be an exciting financial product, since it guarantees a 'no-regrets' result: the best rate is never missed.

The first presentation of how to value these options was given by Goldman *et al.* (1979). They viewed the options as letting the holder 'buy at the low, sell at the high'. Clearly such an attractive prospect is going to be valuable, yet sometimes these options have been given away. For example, at one time in the 1980s buyers of sugar from Brazil could choose, in arrears, the day of the month on which they had made their purchase, thereby obtaining the lowest price in that month.

There are many potential uses. One example would be that of a British fund manager who was going to translate foreign-currency earnings from dollars to pounds. He or she would be very happy to achieve the best rate for the year. However, as we shall see, the cost of a look-back option could be twice that of a simple option, which in turn might be twice that of an Asian option.

In developing a method to value a look-back option, the first step is to demonstrate that it can be replicated, because then it can also be hedged. Following Garman, suppose that a bank has written a 6-month look-back call option on sterling and wants to hedge it. At the time of the sale, the bank buys an ordinary call option which is struck at the original spot price. It holds this option until a new minimum spot price occurs, at which time the option is sold and a new one is purchased with exercise price equal to the new minimum. If this rollover strategy is continued to maturity, then the bank's pay-off will be exactly the same as the pay-off to the look-back option.

Here is an example. Let the original spot price be $1.80 per pound. The bank buys a 6-month call at this exercise price which costs, say, 10 cents. Then the spot price falls to $1.70. The original call is sold for only 3 cents, as it is now out-of-the-money, and a new one is purchased at an exercise price of $1 70, costing 9 cents. The rate then rises to $1.75 at maturity, so exercise gives the bank a final pay-out of 5 cents. The net cost to the bank of the two options was 16 cents and the final pay-out was 5 cents.

Table 14.2 Representative values for look-back call options

L	r	BS	HB	LB
190	0.06	15.19 (0.64)	6.44 (0.28)	21.63 (0.92)
200	0.06	10.24 (0.50)	10.25 (0.38)	20.50 (0.88)
190	0.08	16.36 (0.66)	6.25 (0.29)	22.60 (0.95)
200	0.08	11.19 (0.53)	10.20 (0.40)	21.39 (0.93)
190	0.10	17.57 (0.69)	6.05 (0.30)	23.62 (0.99)
200	0.10	12.18 (0.56)	10.14 (0.42)	22.33 (0.98)

Notes:
1. BS   The Black/Scholes value adapted for currency (Chapter 8)
2. HB   The hedge-bonus option
3. LB   The total look-back call option value (= BS + HB)
4. Bracketed values are hedge ratios.

L = low achieved so far (i.e. exercise price); r = interest rate on domestic currency.

$S = 200$; $\sigma = 0.2$; $R = 0.08$; $T = 28$ weeks.

Each time the bank rolls over in the replication strategy, it buys an option at a lower striking price, so that there is a cash outflow. Suppose that there is another option that pays just these cash outflows. Garman names this a 'strike-bonus' option. Then the value of the original look-back option (C_1) is equivalent to that of an ordinary option (C) *plus* that of a strike-bonus option (C_{sb}):

$$C_1 = C + C_{sb}. \tag{14.10}$$

Because of its 'hedgeability', the strike-bonus option can be valued with procedures similar to the Black/Scholes equation. Garman gives the relevant equation as

$$V_{sb} = \left(\frac{S}{\tau}\right)\left[e^{-rt}\left(\frac{S}{L}\right)^{-\tau} N\left(y_1 + 2\delta\sqrt{\frac{t}{\sigma}}\right) - e^{-Rt}N(y_1)\right], \tag{14.11}$$

where S is the spot rate, L is the achieved minimum, (i.e. the low so far), t is the time to maturity, σ is the volatility of S, r is the dollar interest rate, R is the foreign interest rate, δ ($= r - R$) is the interest-rate differential, $\tau = 2\delta/\sigma^2$, N is the cumulative normal distribution function and

$$y_1 = \frac{-\ln(S/L) - (\delta + \sigma^2/2)t}{\sigma\sqrt{t}}. \tag{14.12}$$

The replication strategy requires that trading be continuous, but so does the simple Black/Scholes equation. It will also be affected by changes in the term structure of interest rates and of volatility. Given the potential magnitude of other errors, these are likely to be minor influences.

Finally, the hedge ratio for the look-back option is equal to the sum of the hedge ratios for the ordinary and look-back options:

$$h_1 = h + h_{sb}. \qquad (14.13)$$

The hedge ratio for the latter is[3]

$$h_{sb} = -\left[e^{-rt}\left(\frac{1-\tau}{\tau}\right)\left(\frac{S}{L}\right)^i N\left(y_1 + 2\delta\sqrt{\frac{t}{\sigma}}\right) - \left(\frac{1}{\tau}\right)e^{-Rt}N(y_1)\right]. \qquad (14.14)$$

Some example values for look-back options are given in Table 14.2, using the same basic data as for the Asian options of Table 14.1. The table gives values for at- and in-the-money calls. Out-of-the-money look-back options cannot exist, because the achieved low cannot be higher than today's spot rate. The total values of the look-back options (LB column) are all in the 20–23 cent range, about one-and-a-half to two times as much as the conventional options (BS column). At-the-money ($L = 200$), the simple (BS) and strike-bonus (SB) calls are almost equal in value. In-the-money ($L = 190$), the simple call value rises and the strike-bonus call value falls, leaving the total almost the same as before. The hedge ratios for the strike-bonus calls are less than for the simple calls, but the total hedge ratios are all close to 1.00.

14.3.1 SUMMARY ON LOOK-BACK OPTIONS

These options always finish in-the-money and so are very safe. They can be hedged, so a pricing formula can be derived along Black/Scholes lines. Because they are so safe, however, they are also very expensive. Nevertheless, some commercial contracts may implicitly incorporate the right to look back and choose a pricing date. With this analysis, the value of such a right can be estimated.

14.4 Options to exchange assets

Any option to exchange one asset for another is an option on a spread, involving the simultaneous purchase of one 'leg' and sale of another. The legs may be *different assets*, such as jet fuel and heating oil, or a corporate bond and a government bond. A convertible bond can be viewed as a spread between a company's debt and its equity. Alternatively, each leg may comprise the same asset except that it is to be delivered at *different maturities*, such as a March/-June spread in Eurodollar futures. The New York Mercantile Exchange is considering the listing of options on spreads in crude-oil futures. British government bonds may have an option to convert them into longer dated bonds. Other, less obvious, examples are: investment advisers' performance fees, general margin accounts, the exchange offer, and the standby commitment (Margrabe, 1978).

Options on oil spreads are discussed in some detail by Heenk *et al.* (1991), who use numerical methods to accommodate the bivariate distribution of the two assets and extend their results to Asian options. A widely used approach is to assume that the spread is lognormally distributed, so that Black/Scholes applies, but a problem is that the spread may take on a negative value. To avoid that a constant may be added. Here we shall use a method developed by Margrabe (1978) and Rubinstein (1991), which applies to spreads where the exercise price is a ratio. We demonstrate that the continuous-time (Black/Scholes type) formulation of this problem is exactly the same as that for a currency option. This means that currency-options models, as outlined in Chapter 8, may be applied. Throughout we shall assume that the option is a call, but puts may be priced with the same models since a call to buy A through the sale of B is equivalent to a put to sell B through the purchase of A.

14.4.1 CONTINUOUS-TIME EQUATIONS

A spread consists of a long position in one asset and a short position in another. Suppose that the two asset prices at time t are respectively S_{1t} and S_{2t}, with the first asset having been purchased and the second asset having been sold. The current value of the spread is $S_{1t} - S_{2t}$. At maturity (time T), the final pay-off to a call option on the spread would be:

$$c_T = \max[0, (S_{1T} - S_{2T})]. \qquad (14.15)$$

The second asset effectively takes on the function played by the exercise price in the conventional options-pricing model.

The difficulty in finding a simple equation for the price of this option is that both assets have stochastic prices. However, Margrabe (1978) demonstrates that by taking ratios the number of stochastic variables may be reduced to one. If both sides of Eq. (14.15) are divided by S_{2T}, then the final pay-off may be re-expressed as

$$\frac{c_T}{S_{2T}} = \max\left[0, \left(\frac{S_{1T}}{S_{2T}} - 1\right)\right]. \qquad (14.16)$$

The transformed option has an exercise price of 1 and an asset price at maturity of S_{1T}/S_{2T}.

More generally, before maturity we may define a new variable S_t^*, which is

$$S_t^* = \frac{S_{1t}}{S_{2t}}.$$

Because the two variables S_1 and S_2 are lognormally distributed, S^* will also be lognormally distributed, with variance σ^{*2} equal to

$$\sigma^{*2} = \sigma_1^2 + \sigma_2^2 - 2\rho\sigma_1\sigma_2,$$

where ρ is the correlation of returns on the two variables.

At this stage it is helpful to consider what this transformed variable represents. Suppose the first asset is oil, with a price in dollars per barrel, and the second asset is gold, with a price in dollars per troy ounce. Then the transformed asset has a price denominated in [($/barrel)/($/troy ounce)], i.e. in troy ounces of gold per barrel of oil. For example, if the price of oil is $20 per barrel ($S_1$) and the price of gold is $400 per troy ounce ($S_2$), then the transformed variable has a price of $20/400 = 0.05$ ounces of gold per barrel of oil.

A useful insight is that this transformed asset is *exactly* comparable to a currency. Quotation of the latter is, by definition, a statement of units of the first currency per unit of the second currency. For example, we might have $2 per pound sterling as S_1 and $1 per dollar as S_2. Then the transformed variable would be quoted as $2/1 = 2$ dollars per pound sterling.

Given that $S*$ is the same as a currency quotation, we know that the currency options model for Chapter 8 may be applied. Let investments in dollars pay r per unit time and investments in pounds sterling pay R per unit time. Then a call option on the pound with an exercise price of E, and which is purchased with dollars, has a price of $\$c*$ per pound sterling, where:

$$c* = S*e^{-R\tau}N(d_1) - Ee^{-r\tau}N(d_2), \tag{14.17}$$

where

$$d_1 = \frac{\log(S_t^*/E) + (r - R + 0.5\sigma^{*2})\tau}{\sigma^*\sqrt{\tau}} \tag{14.18}$$

and

$$d_2 = d_1 - \sigma^*\sqrt{\tau} \tag{14.19}$$

where $\tau = T - t$.

For a call on a spread, the pay-outs on the two assets, r and R, would not be interest rates but any kind of continuous dividend that accrues to holders of the assets. For example, on a share it would be the dividend yield, while on a commodity it would be the convenience yield (if any). The spread is conventionally between one unit of the first asset and one unit of the second, which leads to an exercise price of $E = 1$.

Writing the call-option on spot-spread equations in full we then have

$$\frac{c}{S_{2t}} = \left(\frac{S_{1t}}{S_{2t}}\right)e^{-R\tau}N(d_1) - 1e^{-r\tau}N(d_2), \tag{14.20}$$

where

$$d_1 = \frac{\log(S_{1t}/S_{2t}) + (r - R + 0.5\sigma^{*2})\tau}{\sigma^*\sqrt{\tau}} \tag{14.21}$$

and

$$d_2 = d_1 - \sigma^*\sqrt{\tau}. \tag{14.22}$$

Multiplying both sides of (14.20) by S_{2t} leads to Rubinstein's (1991) expression for dividend-paying assets:

$$c = S_{1t} e^{-R\tau} N(d_1) - S_{2t} e^{-r\tau} N(d_2). \qquad (14.23)$$

Thus far we have only considered spot assets, but in many situations the underlying instruments are likely to be futures contracts. We know that (with constant pay-out rates) the spot price is simply equal to the discounted futures price:

$$S_{1t} = F_{1t} e^{-r\tau} \qquad (14.24)$$

and

$$S_{2t} = F_{2t} e^{-R\tau}. \qquad (14.25)$$

Substituting into the spot equation [Eq. (14.23)] we then have the call option price on futures-spread of

$$c = e^{-r\tau}[F_{1t} N(d_1) - F_{2t} N(d_2)], \qquad (14.26)$$

where

$$d_1 = \frac{\log(F_{1t}/F_{2t}) + 0.5\sigma^{*2}\tau}{\sigma^*\sqrt{\tau}} \qquad (14.27)$$

and

$$d_2 = d_1 - \sigma^*\sqrt{\tau}. \qquad (14.28)$$

These continuous-time solutions apply to European options. However, unless the assets have no pay-out rates (the case considered by Margrabe), there could be value to early exercise, just as there is for currency options (see Chapter 8). To accommodate early exercise, Rubinstein (1991) develops a binomial solution for the spread option, but does not indicate the equivalence of this to the currency-option formulation.

For an option on a spot spread we have:

$$C^*(1 + r) = mC_u^* + (1 - m)C_d^*, \qquad (14.29)$$

where

$$m = \frac{[(1 + r)/(1 + R)] - D}{U - D}. \qquad (14.30)$$

Similarly, for an option on a futures spread we have:

$$C^*(1 + r) = mC_u^* + (1 - m)C_d^*, \qquad (14.31)$$

where

$$m = \frac{1 - D}{U - D}. \qquad (14.32)$$

Pay-out rates disappear in the futures-based equations, (14.31) and (14.32), with the exception that the pay-off still needs to be discounted by the pay-out rate on the first asset (r) because the call price is expressed per unit of this asset.

14.4.2 SUMMARY AND LIMITATIONS OF THIS APPROACH TO VALUING OPTIONS
        TO EXCHANGE ASSETS

Valuing options to exchange assets is very similar to valuing currency options.
The two assets in a spread may be reduced to one by taking one of the assets as
numéraire, as suggested by Margrabe (1978). If asset 1 is purchased and asset 2
is sold, then the pricing model for options on spot currency may be applied with
the following modifications:

(i)   a transformed call price of C/S_2, where C is the call price and S_2 is the price
      of the sold leg of the spread;
(ii) a transformed asset price of S_1/S_2;
(iii) pay-out rates of r and R on assets 1 and 2 respectively;
(iv) exercise price of unity; and
(v)   adjusted variance of $\sigma^{*2} = \sigma_1^2 + \sigma_2^2 - 2\rho\sigma_1\sigma_2$.

The equation for a futures-based spread may be developed analogously.
However, early exercise may have value if the pay-out rates have particular con-
figurations, so numerical solutions may be necessary. Binomial solutions are
found to be relatively simple to derive, as they are the same as for currency options.

  Finally, this approach is accurate only for spreads in which the exercise price
is expressed as a *ratio*. Often a spread has an exercise price which is expressed as
a *difference*. For example, the option might be to buy Brent oil and sell WTI oil
at a spread of $2 per barrel. If Brent is $20 and WTI is $18, then the rate of
exchange is 1.1111. If oil prices then rise to $40 and $38 respectively, the spread
based on the $2 difference is at-the-money. However, the price ratio is now
$40/38 = 1.053$ and the ratio spread is out-of-the-money. The greater the change
in price levels, the larger the error from using the ratio to approximate the
difference. Only if the exercise ratio is 1, which is equivalent to an exercise
difference of 0, will there be no error. For example, if the Brent/WTI option
had been struck at a price difference of $0, the Margrabe approach would have
priced it accurately.

14.5 Summary

This chapter demonstrated the ingenuity of traders in inventing new kinds of
option and of analysts in valuing them. The most general part of the chapter
described the Monte Carlo method. This simple approach can be used on any
option that is hedgeable, because we know that the pay-off may then be
discounted at the risk-free rate. The section on average-rate (Asian) options
demonstrated that an intractable problem (the arithmetic average option) can
be solved if converted into a related problem (the geometric average option).
The sections on look-back options and on options to exchange assets demonstrated how the Black/Scholes approach can be modified, yet again, to apply to
an increasing number of sophisticated situations.

Notes

1. Levy develops a method based upon the following adjustments to the Black/Scholes equation: (i) reduce the exercise price by the average so far; (ii) change the asset price to an expectation of the average for the remaining period of the option; and (iii) adjust the volatility. This method may be even more accurate (see Levy, 1990).
2. These standard errors are particularly small because a further 'trick' has been used known as the *control-variate* method. Monte Carlo results were computed for both geometric and arithmetic average options, thus giving an estimate of the difference. This, rather stable, difference was then added to the correct geometric result as computed from Eq. (14.1).
3. The minus sign appears to be missing in Garman (1989).

References

Bergman, Y. (1985), 'Pricing path contingent claims', *Research in Finance*, **5**, 229–41.

Boyle, P. (1977), 'Options: a Monte Carlo approach', *Journal of Financial Economics*, **4**, 323–38.

Carverhill, A. and Clewlow, L. (1990), 'Valuing average rate options', *Risk*, **3** (4), 25–9.

Garman, M. (1989), 'Recollection in tranquillity', *Risk*, **2** (March), 16–19.

Goldman, M., Sosin, H. and Gatto, M. (1979), 'Path dependent options: "Buy at the low, sell at the high"', *Journal of Finance*, **34**, 1111–27.

Heenk, B., Kemna, A. and Vorst, T. (1991), 'Asian options on oil spreads', *Review of Futures Markets* (forthcoming).

Hull, J. and White, A. (1987), 'The pricing of options on assets with stochastic volatilities', *Journal of Finance*, **42**, 281–300.

Johnson, H. and Shanno, D. (1987), 'Option pricing when variance is changing', *Journal of Financial and Quantitative Analysis*, **22**, 143–51.

Kemna, A. and Vorst, T. (1990), 'A pricing method for options based on average asset values', *Journal of Banking and Finance*, **14**, 113–29.

Levy, E. (1990), *Pricing European Average Rate Currency Options*, Nomura Bank International, London.

Margrabe, W. (1978), 'The value of an option to exchange one asset for another', *Journal of Finance*, **33**, 177–86.

Ritchken, P., Sankarasubramaniam, L. and Vijh, A. (1990), 'Averaging options for capping total costs', *Financial Management*, **19**, 35–41.

Rubinstein, M. (1991), 'One for another', *Risk*, **4** (July/August), 30–2.

Scott, L.O. (1987), 'Option pricing when the variance changes randomly: theory, estimation and valuation', *Journal of Financial and Quantitative Analysis*, **22**, 419–38.

Turnbull, S. and Wakeman, L. (1991), 'A quick algorithm for pricing average options', *Journal of Financial and Quantitative Analysis*, **26**, 377–89.

Vorst, T. (1990), 'Prices and hedge ratios of average exchange rate options', Working Paper, Erasmus University, Rotterdam.

15

The performance of option markets

This final chapter is rather different from the others. It is not concerned with the valuation or use of options, but with the operation of markets. Having studied the technicalities of options in other chapters, we turn our attention to questions of public policy and economics. The chapter is in two sections. The first is a review of what is known about the efficiency of options markets. The second discusses the impact of the existence of options markets on the prices of the underlying assets. Is it benign, harmful or simply irrelevant?

These matters are important. If options markets are inefficient, then either the existing participants are ill informed or there are impediments to competition. There will be a welfare loss. If options have a destabilizing effect on underlying assets, then we may wish to constrain their use.

15.1 Option-market efficiency

'Efficiency' is a term that must be carefully defined before it is used. We shall define it as: *the correct allocation of resources, such that all marginal costs and returns are equated.* For example, if the marginal cost of capital were 10% per annum, then clearly it would be inefficient to forgo investments with returns at the margin of 12%. Under efficient allocation, the net profit to be made on the last additional unit of resource is zero.

It is not easy to make the concept of economic efficiency operational in financial markets. Necessary conditions for the efficient allocation of resources are that prices reflect available information and that transactions costs are minimized. The concepts of 'pricing' efficiency and 'transactions' efficiency have been developed to reflect these two necessary conditions.

Pricing efficiency derives from work by Roberts (1967) and Fama (1970). Fama divides efficiency into different levels, depending on the kind of information reflected in prices. If prices only reflect public information on the past price of that asset, then the market is 'weak-form' efficient. If prices reflect all sorts of public information, not just information on this asset, then the market is 'semi-strong-form' efficient. If prices even reflect unpublished, private information, the market is 'strong-form' efficient. Information can be turned into profit, so the existence of profitable opportunities that are not exploited is evidence of pricing inefficiency. The usual difficulty in testing for unexploited profits, and hence for pricing inefficiency, is in assessing whether profits are sufficient to cover transactions costs and risks.

Transactions efficiency is concerned with the size of bid/ask spreads and commissions. Marketmakers earn at least part of the bid/ask spread as their reward. Brokers earn only commission. Are these rewards at the margin consistent with their marginal costs, taking into account the risks involved? Once again the question reduces to whether marketmakers and other intermediaries make 'excess' profits relative to the risks they bear.

15.1.1 EVIDENCE ON PRICING EFFICIENCY[1]

15.1.1.1 *Simple arbitrages*

The simplest kind of pricing inefficiency that might be investigated is an arbitrage. It has the twin advantages of being both riskless and not dependent on any options-pricing model for its calculation. The main arbitrages, which were discussed in Chapter 3, relate to the minimum bounds on call and put prices and to put/call parity. A series of transactions prices may be observed and lower-bound and parity tests conducted on them.

Minimum bounds   The bound, introduced in Chapter 3, is

$$c \geq S - PV(E). \tag{15.1}$$

There have been many tests of this bound and we shall consider just a few. One of the first, by Galai (1978), found a significant number of call lower-bound arbitrages in the first six months of trading on the CBOE. Similar tests by Bhattacharya (1983), using the Berkeley database of options transactions, found violations to occur, but not large enough to cover transactions costs. Halpern and Turnbull (1985) found violations to occur on the Toronto market, but their study did not take full account of transactions costs. Chance (1988) found insignificant numbers of violations (net of transactions costs) for S&P 100 index options.

Put/call parity   Put/call parity does not lead to a very tight bound for stock options. As discussed in Chapter 3, it only holds perfectly for European stock options. The greater value of American put options make the arbitrage one-sided. Thus, we have

$$P \geq c - S + PV(E). \tag{15.2}$$

In 1969, Stoll tested for put/call parity on US over-the-counter European options, but used a rather peculiar regression analysis. Gould and Galai (1974) used the same weekly dataset to show that violations did not occur after transactions costs. Klemkosky and Resnick (1980) and Brenner and Galai (1984) made tests on transactions data but could not find any significant profits after transactions costs. Similar tests have been made on currency options by (among others) Bodurtha and Courtadon (1986) and on gold/silver options by Ball and Torous (1986).

There have been many other tests on stock, currency and futures options. On the whole, the conclusion is that simple arbitrages are rare. Anyone who has observed a marketmaker at work will know that lower bounds and put/call parity are watched carefully. The absence of arbitrages is not surprising.

15.1.1.2 *Model-based efficiency studies*

More complicated profit opportunities can be attempted with models. In principle, if an option is mispriced then it can be bought (sold) and hedged with the asset or with another option in the model-indicated ratio. The result should be riskless if regularly rebalanced, and so is an arbitrage. One strand of research on options-market efficiency therefore investigates the profit from such procedures. The main difficulty is that such tests are really joint tests of both the appropriateness of the model and the efficiency of the market.

Let us assume that a series of model-based riskless positions has been established. If the outcome is a profit of zero, then what can be concluded? It could indicate that the market is efficient, but it could equally well indicate that the model is inappropriate. If the outcome is a positive profit, then market inefficiency is indicated only if: (i) the model gave the correct hedge ratios for riskless positions; (ii) the full set of transactions costs was taken into account; and (iii) the prices used were a true reflection of those obtainable in the real world.

Early papers on US options markets by Galai (1977) and Chiras and Manaster (1978) indicated inefficiency. However, Phillips and Smith (1980) pointed out that imposing transactions costs would alter this conclusion. Bhattacharya (1983) found a carefully constructed spread strategy to be profitable. Evnine and Rudd (1985) found index options to be inefficiently priced, but Chance (1986) found that they were not if an allowance was made for the bid/ask spread. Whaley (1986) concluded that options on the S&P 500 futures were inefficiently priced.

Studies of markets outside the United States have been less frequent or less well reported. Our review is therefore somewhat 'Eurocentric'. For London, Gemmill and Dickins (1986) found the market in individual options to be inefficient only if transactions costs were not taken into account. Dawson and Gemmill (1991) found evidence that bid/ask spreads in London were being inefficiently set by marketmakers in index options. Gemmill (1992) found that index-option prices in London during the 1987 election did not reflect the opinion-poll information and an almost-riskless arbitrage between index options and individual options could be executed. For Amsterdam, Kemna (1989) found persistent biases between Black/Scholes and market prices, but could not distinguish whether these were due to an inappropriate model or to an inefficient market.

15.1.1.3 *Information in implied volatilities*

Another way to test for inefficiency is to concentrate on information rather than profitable trading opportunities. The question is, to what extent do options prices reflect available information? As the most difficult part of options pricing is deciding on an appropriate volatility, one approach is to examine whether the implied volatilities from options are good forecasts of subsequent volatilities.

Latané and Rendleman (1976) were the first to examine the forecasting performance of implied volatilities with US data. Other studies have been by Schmalensee and Trippi (1978), Macbeth and Merville (1979), Beckers (1981) and Brenner and Galai (1984). Scott and Tucker (1989) studied currency options in this way. Similar European studies have been made by Gemmill (1986) on London data and Kemna (1989) on Dutch data. In order to see whether the implied volatilities capture all the information in historic volatility, most of these papers use a regression of the form

$$OSD_t = a_0 + a_1 ISD_{t-1} + a_2 HSD_{t-1} + e_t$$

where OSD is the observed standard deviation, ISD is the implied standard deviation from the options, HSD is the historic standard deviation and e is an error term.

The period of observation is typically one month. In most studies of this type the coefficient a_1 is significantly different from zero, while a_2 is not significantly different from zero. (An example was given in the appendix to Chapter 6.) The implication of a_2 being zero is that the estimated historic volatility makes no contribution in terms of information in addition to that already reflected in the implied volatility. Of the different options available, in most studies the at-the-money options have been found to give the best predictions in terms of mean-squared error (MSE).

To summarize, implied standard deviations perform well relative to simple projections of volatility based on past data. However, it must be acknowledged that neither historic volatility nor implied volatility gives a good prediction of subsequent volatility. It is just that the implied volatility is a little better in terms of MSE.

15.2 The impact of options on underlying assets

The impact of options on underlying assets is an important subject. If the impact were found to be consistently destabilizing, then the banning of options might be an appropriate policy. It is helpful to distinguish between two potential impacts. The first is a *generally* stabilizing or destabilizing effect. The second is a destabilizing effect *at option maturity*. The latter assumes particular importance for index options, where sudden movements in the whole stock market may arise when arbitrage positions are unwound. The largest effects are likely to occur on so-called 'triple-witching' days, when index futures, options on those futures and options on the index itself all expire. The whole subject of whether options and futures increase market volatility has recently been reviewed by Hodges (1990) and this chapter draws upon his work.

15.2.1 GENERAL IMPACT OF OPTIONS

What can be said in theory about the potential impact of introducing options? The answer is that, depending on the particular assumptions made, the impact could be either stabilizing or destabilizing. An initial problem for the economic theorist is why options (and futures) exist at all. In a Black/Scholes world, in which there are no transactions costs or other 'imperfections', it is possible to replicate any option so perfectly that distinct options contracts are redundant. The continued existence of options must therefore indicate that they help to overcome market imperfections, such as transactions costs, constraints on borrowing or restrictions on short selling.

If options help to overcome 'imperfections', then the cost of speculation is reduced. For example, an investor who has information that a share is overvalued may buy a put option or sell a call option, thus going short of the share. This may be cheaper than selling the share and buying it back later, which in any event is impossible if the investor does not already own the share. Making speculation cheaper seems likely to reduce volatility, but this is not necessarily the case. If speculators are well informed, then prices may move more rapidly to their 'true' levels, leading to an increase in short-run volatility. Destabilization could also occur if there were a rush of ill-informed speculators into the options market. The argument hinges upon the quality of the speculation, as discussed by Stein (1986) in relation to futures contracts. He provides examples in which a few well-informed speculators counteract the destabilizing impact of a much larger number of ill-informed speculators. Even this argument is not completely watertight. There is a recent literature in which investors with rational expectations may generate speculative bubbles, while another literature shows that ill-informed 'noise' traders may consistently make profits.

The theoretical arguments, therefore, give no clear view as to the impact of introducing options, so we must turn to the empirical evidence for guidance.

There have been a few empirical studies of the impact of introducing options trading in the United States. Hayes and Tennenbaum (1979) found that introducing options tended to increase the volume of stock trading. Trennepohl and Dukes (1979) and Klemkosky and Maness (1980) could find no significant change in volatility following the introduction of options. Whiteside *et al.* (1983) found no insignificant impact on either volume or volatility.

More recently, Conrad (1989), Skinner (1989) and Nabar and Park (1988) all found that there were significant impacts on the underlying shares. Their similarity of results may reflect the similarity of their US data. Nabar and Park examined the impact of listing 390 new stock options, using daily price data from 1973 to 1985. In order to detect changes, they used a window spanning from 66 months prior to introduction to 12 months after introduction. The results indicated a 4–8% fall in volatility, which was most pronounced about four months after the options were introduced. They presumed that four months was the 'seasoning' period for a newly listed option.

Conrad examined 96 new options on the CBOE for the period 1974–80, using daily data and a window of from 30 days before introduction to 30 days after. She found that there was on average about a 2% rise in the share price (relative to other shares) at the time an option started to trade. A separate examination for 76 of the shares, of whether there was any rise at the time of announcing that options trading would commence, revealed no impact. Using a 200-day-before/200-day-after window, she found that volatility fell after introduction by about 12%.[2] The beta coefficients of the shares were unchanged, so the reduction in volatility was due to a fall in company-specific risk.

Skinner used 304 new options listings from 1973 to 1986 and windows of ± 100, 250 and 500 days. He found a decline of 10–20% in volatility, which was due to a reduction of specific risk since the betas were not affected. He also found that there was on average a small increase in trading volume following options introduction. As volume and volatility are usually positively correlated, the fall in volatility was the more surprising. His explanation was that the bid/ask spread had probably fallen after listing, as the options led to a larger total market and so enhanced liquidity.

There have been few studies of the impact of introducing options outside the United States. The only European markets with sufficient historic data are those in London and Amsterdam. Gemmill (1989) studied the London market using both a before/after and a paired with/without approach. In the before/after analysis he used a ± 20-week window for 10 shares. There was an average fall of 17% in daily price range (equivalent to volatility) after introducing the options, but this result was only significant at the 10% level. In the paired with/without analysis, 18 shares with options were compared with 18 shares without options, all companies being of approximately equal size. Three months of daily data were used, centred on the Crash of 1987. It was found that the shares with options had larger trading volumes and also higher volatilities. Regression analysis was used to find the impacts of these two variables. The result was that, corrected for volume, options trading was associated with a 4–12% reduction in volatility. This was therefore similar to the US results.

Let us summarize these empirical studies. None of them found that options trading increased volatility, and the more recent studies found a reduction of specific risk to occur. Share volume increased after introduction. What appears to happen is that there is an increase in overall market liquidity after options are introduced. However, the evidence is not strong and is subject to two particular weaknesses. The first concerns 'selection bias'. Exchanges introduce options on the most volatile shares, so shares that have options are, by definition, different from other shares. Any change in volatility from options trading needs to be considered in relation to a long-run view of what volatility might have been in the absence of such trading. The second weakness, detailed by Lamoureux (1990), is that the American studies fail to take account of market-wide movements in specific risk over time. It so happened that most options were introduced in the mid-1970s just prior to a fall in specific risk. Correcting for this fall would lead to the conclusion that introducing options did not have a stabilizing impact. The empirical evidence is therefore inconclusive.

15.2.2   IMPACT OF MATURING OPTIONS

When an option matures, arbitrage positions are unwound and the underlying share market could suffer a bout of 'indigestion' as large blocks of shares are either bought or sold. Prices might be expected to rise or fall temporarily. Sometimes it has been argued that the prices of shares are deliberately manipulated at maturity in order to bring the options either into- or out-of-the-money. If a large options position were held relative to liquidity in the share market, then this might be possible, but that seems unlikely since the share market is usually the more liquid.[3]

Most public concern, mainly in the United States but also in London and Amsterdam, has been about the impact of index options. Stoll and Whaley (1987) made a careful study of this for 1984–85. Their sample included both 'triple-witching' days, on which S&P 500 futures, S&P 500 futures options and S&P 100 options expired, and 'single' days, on which only S&P 100 options expired. On triple Fridays there was an average fall of 0.48% in price over the last hour of trading, but the fall was reversed in the first half hour on the following Monday. Volatility rose on triple Fridays; but on single Fridays there was a very small fall in price and no increase in volatility.

Following this study, from June 1987 the settlement of the US contracts was moved to the Friday opening period of share trading. In a follow-up paper, Stoll and Whaley (1990) found that there was now a change in price of about 0.3% at the Friday opening, so the effect had shifted from the close to the open. As the bid/ask spread in the S&P 100 stocks is about 0.5%, the price impact of the futures and options expiring is only about half of the full spread.

Pope and Yadav (1992) examined individual option expirations in London for the period October 1982 to September 1987. There were 46 expiration dates and 465 individual firm expirations. Using a 4-days-before/5-days-after window, they found that there was an average 0.5% fall in price at the time of expiration. Van den Bergh and Kemna (1988) made a study of expirations for options on 13 Dutch shares in Amsterdam for the period January 1984 to October 1987. Surprisingly, they found that volatility was smaller than normal at expiration.

To summarize this section, it appears that expiration of options may have a temporary influence on share prices and on volatility. The effect is relatively small and reverses after expiration.

15.3 Summary

There is not much evidence of pricing inefficiency in options markets. Arbitrages are fleeting and profits from continuously hedged positions are too small to cover transactions costs. Implied volatilities do not forecast subsequent volatilities very well, but they do so better than simple projections of past volatility.

The impact of options on the markets for underlying assets is small. Some evidence suggests that they have a slight stabilizing influence on asset prices, but this result is controversial. When the options mature, there appears to be a very brief destabilizing effect.

None of the above findings imply that more regulation of options markets would be desirable.

Notes

1. This section draws upon an unpublished review by Paul Dawson, entitled 'A review of empirical studies of exchange-traded stock and stock-index options', City University Business School, London, 1990. It also draws upon Galai (1983, 1987).
2. She found that the *variance* of excess returns declined from 2.28% to 1.79% over the 200-day periods, which is equivalent to a 12% reduction in *volatility*.
3. There may be a different level of impact in an order-driven market, such as that in Paris, as compared with a competitive-marketmaker system, such as that in London.

References

Ball, C. and Torous, W. (1986), 'Futures options and the volatility of futures prices', *Journal of Finance*, **41**, 857–70.

Beckers, S. (1981), 'Standard deviations implied in option prices as predictors of future stock price variability', *Journal of Banking and Finance*, **5**, 363–81.

Bhattacharya, M. (1983), 'Transactions data tests of efficiency of the Chicago Board Options Exchange', *Journal of Financial Economics*, **12**, 161–85.

Bodurtha, J. and Courtadon, G. (1986), 'Efficiency tests of the foreign currency options market', *Journal of Finance*, **41**, 151–62.

Brenner, M. (ed.) (1983), *Option Pricing*, D.C. Heath, Lexington, Mass.

Brenner, M. and Galai, M. (1984), 'On measuring the risks of common stocks implied by options prices: a note', *Journal of Financial and Quantitative Analysis*, **19**, 403–12.

Chance, D. (1986), 'Empirical tests of the pricing of index call options', *Advances in Futures and Options Research*, **1a**, 141–66.

Chance, D. (1988), 'Boundary condition tests of bid and ask prices of index call options', *Journal of Financial Research*, **11**, 21–31.

Chiras, D. and Manaster, S. (1987), 'The information content of options prices and a test of market efficiency', *Journal of Financial Economics*, **6**, 213–24.

Conrad, J. (1989), 'The price effect of options introduction', *Journal of Finance*, **44**, 487–98.

Dawson, P. and Gemmill, G. (1991), 'The profitability of marketmaking on the London Traded Options Market', *Review of Futures Markets* (forthcoming).

Evnine, J. and Rudd, A. (1985), 'Index options: the early evidence', *Journal of Finance*, **40**, 743–56.

Fama, E. (1970), 'Efficient capital markets: a review of theory and empirical work', *Journal of Finance*, **25**, 383–417.

Galai, D. (1977), 'Tests of market efficiency of the Chicago Board Options Exchange', *Journal of Business*, **50**, 167–97.

Galai, D. (1978), 'Empirical tests of boundary conditions for CBOE options', *Journal of Financial Economics*, **6**, 187–211.

Galai, D. (1983), 'A survey of empirical tests of option pricing models', in Brenner (1983), pp. 45–80.

Galai, D. (1987), 'An updated survey of empirical tests of options pricing models', Joint AMEX/SOFFEX Seminar, Zurich.

Gemmill, G. (1986), 'The forecasting performance of stock options on the London Traded Options Market', *Journal of Business Finance and Accounting*, **13**, 535–46.

Gemmill, G. (1989), 'Stock options and volatility of the underlying shares', *Journal of International Securities Markets*, **3**, 15–22.

Gemmill, G. (1992), 'Political risk and market efficiency: stock and options markets in the 1987 election', *Journal of Banking and Finance*, **16**, 211–31.

Gemmill, G. and Dickins, P. (1986), 'An examination of the efficiency of the London Traded Options Market', *Applied Economics*, **18**, 995–1010.

Gould, J. and Galai, D. (1974), 'Transactions costs and the relationship between put and call prices', *Journal of Financial Economics*, **1**, 105–29.

Guimaraes, R., Kingsman, B. and Taylor, S. (eds) (1989), *A Re-appraisal of Market Efficiency*, Springer-Verlag, Berlin.

Halpern, P. and Turnbull, S. (1985), 'Empirical tests of boundary conditions for Toronto stock exchange options', *Journal of Finance*, **40**, 481–500.

Hayes, S. and Tennenbaum, M. (1979), 'The impact of listed options on the underlying shares', *Financial Management*, **8**, 72–6.

Hodges, S. (1990), 'Do derivative instruments increase market volatility?', Futures and Options Research Centre, University of Warwick.

Kemna, A. (1989), 'An empirical test of the options pricing model based on EOE transactions data', in Guimaraes *et al.* (1989), pp. 745–68.

Klemkosky, R. and Maness, T. (1980), 'The impact of options on the under-lying securities', *Journal of Portfolio Management*, **6**, 12–18.

Klemkosky, R. and Resnick, B. (1980), 'An ex-ante analysis of put–call parity', *Journal of Financial Economics*, **8**, 363–78.

Lamoureux, C. (1990), 'Systematic patterns in nonsystematic return variances', Working Paper, Washington University.

Latané, H. and Rendleman, R. (1976), 'Standard deviations of stock price ratios implied in options prices', *Journal of Finance*, **31**, 369–81.

Macbeth, J. and Merville, L. (1979), 'An empirical examination of the Black-Scholes call option pricing model', *Journal of Finance*, **34**, 1173–86.

Nabar, P. and Park, S. (1988), 'Options trading and stock price volatility', paper presented at the 8th AMEX Options Colloquium, New York.

Phillips, S. and Smith, C. (1980), 'Trading costs for listed options', *Journal of Financial Economics*, **8**, 179–201.

Pope, P. and Yadav, P. (1992), 'The impact of option expiration on underlying stocks: the UK evidence', *Journal of Business Finance and Accounting*, **19**, 329–44.

Roberts, H. (1967), 'Statistical versus clinical prediction of the stock market', Seminar on the Analysis of Security Prices, University of Chicago.

Schmalensee, R. and Trippi, R. (1978), 'Common stock volatility expectations implied by options premia', *Journal of Finance*, **33**, 129–47.

Scott, E. and Tucker, A. (1989), 'Predicting currency return volatility', *Journal of Banking and Finance*, **13**, 839–52.

Skinner, D. (1989), 'Option markets and stock return volatility', *Journal of Financial Economics*, **23**, 61–78.

Stein, J. (1986), *The Economics of Futures Markets*, Blackwell, Oxford.

Stoll, H. (1969), 'The relationship between put and call option prices', *Journal of Finance*, **24**, 801–24.

Stoll, H. and Whaley, R. (1987), 'Program trading and expiration day effects', *Financial Analysts Journal*, **43**, 16–28.

Stoll, H. and Whaley, R. (1990), 'Program trading and individual stock returns: ingredients of the triple witching brew', *Journal of Business*, **63**, S165–92.

Trennepohl, G. and Dukes, W. (1979), 'CBOE options and stock volatility', *Review of Business and Economic Research*, **18**, 36–48.

Van den Bergh, W. and Kemna, A. (1988), 'The impact of option trading on stock prices' (in Dutch), *Economische Statistische Berichten*, **3652**, 372–6.

Whaley, R. (1986), 'Valuation of American futures options—theory and empirical tests', *Journal of Finance*, **41**, 127–50.

Whiteside, M., Dukes, W. and Dunne, P. (1983), 'Short term impact of option trading on underlying securities', *Journal of Financial Research*, **6**, 313–21.

Areas under the standard normal distribution

x	0	1	2	3	4	5	6	7	8	9
-3.0	.0013									
-2.9	.0019	.0018	.0018	.0017	.0016	.0016	.0015	.0015	.0014	.0014
-2.8	.0026	.0025	.0024	.0023	.0023	.0022	.0021	.0021	.0020	.0019
-2.7	.0035	.0034	.0033	.0032	.0031	.0030	.0029	.0028	.0027	.0026
-2.6	.0047	.0045	.0044	.0043	.0041	.0040	.0039	.0038	.0037	.0036
-2.5	.0062	.0060	.0059	.0057	.0055	.0054	.0052	.0051	.0049	.0048
-2.4	.0082	.0080	.0078	.0075	.0073	.0071	.0069	.0068	.0066	.0064
-2.3	.0107	.0104	.0102	.0099	.0096	.0094	.0091	.0089	.0087	.0084
-2.2	.0139	.0136	.0132	.0129	.0125	.0122	.0119	.0116	.0113	.0110
-2.1	.0179	.0174	.0170	.0166	.0162	.0158	.0154	.0150	.0146	.0143
-2.0	.0228	.0222	.0217	.0212	.0207	.0202	.0197	.0192	.0188	.0183
-1.9	.0287	.0281	.0274	.0268	.0262	.0256	.0250	.0244	.0239	.0233
-1.8	.0359	.0351	.0344	.0336	.0329	.0322	.0314	.0307	.0300	.0294
-1.7	.0446	.0436	.0427	.0418	.0409	.0401	.0392	.0384	.0375	.0367
-1.6	.0548	.0537	.0526	.0516	.0505	.0495	.0485	.0475	.0465	.0455
-1.5	.0668	.0655	.0643	.0630	.0618	.0606	.0594	.0582	.0571	.0560
-1.4	.0808	.0793	.0778	.0764	.0750	.0735	.0721	.0708	.0694	.0681
-1.3	.0968	.0951	.0934	.0918	.0901	.0885	.0869	.0853	.0838	.0823
-1.2	.1151	.1131	.1112	.1093	.1075	.1056	.1038	.1020	.1003	.0985
-1.1	.1357	.1335	.1314	.1292	.1271	.1251	.1230	.1210	.1190	.1170
-1.0	.1587	.1562	.1539	.1515	.1492	.1469	.1446	.1423	.1401	.1379
-.9	.1841	.1814	.1788	.1762	.1736	.1711	.1685	.1660	.1635	.1611
-.8	.2119	.2090	.2061	.2033	.2005	.1977	.1949	.1921	.1894	.1867
-.7	.2420	.2389	.2358	.2327	.2296	.2266	.2236	.2206	.2177	.2148
-.6	.2743	.2709	.2676	.2643	.2611	.2578	.2546	.2514	.2483	.2451
-.5	.3085	.3050	.3015	.2981	.2946	.2912	.2877	.2843	.2810	.2776
-.4	.3446	.3400	.3372	.3336	.3300	.3264	.3228	.3192	.3156	.3121
-.3	.3821	.3783	.3745	.3707	.3669	.3632	.3594	.3557	.3520	.3483
-.2	.4207	.4168	.4129	.4090	.4052	.4013	.3974	.3936	.3897	.3859
-.1	.4602	.4562	.4522	.4483	.4443	.4404	.4364	.4325	.4286	.4247
-.0	.5000	.4960	.4920	.4880	.4840	.4801	.4761	.4721	.4681	.4641

x	0	1	2	3	4	5	6	7	8	9
.0	.5000	.5040	.5080	.5120	.5160	.5199	.5239	.5279	.5319	.5359
.1	.5398	.5438	.5478	.5517	.5557	.5596	.5636	.5675	.5714	.5753
.2	.5793	.5832	.5871	.5910	.5948	.5987	.6026	.6064	.6103	.6141
.3	.6179	.6217	.6255	.6293	.6331	.6368	.6406	.6443	.6480	.6517
.4	.6554	.6592	.6628	.6664	.6700	.6736	.6772	.6808	.6844	.6880
.5	.6915	.6950	.6985	.7019	.7054	.7088	.7123	.7157	.7190	.7224
.6	.7257	.7291	.7324	.7357	.7389	.7422	.7454	.7486	.7517	.7549
.7	.7580	.7611	.7642	.7673	.7704	.7734	.7764	.7794	.7823	.7852
.8	.7881	.7910	.7939	.7967	.7995	.8023	.8051	.8078	.8106	.8133
.9	.8159	.8186	.8212	.8238	.8264	.8289	.8315	.8340	.8365	.8389
1.0	.8413	.8438	.8461	.8485	.8508	.8531	.8554	.8577	.8599	.8621
1.1	.8643	.8665	.8686	.8708	.8729	.8749	.8770	.8790	.8810	.8830
1.2	.8849	.8870	.8888	.8907	.8925	.8944	.8962	.8980	.8997	.9015
1.3	.9032	.9049	.9066	.9082	.9099	.9115	.9131	.9147	.9162	.9177
1.4	.9192	.9207	.9222	.9236	.9251	.9265	.9279	.9292	.9306	.9319
1.5	.9332	.9345	.9357	.9370	.9382	.9394	.9406	.9418	.9429	.9441
1.6	.9452	.9463	.9474	.9484	.9495	.9505	.9515	.9525	.9535	.9545
1.7	.9554	.9564	.9573	.9582	.9591	.9599	.9608	.9616	.9625	.9633
1.8	.9641	.9649	.9656	.9664	.9671	.9678	.9686	.9693	.9700	.9706
1.9	.9713	.9719	.9726	.9732	.9738	.9744	.9750	.9756	.9761	.9767
2.0	.9772	.9778	.9783	.9788	.9793	.9798	.9803	.9808	.9812	.9817
2.1	.9821	.9826	.9830	.9834	.9838	.9842	.9846	.9850	.9854	.9857
2.2	.9861	.9864	.9868	.9871	.9875	.9878	.9881	.9884	.9887	.9890
2.3	.9893	.9896	.9898	.9901	.9904	.9906	.9909	.9911	.9913	.9916
2.4	.9918	.9920	.9922	.9925	.9927	.9929	.9931	.9932	.9934	.9936
2.5	.9938	.9940	.9941	.9943	.9945	.9946	.9948	.9949	.9951	.9952
2.6	.9953	.9955	.9956	.9957	.9959	.9960	.9961	.9962	.9963	.9964
2.7	.9965	.9966	.9967	.9968	.9969	.9970	.9971	.9972	.9973	.9974
2.8	.9974	.9975	.9976	.9977	.9977	.9978	.9979	.9979	.9980	.9981
2.9	.9981	.9982	.9982	.9983	.9984	.9984	.9985	.9985	.9986	.9987
3.0	.9987									

Approximation for the cumulative normal distribution

The objective is to find the cumulative probability of x, where x is normally distributed. This is written $N(x)$.

Let

$$q = \frac{1}{\sqrt{2\pi}}\, e^{-x^2/2}$$

$$y = \frac{1}{1 + [0.33267\ \text{abs}\ (x)]}$$

where 'abs' is an absolute value.

Let

$$w = 0.5 - q(0.436184y - 0.120168y^2 + 0.937298y^3).$$

Then

$$N(x) = 0.5 + w \quad \text{for } x \geq 0$$

and

$$N(x) = 0.5 - w \quad \text{for } x < 0.$$

For example, if $x = -0.1547$, then

$$q = 0.39420$$
$$y = 0.95105$$
$$w = 0.06148$$

and

$$N(x) = 0.5 - 0.06148 = 0.43852.$$

Subject index

Author index